ULYSSES KAY

Ulysses Kay.

ULYSSES KAY

A Bio-Bibliography

Compiled by

Constance Tibbs Hobson

and

Deborra A. Richardson

Bio-Bibliographies in Music, Number 53
Donald L. Hixon, Series Adviser

GREENWOOD PRESS
Westport, Connecticut • London

Library of Congress Cataloging-in-Publication Data

Hobson, Constance Tibbs.
    Ulysses Kay : a bio-bibliography / compiled by Constance Tibbs
Hobson and Deborra A. Richardson.
        p. cm.—(Bio-bibliographies in music, ISSN 0742–6968 ; no.
53)
    Includes bibliographical references (p.   ) and index.
    Discography: p.
    ISBN 0–313–25546–6 (alk. paper)
    1. Kay, Ulysses, 1917- —Bibliography. 2. Kay, Ulysses, 1917–
—Discography. I. Richardson, Deborra A. II. Title. III. Series.
ML134.K3H6 1994
016.78′092—dc20   93–45940

British Library Cataloguing in Publication Data is available.

Library of Congress Catalog Card Number: 93–45940
ISBN: 0–313–25546–6
ISSN: 0742–6968

First published in 1994

Greenwood Press, 88 Post Road West, Westport, CT 06881
An imprint of Greenwood Publishing Group, Inc.

Printed in the United States of America

The paper used in this book complies with the
Permanent Paper Standard issued by the National
Information Standards Organization (Z39.48–1984).

10 9 8 7 6 5 4 3 2 1

COPYRIGHT ACKNOWLEDGMENTS

To the memory of
Mark Fax and Thomas Kerr

Contents

Preface

Ulysses Kay is one of the most prominent American composers living today. Born in the second decade of the twentieth century, this distinguished and eminent composer belongs to a musical generation that boasts such renowned composers as William Schuman (1910-92), Roque Cordero (b. 1917), Margaret Bonds (1913-70), Gian Carlo Menotti (b. 1911), Leonard Bernstein (1918-90), and Alberto Ginastera (1916-83), among others. His compositions, totalling more than 135, encompass a wide variety of forms and media, and have been heard from "Kiev to Kennebunkport," as Oliver Daniel has stated so descriptively. As a composer, conductor, educator, writer, and consultant, Kay has made a significant contribution to the cultural life of world-wide audiences, and his compositions have enriched the repertory of contemporary music by American composers.

The present volume, which celebrates the achievements of Ulysses Kay through 1992, consists of four major sections:

1) A brief biography which highlights major events in the composer's life and career;

2) A complete list of works and performances, arranged chronologically by date of composition. Each title is followed by descriptive information including medium, duration, alternate titles, movements, instrumentation, names of librettists/literary sources, performers, and publication. Where applicable, pertinent data relating to awards, dedications, commissions, or prizes are provided, and followed by information relating to premiere and other selected performances. Each title entry is preceded by the mnemonic "W" (W1, W2, W3, etc.), and each successive performance is identified by a lower case letter, e.g., W1a, W1b, W1c, etc., thereby giving the reader an idea of the magnitude of performances, nationally and internationally. The reader is also able to ascertain those compositions which have emerged as standard concert repertory. Orchestral parts, identifying instrumentation, list woodwinds first,

followed by brasses, timpani, percussion, and strings. Instrumentation, e.g., 2-3-3-1, 4-2-2-1, timp, perc, str, means that the composition is written for 2 flutes, 3 oboes, 3 clarinets, and 1 bassoon; 4 horns, 2 trumpets, 2 trombones, and 1 tuba; timpani; percussion; and the customary string section of violins, violas, violoncellos, and contrabasses. References to recordings or commentaries on performances located in the "Discography" and "Bibliography" sections are designated by the phrase, *See also*;

3) A discography of all commercially produced sound recordings of Kay's works (disc and tape). Reference to privately produced records will be found in the "Works and Performances" section. Each entry is preceded by the mnemonic "D" (D1, D2, D3, etc.) and includes full information of title, date of composition, duration of recorded performance, record company, date of release, record number, title, type of recording (stereo or mono), and performing artists. Names of other composers whose works appear on the recording are also noted. References to commentaries of recordings located in the "Bibliography" and "Works and Performances" sections are indicated by the term, *See*;

4) An annotated bibliography of writings by and about Ulysses Kay. It is divided into two parts: (a) articles by Kay and (b) references to Kay, his style, and his music. In the first part, each entry is preceded by the mnemonic "K" (K1, K2, K3, etc.); in the second part, each entry is preceded by the mnemonic "B" (B1, B2, B3, etc.). This part is further augmented by "Additional Resources," entries from general sources, catalogs, and libraries. References to "Works and Performances" and other sections of this volume are indicated by the term, *See*. In a few instances, the reader is referred to related references within this section. Some brief entries have been included, especially, to direct the reader to African American sources and to provide a view of the variety and extent of coverage afforded Kay in scholarly publications. The citations succinctly describe the content of the bibliographic sources as they relate to the composer and follow *The Chicago Manual of Style* (1982) for format.

In addition, two appendices are provided. The first consists of an alphabetical arrangement of compositions and the second lists them by classification or genre. A complete index of names, personal and corporate, as well as titles, concludes this volume. Readers are encouraged to send additional information or corrections to the compilers in care of Greenwood Press Music Editor.

The compilers feel that the identification of African American personalities and others of African descent is germane to the information in this volume and will be of extreme benefit to the reader. The names, therefore, of significant African American composers, performers, scholars, conductors, authors, or journalists have been indicated with an asterisk (*) in the index.

In publications that involve much research, there are always many persons and institutions who have contributed to its preparation. The compilers are, indeed, grateful to all who gave assistance. First, we are extremely indebted to the composer, Ulysses Kay, and to his gracious wife, Barbara, for their unstinting cooperation in providing detailed information through a personal interview and lengthy telephone conversations.

Persons at Greenwood Press, Westport, CT, whose support and assistance are deeply appreciated, include Marilyn Brownstein, former Humanities Editor, Maureen Melino, Coordinating Editor, Alicia Merritt, Acquisitions Editor, and Donald L. Hixon, Series Adviser, and former Fine Arts Librarian of the University Library of the University of California at Irvine.

In addition, we would like to acknowledge the invaluable assistance provided by the staffs of the following institutions:

The Library of Congress, Washington, DC, especially Elmer Booze and Wayne Shirley, Music Specialists; The Schomburg Center for Research in Black Culture, The New York Public Library, New York, NY; The E. Azalia Hackley Collection, The Detroit Public Library, Detroit, MI; The Center for Black Music Research of Columbia College, Chicago IL, Samuel A. Floyd, Jr., Director, and Marsha Reisser, Assistant Director; The Voice of America, Michael Gray, Music Librarian, Washington, DC; Helen Cheng and Mercedese M. Miller, Consultants; and the University of Arizona Music Library, Tucson, AZ.

Special thanks is extended to the staff of the Moorland-Spingarn Research Center, Howard University, Washington, DC, for general support, encouragement, and clerical assistance, with particular mention of Thomas C. Battle, Director; Karen L. Jefferson, Curator; and staff members, Gladys O. Toney, and Monica M. Beckles.

Finally, we are especially grateful to personal family members and friends, namely Craig A. Hobson, Agnes R. and Ernest E. Boyd, Alexander F. Richardson, Aridell M. Butler, and Hortense R. Kerr, whose day-by-day encouragement, patience, and enthusiasm enabled us to complete this volume.

ABBREVIATIONS

Usual and standard abbreviations have been used throughout the volume. Months of the year are abbreviated by the first three letters, and the two-letter postal abbreviation is used for names of states. An explanation of musical terms and instruments follows, along with separate directories of publishing and recording companies, complete with current addresses as found in *Billboard's International Buyers Guide* (1988) and the annual booking issue of *Musical America: The International Directory of the Performing Arts* (1988). Explanations of further abbreviations may be found in the "Index."

In addition, the following abbreviations for musical terms and instruments have been incorporated in this volume:

MUSICAL TERMS AND INSTRUMENTS

A, alto
annot, annotator
B, bass
bar, baritone horn
bcl, bass clarinet
bsn, bassoon
cb, contrabass
cel, celesta
cl, clarinet
cond, conductor
cor, French horn
crnt, cornet
D, difficult
des, designer
dir, director
Eng hn, English horn

fl, flute
hn, horn
hp, harpsichord
M, medium
MSS, manuscript
PR, parts on rental
prod, producer
S, soprano
sax, saxophone
str, strings
T, tenor
timp, timpani
trb, trombone
trp, trumpet
vib, vibraphone
vln, violin

DIRECTORY OF PUBLISHERS

Publishers cited throughout this volume have been abbreviated as indicated below.

AMP, Associated Music Publishers, Inc., 866 Third Avenue, New York, NY 10022

BEL, Belwin-Mills Publishing Corp., 250 Deshon Drive, Melville, NY 11747

CFP, C.F. Peters Corp., 373 Park Avenue South, New York, NY 10016

CAN, Canyon Press, P.O. Box 1235, Cincinnati, OH 45201

CF, Carl Fischer, Inc., 62 Cooper Square, New York, NY 10003

DUCH, Duchess Music Corp., 221 Park Avenue South, New York, NY 10016

DUCH/LEEDS, Duchess/Leeds Corp. (see MCA)

DUCH/MCA, Duchess/MCA Music Corp. (see MCA)

FC, Franco Columbo (see GR)

GR, G. Ricordi (F. Columbo)/Belwin-Mills (see BEL)

HWG, H.W. Gray Publications/Belwin Mills (see BEL)

JCP, JCPenney Bicentennial Music Project, c/o Joan Gosnell, Archives and Research Service, P.O. Box 659000, Dallas, TX 75265-9000

LEEDS, Leeds Music (see MCA)

MCA, MCA Music Corp., 445 Park Avenue, New York, NY 10022

MCA/BEL, MCA Music Corp./Belwin-Mills (see BEL)

PEER, Peer International (see PEER/SO)

PEER/SO, Peer International-Southern Organization, 1740 Broadway, New York, NY 10019

PEM, Pembroke Music Co., Inc. (see CF)

PEM/CF, Pembroke Music/Carl Fischer (see CF)

DIRECTORY OF RECORD COMPANIES

The following record companies are cited throughout this volume.

CBS Records, Inc., 51 West Fifty-second Street, New York, NY 10019
Cambridge Records, Inc., 125 Irving Street, Farmington, MA 01701
Century Record Company, c/o University of Arizona, Tucson, AZ 85700
Columbia Records (see CBS)
Composers Recordings, Inc., 170 West Seventy-fourth Street, New York, NY
    10023
Crystal Records, Inc., 2235 Willida Lane, Sedro Wooley, WA 98284
Desto, c/o C.M.S. Records, Inc., 226 Washington Street, Mount Vernon, NY
    10553
Eastern Records (information unavailable, company no longer exists)
Folkways Records and Service Corp., 632 Broadway, New York, NY 10012
Gothic Records, Inc., c/o George Dickey, P.O. Box 1576, Tuftin, CA 92681
Grenadilla Productions, c/o Richard Gilbert, 217 East Eighty-fifth Street,
    Suite 263, New York, NY 10028
JCPenney Bicentennial Music Project, Archives and Research Service, P.O.
    Box 659000, Dallas, TX 75265-9000
London, c/o Polygram Records, Inc., 810 Seventh Avenue, New York, NY 10019
Louisville Orchestra/First Edition Records, 609 West Main Street,
    Louisville, KY 40202
Opus One, Box 604, Greenville, ME 04441
Orion Master Recordings, Inc., Box 4087, 5840 Bursch Drive, Malibu, CA
    90265
Remington Musirama (information unavailable, company no longer exists)
Turnabout, Distributor: Moss Music Group, 200 Varick Street, New York, NY
    10014
Turnabout, c/o Moss Music Group, 48 West Fifty-eighth Street, New York, NY
    10018
Varese Sarabande Records, Inc., 13006 Saticoy Street, North Hollywood, CA
    91605

ULYSSES KAY

Biography

In the past five decades, Ulysses Kay has produced more than 135 compositions, representing a tremendous outpouring of divergent forms—five operas, over twenty large orchestral works, more than thirty choral compositions, fifteen chamber works, a ballet suite, and numerous other compositions for voice, solo instruments, film, and television. His compositions, part of mainstream concert repertory, have received extensive performances by major orchestras and ensembles throughout the world and have earned for him a prodigious number of awards, fellowships, grants, and commissions.

Kay, the recipient of an inordinate number of honorary degrees, is one of America's well published and frequently performed composers and has worked closely with most of the renowned conductors of this century. In addition, he is probably the most published and commissioned African American composer. Kay acknowledges that 98 percent of his compositions have been performed, about 65 percent published, and approximately 18 percent recorded.[1] His quiet, soft-spoken demeanor reflects a deep reverence and humility which belies the intensity and drive he brings to his craft.

Unlike many of his contemporaries, he is a composer whose works can be categorized in neither "technical, racial, nor stylistic" terms. In explanation, Nicolas Slonimsky, renowned Russian American musicologist, further states that Kay "writes music that corresponds to his artistic emotions within a framework of harmony, counterpoint and orchestration that provides him with the broadest sense of expression." Continuing, he affirms that "the musical language of Ulysses Kay is that of enlightened modernism. This is the only 'ism' that he accepts, and even that only as a matter of chronological placement."[2]

Born in Tucson, Arizona, on January 7, 1917, Kay's musical talent was encouraged and his interest heightened by the music-centered activities in the home, church, and community. He was the only son of a second marriage which united Ulysses Simpson Kay, Sr. and Elizabeth Davis. Named after his father, he did not use the customary "junior." Later, he dropped the middle name and, ultimately, the middle initial.

The entire family pursued various musical interests. His father, a former cowboy and jockey in Texas, was a barber who sang around the house to the accompaniment of his own rhythmic hand-drumming. His mother, originally from Louisiana, enjoyed playing the piano and singing at home and in the church. His stepbrother played violin and saxophone, and his stepsister studied piano. Her repertoire consisted of many of the standard classical works but, for the young Kay, the marches she played were his favorites.

Faced with the dilemma of choosing between trumpet and piano as a beginner's instrument, his mother consulted with his uncle in Chicago—the celebrated jazz musician and cornetist, Joe "King" Oliver—to decide the issue. His uncle advised that he take piano lessons in order to learn the rudiments and then decide in which direction to go musically. The advice was confidently accepted by the young Kay, for he was fascinated by Uncle Joe's life and regarded his work as "magical."[3]

For the young Ulysses, piano study began at age six with William A. Ferguson. However, the magic, the fascination, and the inspiration were not powerful enough to offset the routine of daily practice. Ulysses found other things to do, and his sister had to admonish him to practice. She did this with the tenacity and vigilance of a task-master, reporting, on many occasions, that he was "goofing off."

In a few years, the study of violin was added and, around age fourteen, he began playing the alto saxophone, a Christmas gift from his sister. Kay recalls his astonishment and wonder. "WOW! Everything went out the window—the piano AND the violin. The sax is fascinating, well, it's beautiful, and then it is so different."[4] So the young Kay, with his saxophone, another friend with his clarinet, another with a trumpet and violin, and another with drums, formed a combo which "drove everyone wild." Thus began Kay's first step toward orchestrating, arranging, and compositing. He explains that:

> at the music store, you could buy sheet music for piano, or study books on orchestration—a six and a half by eight guide—selling for fifty cents. These were stock arrangements for three saxophones, three trumpets, and three trombones. Everyone had an introduction, chorus, repeat, modulation, chorus, modulation, and out chorus—just stock.[5]

Because the combo wanted to achieve sounds like those heard on radio, the stock arrangements were found lacking to their ears:

> I was a radio fiend and listened to Cab Calloway, Duke Ellington, Benny Goodman . . . and we'd try to make these arrangements SOUND like something,

which, of course, they never did! I started to try to adapt them but arranging them was never very satisfactory. So I began to have melodies of my own and to write pieces for the group.[6]

Kay soon discovered that his early attempts at rudimentary composition were sorely hampered by his lack of compositional technique and knowledge of the instruments:

I'd get what I thought was a very good melodic idea with some rhythmic things, but I didn't know what to do with it. I'd get hung up in terms of what you do with melodies in the violin, in the trumpet . . . I really became preoccupied with how the music was put together—what makes it work—not just play my part. And this has been a kind of recurring motif in all my work through life.[7]

His musical efforts continued and he participated in the glee club, the marching band, and a dance orchestra while in school.

Tucson was a city of about thirty thousand by the time Kay was ready to enter college—quite a different city from the Tucson he knew as a child. Kay remembers that when he was young:

Tucson was really a country town with dirt streets in quite a few neighborhoods—even in some of the white neighborhoods. The streetcar ran right in front of our house, and it made a "gyro," a circle, which surrounded the business corridor and the residential district. There was a black neighborhood with some Mexicans and very few whites. I don't think that it was segregated as such; the separation was due to economics and the location of the churches. There were two principal churches in the area, a Methodist Church and a Baptist Church. They were across town from each other. My father belonged to the Methodist one, and my mother belonged to the Baptist one. I grew up attending some church all of the time. By the time I was in high school, blacks had started moving into more affluent neighborhoods. We had separated schools up through the ninth grade, then we all went to one high school.[8]

Nevertheless, there were many persons and events in Tucson that influenced and inspired the young Kay. The principal of the secondary school was a graduate of Tuskegee Institute (Alabama) and was succeeded by a graduate of Fisk University (Nashville, Tennessee), both bastions of higher education among blacks. Additionally, summer activities in the park offered a variety of concerts, including a type of music known as "Típica," which was performed by a Mexican orchestra. Appearing also was Arizona University's band director, Joseph Di Lucca, a euphonium virtuoso, who had studied with the famous John Philip Sousa. Other concerts held at the Temple of Music and at the Carnegie Library enabled the young Kay to hear some of the great artists of the era, e.g., Jascha Heifetz, violinist, and Marian Anderson, contralto. Further musical opportunities were afforded by the Tucson Symphony and the unique Jooss Ballet, directed by Kurt Jooss, a famous German expressionist dancer.[9]

Although these forces fed his musical interest, Kay entered the University of Arizona in 1934 as a liberal arts major, feeling at the time that a Bachelor of Arts degree was desirable. Soon, however, he found that he missed participating in music and, subsequently, changed his major to public school music. Another influence upon his decision to pursue a musical career occurred during the summers of 1936 and 1937. Kay met the celebrated composer, William Grant Still, who "both inspired him and encouraged him to become a composer."[10] Still was quite impressed with Kay's potential and recommended him for various fellowships later in his career.[11]

At the university, Kay's musical insight and knowledge were sharpened and broadened by two of his professors. One, Julia Rebeil, his piano teacher, introduced him to the works of Béla Bartók and other contemporary composers. The other, John L. Lowell, his theory teacher, "conjured up the mystical world of creating music in an organized theoretical manner."[12]   He received the Bachelor of Music degree in 1938, and entered the Eastman School of Music on scholarship. For the next two years, 1938-40, Kay studied composition with Bernard Rogers and Howard Hanson. His earliest compositions, *Ten Pieces for Children* (admittedly, his first) and *Sinfonietta for Orchestra*, were written in 1938, at age twenty-two. The piano pieces were "charming miniatures along modal lines, redolent of European folk songs and incongruously close to Liadov's harmonizations of Russian songs."[13] The *Sinfonietta*, acknowledged as his first important orchestral work, was performed at Eastman during the 1939 annual spring symposium of selected students' works. Howard Hanson conducted the Rochester Civic Orchestra in what was Kay's first opportunity to hear his orchestral work performed!

A favorable review of *Sinfonietta* by John Dwyer in the *Rochester Times Union* (April 21, 1939) brought Kay's name to the attention of the public and press:

> The Andante movement of the *Sinfonietta* . . . was tuneful, possibly pastoral in the manner of Debussy's string technique. A dipping counter figure to the diatonic melody gave the work a pleasing implication of gradual harmonic transition. The return to the original tasteful material of the beginning was gratefully observed.

Kay concurs that "the *Sinfonietta* was very musical and very honest. It wasn't fancy orchestration, not trying to make a joyful noise unto the Lord, it was just what it was—just right, a little rare, and so everyone was charmed by it, and it made a place for me."[14]

Compositions performed at succeeding symposia were *Concerto for Oboe* (1940), composed at age twenty-three, and a ballet suite, *Danse Calinda*, first scene for orchestra, based on a story by Ridgeley Torrence (1941). Kay subsequently added a second scene. The complete work was premiered in New York in 1947 and received the Anna Bobbit Gardner Award. Slonimsky reveals that "in his *Oboe Concerto* . . . and in *Five Mosaics* for chamber orchestra of the same period, Ulysses Kay is still a lyric composer, evoking well-proportioned landscapes of sound, and amply succeeding in this modest undertaking."[15]

Study at Eastman provided invaluable and stimulating experiences. Kay found that his teachers were very fair and treated everyone in the same manner, as long as one showed interest, did one's work, and demonstrated talent. Friendships that lasted through the years were formed with the few other black musicians who were students—Mark Fax, Thomas Kerr, and Raymond Morris, all composers; William Warfield, Kenneth Spencer, and Irma Allen, all singers:

> Rochester was a very cold place, and the big industry was the Eastman Kodak Company. My friend, Tommy Kerr, who had been in Rochester several years, showed me around the city. He introduced me to a few families, and I inherited two or three of his piano students after he graduated. Tommy accompanied Kenneth, a marvelous bass-baritone, who had finished Eastman, but who returned periodically for engagements in some of the night clubs. He was a serious singer, but accepted this type of engagement to help him through school. Bill Warfield, from Rochester, was a freshman in my last year of graduate school and was known all over town. He exuded all this enthusiasm and warmth; nothing "phased" him. He was an excellent musician and, with this personality, into everything.[16]

Aside from these few encounters, social life was limited to a few restaurants and clubs. On one occasion, at a favorite "soul food" restaurant, Kay met Count Basie, over half of Basie's orchestra, and "Mr. Five by Five" (Jimmy Rushing), a real "gutsy" singer. Kay was quite impressed with them and thoroughly enjoyed this rare social exchange.

Kay completed his studies at Eastman in 1940, graduating with a Master of Music degree in composition. During 1941 and 1942, scholarships enabled him to study with Paul Hindemith, first at Tanglewood at the Berkshire Festival during the summer, and continuing at Yale University in New Haven. A brief insight into Hindemith's methodology is provided by Kay's personal observations:

> Hindemith insisted we write away from the piano. And we did various things in class. He [would] put a text on the board of about 4 or 8 lines and say: "OK, let's write a piece." Twenty minutes later, he wanted to see it, and he'd write one too. And that didn't mean a piece ready for performance or publication, but a first sketch. And nobody used a piano (unless he'd play it over for the class); but it was just fantastic. . . .[17]

Robert Herrema suggests that "it was Hindemith—certainly no stranger to vocal music—that cultivated Kay's heretofore undeveloped gift of melody and literary sensitivity into the fertile soil of choral singing."[18]   However, Richard Hadley maintains that "even though the influence of Hindemith . . . is evident, this has not precluded the development of a personal style."[19] Eileen Southern submits that "Kay's mature style continued the emphasis on lyricism and was distinctive for its rhythmic vitality, sensitivity for contrasting sonorities, and predilection for crisp, dissonant counterpoint, though not necessarily atonal. . . . He represented modern traditionalism with its roots in romanticism and expressionism of the early twentieth century."[20]   Herrema described the dichotomy present in Kay's music as a "marvelous" one.   There is "craftsmanship and romanticism, reason and emotion. . . . His craft is at once Hindemithian, classical, and Netherlandish; his expressiveness is incredibly romantic and Madrigalian."[21] Kay views his own compositional style as one that is "traditional in terms of materials and attitudes toward them, but personal in expression."[22]

Kay freely admits that composing is not easy for him, and that it takes considerable work:

> I'm not of the type with the ability to compose right out like Mozart or like some "pop" people do. I begin to sketch, usually a quick one-line sketch. Occasionally, I might have need to add a bass note or harmony.   This would apply to any medium—orchestra or band. When it gets around to chorus or vocal things, words condition the kind of sketch I do, mainly because it happens that way. The quick sketch is of great advantage because you get a shape—a scope of seeing music down. If you come up with six or eight bars or twenty, thirty bars, at least you have a shape and a body of material to work with.[23]

When writing for chorus or solo voice, he confides:

> I'll read a lot; I'll just get an anthology of poetry or,
> if going through an anthology I run across several
> poets who sort of interest me, I'll get their collected
> works and scan the poems. . . . Ordinarily, especially
> in an anthology, I'll read two or three lines and if the
> poetry doesn't grip me, then forget it. Poetry is a
> special medium, and to compose, I need a special
> kind of poetry; if I don't have some kind of reaction
> within three or four lines, then I'm convinced that
> the poem isn't for me. I could read the other twenty
> lines or ten pages; I've tried it many times, to be fair
> to the author or to the poetry, but inevitably I've
> very seldom found this intuitive reaction to be wrong.
> If it grips me immediately, I can pursue it. Once I've
> chosen the text, I really work melodically . . . I usual-
> ly carry the text around with me in the sense of
> practically memorizing it; I kind of live with it. Then
> it sort of germinates, and thematic ideas come to
> me.[24]

In a much simpler statement, reported by Hope MacLeod (*New York Post*, June 13, 1968), Kay "described the creative process as starting with a sketch of 'an idea, a line, on a pad of music paper.' After which, you 'clothe it in a realized form and mixture. If a lot flows out, like a Mozart, why wonderful! Otherwise you plug at the piano, like Stravinsky.'"

Kay's catalog of works, from 1939 through 1942, represents a conscious effort to write for varying media. He wrote for orchestra, *Sinfonietta* (1939); for chamber orchestra, *Five Mosaics* (1940); for oboe and orchestra, *Concerto for Oboe and Orchestra* (1940); and for theater orchestra, *Danse Calinda* (1941). For piano, he composed *Ten Pieces for Children* (1939) and *Piano Sonata* (1940); for chorus, *Four Pieces for Male Chorus* (1941); for strings, *Sonatine for Viola and Piano* (1939); and *Sonatina for Violin and Piano* (1942); and for brass, *Three Fanfares for Four Trumpets* (1942). Several have been performed while others have been withdrawn by the composer. Kay offers no apologies for withdrawing a composition or for not offering it for publication. He remains his best critic and is not "automatically satisfied with every piece he writes simply because it is his." "Some of his music," confides Slonimsky, "causes him acute embarrassment for no more specific reason than his detachment from that particular phase of his work. Some of the material he rejects is of excellent quality and it would be a pity if he would physically destroy the manuscripts. He has not been driven to that yet . . ."[25]

The outbreak of World War II precipitated a change in Kay's life. Rather than wait to be drafted, he enlisted in the United States Navy in 1942, and was assigned to a band at Quonset Point, Rhode Island. The multi-talented Kay played the alto saxophone, flute, and piccolo; he played piano in a dance orchestra; and devoted as much time as possible to arranging and composing. Although his schedule was demanding, Kay was able to conceive several choral works during his service years, 1942-46. They were *As Joseph Was A-Walking*, for mixed chorus (1943); *Christmas Carol*, for women's chorus (1943); and *Come Away, Come Away Death* for male chorus (1944). In addition, he wrote several compositions for oboe, brass choir, flute, and chamber orchestra—*Flute Quintet*, *Prelude for Unaccompanied Flute*, *Suite in B* (oboe and piano), *Suite for Brass Choir*, and *Duo for Flute and Oboe*—all written in 1943. In 1944, he composed *Evocation*, for concert band, and *Of New Horizons*, an overture for orchestra.

It is the latter composition that has become one of Kay's most celebrated orchestral works and has received a number of performances in the United States, Spain, Sweden, Russia, and Peru. *Of New Horizons* was commissioned by Thor Johnson and performed by the New York Philharmonic with Johnson conducting. The premiere took place in the Lewisohn Stadium in New York City in July 1944. Two years later, in 1946, it was awarded the American Broadcasting Prize, and it was performed by the Detroit Symphony and the Juilliard Orchestra in 1947. Ten years later (1954), in a triumphant return to his hometown, Kay conducted the Tucson Symphony in a performance of the overture before a record audience of twenty-four hundred.

The following journalists had this to say of its premiere performance:

Robert Bagar (*New York World Telegram*, July 31, 1944):

> A new work was given its premiere at this concert, providing still another source of enjoyment and variety to the proceedings. This was *Of New Horizons* by Ulysses Kay, Musician 2-C, USN. The composition is unusually well constructed, its developments are secure and interesting and its thematic material most agreeable.

Grena Bennett (*New York Journal-American*, July 31, 1944):

> A notable feature of the program was the first performance of *Of New Horizons* by the young Negro composer, Ulysses Kay. The work made a favorable impression because of its interesting language and praiseworthy orchestral treatment.

And at the later performance of the overture by Thor Johnson and the Juilliard School Orchestra in Carnegie Hall on March 10, 1947, John Briggs (*New York Post*, March 11, 1947) reported:

> *Of New Horizons*, by Ulysses Kay, suggests a young, vigorous talent which is growing and will continue to grow. Mr. Kay has a knack for melodic invention and a sense of tradition. His piece was effective,

which in any art involving public performance is half
the battle.

In 1945, Kay produced *Suite for Orchestra* which received the BMI
Orchestral Award in 1947. This early work captured the attention of Ross
Parmenter who reviewed its performance (*New York Times*, May 22, 1950) at
Town Hall, New York City, on May 21, 1950. "Mr. Kay's *Suite for Orchestra*
was the most inventive and individual of the works, being cleverly orchestrated
and with each section being well set off from the other." The performance,
sponsored by the African Aid Committee and chaired by the revered W. E. B.
DuBois, featured the music of six black composers from five countries—Samuel
Coleridge-Taylor (England); Amadeo Roldán (Cuba); Michael Moerane (Union
of South Africa); Ingram Fox (British Guiana); and from the United States,
William Grant Still and Ulysses Kay.[26] "The Kay work," added Arthur Berger
in another review (*New York Herald Tribune*, May 22, 1950), "stood out on this
program, despite its repetition of catchy phrases and its Shostakovitch-like [sic]
close. Mr. Kay is a young man with big talent and much skill, and his work had
finish and excellent orchestration."

Kay's naval career ended in 1946 when he was honorably discharged.
That same year, he was awarded the Alice M. Ditson Fellowship for creative
work at Columbia University, where he studied with Otto Luening from 1946
to 1947. During the summers, he was a resident at the Yaddo Festival in
Saratoga Springs, New York, where efforts were being made to improve the
status of the American composer through performance of contemporary
compositions.

Additions to his catalog in 1946 included *Brief Elegy, Dedication, Four
Inventions, The Rope, A Short Overture* and, in 1947, *Ancient Saga* (a revision
of *The Rope*), *Danse Calinda Suite, Song of Jeremiah*, and *Suite for Strings*. In
1948, Kay composed *Concerto for Orchestra, Portrait Suite, The Quiet One* (his
first film score), and *Suite from "The Quiet One*," for orchestra.

It was said of a later recording of *Concerto for Orchestra*, (Remington
label), performed by the Teatro La Fenice Symphony with Jonel Perlea
conducting, that the work was a strong contemporary American piece. The
Argonaut (San Francisco, May 21, 1954) observed:

> Listening to Remington Records' recent release of
> Ulysses Kay's CONCERTO FOR ORCHESTRA, a
> piece that explores with remarkable imaginative
> freedom the structural and coloristic problems posed
> by Kay's idiom and choice of instruments, one
> wonders how any conductor able and willing to meet
> his responsibilities could ignore a work, even if he
> didn't like it. A great conductor ought to be able to
> present all kinds of music irrespective of his own
> preferences, and it is certainly ironic that we had to

wait for an Italian orchestra and Czech conductor to
record it.

Meanwhile, Kay "began to receive recognition from his fellow musicians
and from the various executive and legislative musical bodies. His name
appeared on the programs of contemporary music festivals in the United States;
Leonard Bernstein played the piano part in his Sonatina for Violin and Piano
at a New York concert of the League of Composers . . ."[27] The press was
generous, his compositions were awarded prizes; and fellowships were granted
him for the next five years.

From 1946 to 1951, he received, not only a Fulbright Scholarship, but
was awarded the *Prix de Rome*, a fellowship of three thousand dollars for study
at the American Academy in Rome. Additionally, he was awarded grants from
the American Academy and the National Institute of Arts and Letters, and a
Julius Rosenwald Fellowship.

In 1947, *A Short Overture* (1946) won the Third Annual George Gershwin
Memorial Award. Its premiere performance at the Brooklyn Academy of Music
on March 31, 1947, was by the New York City Symphony Orchestra with
Leonard Bernstein conducting.

In 1948, the Phoenix Symphony Orchestra Award, given by the Arizona
Musicians Club for the best composition by a native Arizonan, was presented
to his *Portrait Suite*. This suite was inspired by four sculptures: *Kneeling
Woman* and *Rising Youth* by Wilhelm Lehmbruch, *Reclining Figure* by Henry
Moore, and *Blossoming* by Jacques Lipchitz.

In 1949, Kay was awarded a Fulbright scholarship and another *Prix de
Rome*. The awards, which ran concurrently, enabled him to travel and study
in Italy from 1949 to 1952. However, the young composer did not go alone. On
August 20, 1949, in Columbus, Ohio, Kay married Barbara Harrison of Chicago.
His wife, who had been a music major and school teacher of ungraded children
in Chicago, accompanied him to Italy where she continued teaching music at the
Anglo-American Overseas School. And there, also, the young couple had their
first child, Virginia, in 1951. Kay recalls with extreme pride his attendance at
her birth in the Italian Clinicia, a private hospital.[28]

For the next three years, Kay was to make his "home" at the august
American Academy in Rome, which in reality, consisted of a "grand Palazzo, an
accompanying 17th-century villa and the complex of manicured gardens, artists'
studios and apartments."[29] The academy, created at the turn of the century
by Charles Follen McKim and financed by J. P. Morgan, John D. Rockefeller,
and William Vanderbilt, was a "place for select U.S. scholars and artists to
gather in Rome to commune, exchange ideas, think, create and generally be
exposed to the great cultural repository that is Rome and its history-steeped
surrounding countryside."[30] Kay, the first black so honored and twice a
winner, joined the ranks of this elite "embassy."

While in Italy, Kay not only visited Rome, but also Perugia, Naples, Genoa, Torino, Florence, and Arezzo, pursuing his interest in liturgical music. Articles published after his return to New York reflected his impressions of the state of music in Italian churches.

In 1949, he wrote *Piano Quintet* which was premiered at the academy, *String Quartet No. 1*, and *Solemn Prelude*; in 1950, he composed *Brass Quartet*, *Fugitive Songs*, *Partita in A* (also premiered at the academy), *Pietà*, *Short Suite*, *Sinfonia in E*, *Song of Ahab* (a cantata for baritone and ten instruments), and *Two Meditations for Organ*. A film score, *The Lion, the Griffin and the Kangaroo*, was written in 1951 for a documentary film in Italy. It was commissioned by Peter Hollander of Hollander-Tait Productions, Inc. In 1952, he wrote *Three Pieces After Blake*, for dramatic soprano and orchestra.

Kay was to call upon his storehouse of memories of Italy in a later composition, *Umbrian Scene* (1963). As part of a project to write "tranquil music," Kay was commissioned by Edward B. Benjamin to produce such a work for the New Orleans Philharmonic Symphony:

> While I was clear about the mood of the piece, I found it difficult to imagine the scope of form. . . . Then suddenly, and this was four months later, I remembered the wonder and magic I had felt while attending the Festival of Sacred Music near Perugia, Italy, in the fall of 1950. I recalled the antiphonal instrumental music, the glorious choral singing there in the old chapels of Umbria . . . I thought of my visit to the historic towns of Arezzo, Assisi, and Narni, of the rugged hills and beautiful valleys . . . and so came the inspiration. . . .[31]

Their three-year hiatus in Italy over in 1953, the couple returned to New York, where Barbara taught music in Manhattan, and Ulysses accepted a position with Broadcast Music, Inc. The family grew to include two more daughters, Melinda, born in 1957, and Hillary, born in 1959.

Kay's liaison with BMI was to last for fifteen years (1953-68). Beginning as an editorial advisor of concert music, he later became a consultant. During this time, several teaching offers from well-known schools were extended him. But Kay elected to maintain a solid "nine to five" position enabling him to compose on a regular schedule. He felt that it was important to have the time to write as much as possible, for the market was beckoning, conductors were asking for new works, and commissions were pouring in.

And write he did! A total of sixteen works were written between 1953 and 1958. For chorus, he composed *A Lincoln Letter* and *Triumvirate* in 1953; *Two Madrigals* (*How Stands the Glass Around?* and *What's In a Name?*) and *A Wreath for Waits* in 1954; and *Grace to You, and Peace* and *A New Song* in 1955. Orchestral works included *Serenade for Orchestra* and *Six Dances for*

String Orchestra in 1954. Other works completed were *String Quartet No. 2* in 1956; *Ten Short Essays* and *Two Short Pieces*, both for piano, and *Serenade No. 2* for four horns, all in 1957.

Among major works written in 1953 was *Fantasy Variations* for orchestra. A detailed analysis of this work has been published by Lucius R. Wyatt, among others. Wyatt allows that *Fantasy Variations* "has been regarded as one of the most successful American works of the mid-twentieth century utilizing the theme and variations idea." Further, he adds that "the *Fantasy Variations* is characterized by the composer's ingenious handling of the resources of the orchestra and his skillful organization of the melodic, harmonic, formal, rhythmic, and textural details. The composition, although employing compositional techniques indicative of the twentieth century, illustrates the composer's appreciation and understanding of the music of the past."[32]

In consecutive years, Kay completed two one-act operas, *The Boor* (1955) and *The Juggler of Our Lady* (1956). *The Boor*, commissioned by the Koussevitsky Foundation of the Library of Congress and dedicated to the memory of Serge and Natalie Koussevitsky, was premiered in 1968 at the University of Kentucky in concert performance. This work, based on Chekhov's comical libretto, demonstrates Kay's gift for dramatic expression. *The Juggler of Our Lady*, on the other hand, was premiered in full production by the Xavier University Opera Workshop under the sponsorship of Sister M. Elise, S.B.S., on February 23 in New Orleans, Louisiana, and later performed by Opera/South in Jackson, Mississippi, November 17 and 19, 1972. Based on a story taken from a French morality play used earlier in the century by Massenet, the libretto, by author Alexander King, tells the story of a street entertainer—a juggler—who offers his talent as a gift to a statue of the Virgin in thanks for her protection. The statue comes to life and blesses him. Frank Gagnard (*New Orleans Times-Picayune*, February 24, 1962) reported that "in the new operatic telling, there is a staging opportunity for colorful street crowds, and the introduction of musically atmospheric characters. . . . Within this dramatic framework, composer Kay presents a ballet, ariettas and choral sections, and such telling sections as a satiric discourse between two friars and the juggler's lyrical reverie on a luxurious occasion when he enjoyed the comfort of a bed."

Two very significant events occurred during the next two years which served as catalysts to Kay's rising prominence on both the national and international scenes. In 1958, Kay was the featured composer in volume seven of the *American Composers Alliance Bulletin*. His picture was displayed on its cover, and an extensive article was written by Nicolas Slonimsky. The article included a biographical essay, a catalog of works to that time, and a style analysis of his compositions. For its preparation, Slonimsky visited the Kays, interviewing the composer at great length and closely perusing his compositions. The depth of his research and the seriousness of the undertaking, Kay fondly reflects, were tempered by Slonimsky's fabulous musicianship, witticism, and joviality.[33] Although written some thirty years ago, the article remains today one of the most definitive and authoritative discussions of Kay's early period.

The second catalystic event was Kay's selection as delegate to the Soviet Union the year after "Sputnik" was launched. In 1958, the State Department initiated a cultural exchange program of U.S. and Russian composers, a part of the U.S. State Department's Cultural, Educational and Technical Exchange Agreement. The first delegation to the Soviet Union, by official invitation, included Roy Harris, Ulysses Kay, Peter Mennin, and Roger Sessions. The program provided a rare opportunity for the exchange of ideas, a closer view of Russian musical life, and a chance to hear many Russian compositions. Dwight D. Eisenhower, then President of the United States, referred to the Americans as good-will ambassadors. In a letter to Kay, he affirms that Kay and his colleagues "represent us all in bringing assurance to the people you meet that the United States is a friendly nation and one dedicated to the search for world peace and to the promotion of the well-being and security of the community of nations."[34]

In a diary, Kay logged the daily events of the month-long visit to Moscow, Leningrad, Tbilis (Tiflis), and Kiev. The U.S. team was met at the airport by "Tikhon Khrennikov, general secretary of the Moscow Composers' Union, three members of the Soviet Ministry of Culture, our interpreter, Tamara, two members of the American Embassy, and four press and radio people. Several of the Russians spoke English, and our welcome was most friendly."[35]

Concerts and tapes of performances were plentiful and the level of musical activity high. Noting that all concerts were controlled and booked by the Philharmonic Society through a highly-organized structure, Kay resolved to seek more information concerning this procedure. The first meeting with Soviet composers at the House of Composers of the Moscow Composers' Union occurred on September 19, 1958. With approximately thirty composers and five musicologists (musicaveds) present, an itinerary was planned and assurances granted as to attendance at productions, rehearsals, and visits to educational centers, etc. The U.S. Team, then, embarked upon a whirlwind routine—conversing with Soviet composers, listening to symphonies, chamber music, operas and ballet, attending schools, sight-seeing, and being "wined and dined." Among the many works they heard were the familiar symphonies of Dmitri Kabalevsky, Aram Khachaturian, and Khrennikov. Newer works included an opera, *The Mother*, by Khrennikov; a ballet, *Spartacus*, by Khachaturian; and works by Arno Babadjanian, E. Tamberg, Karen Khachaturian (Aram's nephew), A. Eshpai, and the second opera of ten-year-old Kyril Molchanov.[36]

The Americans became increasingly aware of the fact that "socialistic realism"—a view that music should reflect the ideals of the state and the spirit of the people—permeated all aspects of musical activity, music education, performance, production, and composition.[37] To insure and maintain this policy, new works were screened, evaluated, and judged through a committee system of a "Composers' Union" (one in each city). Success meant wide performances and publication by the state. Failure meant a series of changes and revisions.

During many sessions of open dialogue, Kay and his colleagues explained that American composers were free to use or ignore experimentation. Thus, no one "direction" or no one "school" existed among them. This revelation surprised Zaven Vartanian, Chief of the Music Division of the Ministry of Culture, who thought that every American composer worked with dodecaphonic materials![38]

Kay was also interested in the effect of American jazz upon Russian composers. Earlier, letters to David Diamond of Radio Free Europe, from other sources, and accounts of Dave Brubeck's successful tour in Poland gave evidence to increased jazz interest in the Soviet Union. To this end, Kay took with him recordings of compositions by prominent and predominantly black jazz "greats." The collection consisted of "Miles Davis-Gil Evans' *Miles Ahead* LP, Duke Ellington's *In A Mellotone*, the Columbia LP of the Brandeis commissions, *Louis Armstrong Plays W. C. Handy*, Thelonious Monk's *Monk's Music* and *Wide Range* by John Richards."[39]   Kay's amusing encounter with a Russian "jazz buff" was recounted by Ralph Gleason in the *San Francisco Chronicle*. "As for jazz interest in the Soviet Union, I would say it is definitely increasing. At our first meeting at the Moscow House of Composers, a young legit composer eagerly approached me with many questions about new jazz trends in America. [']What is Ellington doing? What's with Kenton['], etc., etc.? The composer then began playing some *A-Train* on the piano, and Kay asked where he'd learned it. 'Oh, we hear a lot of good jazz—two hours a day on the Voice of America!'"[40]

The high point of the Americans' visit was a concert of their works by the Moscow State Radio Orchestra in Tchaikovsky Hall on October 15. The concert, planned during their first stay in Moscow, was well publicized, and the house sold out. Ambassador and Mrs. Llewellyn E. Thompson, along with other American Embassy personnel, were among the fifteen hundred in the audience. After Khrennikov introduced the composers and spoke of the aims and achievements of their visit, the concert of American works began. Presented were Mennin's *Sixth Symphony*, Harris's *Fifth Symphony*, Sessions's *Suite from "Black Maskers,"* and Kay's *Of New Horizons*. Roy Harris conducted his own work; however, the rest of the program was conducted by Gennady Rozhdestvensky, the promising young conductor of the Bolshoi Theater. The compositions were well-received, and the composers were honored at a post-concert buffet supper given by the Thompsons. Among the many compliments was one by a Swedish diplomat who "considered their type of cultural exchange a strong force for forging international good will."[41]

On October 17, the U.S. Team departed for home "to continue their individual work and to await the visit in the U.S. of the Soviet composers, Shostakovich, Khrennikov, Dankevich and others."[42]   In a narrative summarizing his impressions, Kay acknowledges:

> the Russian people love music and greatly appreciate the
> artist. The government realizes the value of the arts and
> supports them completely . . . The system seems to provide

controls which affirm the viewpoint of the government. But mass support of this program . . . is resulting in a phenomenal amount of music. . . . To my taste, there was an undesirable sameness and a lack of experimentation noticeable in most of the contemporary scores we heard. Undoubtedly these qualities reflect some official view, which the passing visitor can only speculate about. However, various trends seem to indicate a coming change. . . . First, delegations of composers from many countries are visiting the U.S.S.R. Second, Soviet composers are visiting various countries and taking note of techniques and trends in contemporary music. And third, the Soviet Union is exporting really fine performers who are challenging figures on the world musical scene.[43]

The next decade (1958-68) has been dubbed "the prolific decade" by Richard Hadley, who observed that Kay composed a number of choral works, received many commissions, and was awarded two honorary degrees.[44] Commissions were received from The International Music Council of New York City; Broadcast Music, Inc.; Youth Concerts Committee for the Tucson Symphony; the Stanley Quartet of the University of Michigan; The American Wind Symphony; the Tercentary Commission of the State of New Jersey; the New Jersey Symphony Orchestra; the Greater Boston Youth Symphony; the New York Society for Ethical Culture; and the Meadow Brook Festival. Institutions commanding compositions included Fisk University; the Juilliard School of Music; West Virginia State College (seventy-fifth anniversary); the Chicago Musical College of Roosevelt University (one hundredth anniversary); and the Illinois Sesquicentennial Commission. Among individuals who commissioned works were: John Solum, Marilyn Mason, Vinnie Burrows, Arthur Bennett Lipkin, Peter Hollander, David Susskind, Kermit Moore, Daniel Pinkham, Edward B. Benjamin, and Burton A. Cleaves.

Kay wrote a total of forty-one compositions during the decade, among which were several film and television scores: *FDR: From Third Term to Pearl Harbor* (1958), *New York: City of Magic* (1958); *The Fall of China* (1959), *Submarine!* (1959); *Admiral Byrd* (1960), *The Shape of Things* (1960), *The Three Musketeers* (1960); *Going Home, The Land,* and *Nosotros* (all in 1962); *Essay on Death* (1964); and *A Thing of Beauty* (1966). Significant among the choral works of this period is *Phoebus, Arise* (1959), a cantata for soprano and bass soli, mixed chorus, and orchestra. The words, selected from works of seventeenth century poets, were augmented by Kay's own prelude and postlude. The premiere performance was held in Town Hall, New York, May 17, 1959, by the Interracial Fellowship Chorus and Orchestra with Harold Aks conducting. Featured soloists were Louise Natale, soprano, and Lee Cass, bass. The reviews were uniformly positive.

"The words," wrote Harriett Johnson (*New York Post*, May 18, 1959), "were singularly appropriate to the occasion, exalting the joy of music in the midst of human experience which is less joyous. The final words of the epilogue, 'We glory in music and song!' proved reminiscent of the seventeenth century madrigal style and idiom, while the addition of a colorful orchestration, dramatizing the percussion, added a modern flavor."

Francis D. Perkins, (*New York Herald Tribune*, May 18, 1959), confirms that:

> the music has vigor, color and definite moods which often, while not always, correspond to those of the texts. The projection of vocal and instrumental hues is skillful and usually effective . . . Mr. Kay's cantata is not simplified music, but its details as well as its colors and sonority were well revealed in a unified and balanced interpretation which was marked by pervasive vitality and spontaneity.

Another review, equally as generous, was published in the *N.Y. Staats-Zeitung und Herold*, May 20, 1959. In referring to Kay, the reviewer extols that "this American musician has the inborn faculties of a strong personal talent and an almost inexhaustible creative gift of instrumentation."

Significant among instrumental works during this period are *Trigon* (1961) for wind orchestra; *Forever Free* (1962) for band; *Concert Sketches* (1965) for band; and *Aulos* (1967) for solo flute, two horns, string orchestra, and percussion. *Hymn-Anthem on the Tune "Hanover"* (1959), *Flowers in the Valley* (1961), *Choral Triptych* (1962), and *Inscriptions from Whitman* (1963) are representative of his well-known choral compositions.   Outstanding organizations such as the Tanglewood Festival Chorus; The Eastman School of Music Chorus; the Sigma Alpha Iota Chorus with Margaret Hillis, conductor; the King's Chapel Choir of Boston, Daniel Pinkham, conductor; the Master Institute Chorus and Orchestra with David Labovitz, conductor; the Oberlin Conservatory Choir; the Coorhees Chapel Choir; and the New Jersey Oratorio Society Male Chorus contributed greatly to the success and publication of works from Kay's choral catalog.

Perhaps the most memorable composition during this period was his orchestral work, *Markings* (1966). Written in memory of Dag Hammarskjöld, the distinguished U. N. Secretary from Sweden, this eloquent score was premiered by the Detroit Symphony with Sixten Ehrling conducting at the Meadow Brook Festival, Oakland University, in Rochester, Minnesota, on August 18, 1966. Howard Klein (*The New York Times*, August 20, 1966) called the work "a masterpiece of conservative modern orchestral writing." In 1972, WNET-TV (Channel 13) in New York City, featured *Markings* on a program entitled "The Black Composer." The program included scenes from the life of Hammarskjöld and was produced for educational television.

Toward the end of the decade, in 1965, Kay accepted a visiting professorship at Boston University, where he taught composition and theory.   The following year, from 1966 to 1967, he was Visiting Professor at the University of California at Los Angeles. In 1968, at age fifty-one, Kay joined the staff of the Herbert H. Lehman College of the City University of New York, as Professor of Music, teaching theory and composition to "budding musicians" on a full-time basis.

Kay considers teaching to be challenging and gratifying. In view of the many changes that occur within the music field, he feels that "teaching is right in the thick of it, and the young people are very vitally concerned and interested."[45] He also was pleased that he waited to enter the field at a later date than is customary—a time when he was secure in his work as a composer and "less likely to get tired of it."[46] Although Kay has spent the last twenty-odd years teaching, he has found time to participate in related musical activities. His routine is one of composing, conducting, serving as adjudicator and consultant, appearing as lecturer, and participating as a member of composer panels and forums.

Three operas were created from 1968 through 1986—*The Capitoline Venus* (1969), librettist, Judith Dvorkin; *Jubilee* (1976), librettist, Donald Dorr; and *Frederick Douglass* (1979-85), also with Donald Dorr, librettist. *The Capitoline Venus*, a one-act opera, was commissioned by the Quincy Society of Fine Arts and premiered by the University of Illinois Opera Group at the Krannert Center for the Performing Arts (Champaign-Urbana) in 1971. The libretto is based on an episode from the literature of Mark Twain, *Legend of the Capitoline Venus*. "Metrical changes, often sequential motivic groupings, pedal points and a chromatic bass line are all characteristic of this opera which ends on a happy note."[47]

Jubilee and *Frederick Douglass* are two works extracted from the African American idiom. The first is based on Margaret Walker's novel, *Jubilee*, which depicts Georgian life from the black perspective—before, during, and after the Civil War. The premiere production, commissioned for the Jackson State University Centennial Anniversary and performed by Opera/South in Jackson, Mississippi, November 20, 1976, lasted approximately two hours. The three-act work included a large integrated cast with thirteen principals, double chorus, orchestra, and a production staff of renown. The principals, Hilda Harris, Marcia Baldwin, Vinson Cole, Clyde Walker, John West, Raymond Bazemore, Adelaida Acevedo-Anderson, Richard Mundt, and Alfred Anderson, among others, were supported by a large chorus of area college students. Remarkably, *Jubilee* was pulled together in ten days. It played to a capacity audience and was reviewed as one of the company's best efforts to date.

According to Bruce Eggler of *Opera News* (January 22, 1977), "the novel loses much of its richness and power in the severe compression of a libretto." However, he maintains, "Kay has provided some of the book's key points. The moral obtuseness of the slave owners, the need for interracial cooperation, did emerge forcefully aided by the cast's exemplary enunciation. The score is melodic, generally suited to the text and grateful to the voices if not especially original. Conductor James DePriest shaped it persuasively, drawing good work from singers and orchestra."

Frederick Douglass, another large opus, took a long time to devise. With the aid of a grant from the National Endowment for the Arts in 1979, Kay was able to create a full length opera based on the life of the famous abolitionist and statesman:

> Now, the opera has to be conceived of first. Then it starts its long, long journey to work it[self] out. It's both wonderful and terrible! For one thing, we have very few librettists, unlike in Mozart's time. Then, there were librettists who would do some work for Rossini, some for another composer, etc., and apparently, in France, there was a whole "nother" bunch of them. They were people who knew the literature; knew the stage; and could turn a hand to maneuver these fantastic ideas into a worthy vehicle for the composer to use. The answer is to be your own librettist, like Wagner and Menotti. For whatever people say about Menotti's music, he is worlds ahead of all the rest of us, because he is a real theater person—one who lives it and knows it inside out. And that's what it takes.[48]

Further, he adds, "I started *Frederick Douglass* in June 1979, and it took me almost forever. I finished it in March 1985. This cut down on my production. I found it very draining—quite a few notes. It has a lot of choruses—a double chorus, a women's chorus, a big SATB, and a children's chorus."[49]

The music for *Frederick Douglass* was completed in 1983, with additional details worked out from 1983 to 1985:

> There's nothing like the opera to really put a searchlight on you as a composer. Writing for the theater or for the opera is so much more complicated. The elements—the down-to-earth elements—are not just how good it is or how pretty it is, but how it works. (She's singing about her loss of life and happiness and he's twenty feet across the stage doing something else. But they have to jibe in the next six measures!) So it is necessary to imagine the matter of time and the movement within all this. It's terrific, and you only learn it by doing it. You might say, "Well, the old masters did it overnight. Why can't somebody do it now?" But they grew up in that—playing and singing; observing and learning. When you really come down to it, it was another time, and it seems that opera is not the medium for our time.[50]

Between 1968 and 1972, Kay completed four works for orchestral and band ensembles: *Bleeker Street Suite* (1968), *Scherzi Musicali* (1968), *Theater Set* (1968), and *Four Silhouettes* (1972); three instrumental works: *Heralds I* (1968), *Facets* (1971), and *Five Portraits* (1972); and four choral works: *Once There Was A Man* (1969), *Parables* (1969), *Triple Set* (1971), and *Pentagraph* (1972).

Of the four instrumental ensembles, two were written for school groups. *Bleeker Street Suite*, for elementary orchestra, appears in manuscript only and has been withdrawn by the composer. *Four Silhouettes*, suitable for junior and senior high school bands, was premiered by the Lehman College Band with J. Dellicarri, conductor. *Scherzi Musicali*, a work for chamber orchestra, is "an exuberant piece . . . which celebrates the composer's 'admiration of the early 17th century Italian vocal pieces of the same name, meaning literally *musical jests.*'"[51] A descriptive review by Arthur Custer of the Rhode Island State Council on the Arts follows:

> The instrumental writing is gracious and practical. (The woodwind quintet and the string orchestra are congruent partners, but provide a limited sonorous framework for Kay's ideas. He has, however, used the timbral resources to the fullest, and with great imagination.). . . . There are blocks of sound built up bell-tone fashion, and saucy tunes given depth by contrapuntal reinforcement. There are big tuttis and contemplative cantilenas; passionate, robust statements and quiet roulades, often running harp-like through the strings; passages of woodwinds alone and of strings alone and all of the combinations one might imagine. All of this . . . enriches the chamber orchestra repertoire.[52]

Theater Set, written for full orchestra, reflects Kay's enjoyment of music played by live show orchestras. It is a "tribute to 'show music without quoting any popular theater tunes.'"[53]

The three instrumental ensembles from this period exemplify works for differing media: *Heralds I*, for brass ensembles, was first performed in New York for the International Music Congress. *Facets*, for woodwind quintet and piano, was commissioned to celebrate the fiftieth anniversary of the Eastman School of Music, and *Five Portraits*, for violin and piano, was commissioned by the McKim Fund of the Library of Congress.

Among the choral works written from 1968 to 1972, *Once There Was a Man*, a work requiring narrator, appears to have received the most acclaim. Its world premiere was held on September 18, 1969, in Detroit, Michigan, where Sixten Ehrling conducted the Detroit Symphony and the thirty-six voices of the Kenneth Jewell Chorale. William Warfield, Kay's Eastman classmate, provided the narration.

From 1973 through 1977, Kay added an impressive list of thirteen works. These included four for solo instruments, two for brass ensemble, two for orchestra, two for chorus, one for concert band, and two operas. One of the piano solos, *Visions* (1974), was written to commemorate the eightieth anniversary of William Grant Still's birth. Another, *First Nocturne* (1973), "shows creative command of structural organization, for it reads like a painting, ever-changing and ever-revealing at each scrutiny."[54]

Five compositions were the result of commissions to celebrate America's Bicentennial (1975-77): *Jubilee, Southern Harmony, Two Folk Settings, Western Paradise*, and *Epigrams and Hymn*. In *Southern Harmony*, commissioned by the Southeastern Regional Metropolitan Orchestra Managers Association, Kay pays tribute to the American musical heritage of the mid-nineteenth century South. Based on the motives and themes from *The Southern Harmony* of William Walker, a white itinerant singing teacher (1809-75) from Spartanburg, South Carolina, the composition revealed Kay's fascination for tales of the old South's circuit riders and revival meetings.[55]

The *Two Folk Settings—Sally Anne* and *Blow, Ye Winds in the Morning*—were based on other examples of folklore. *Sally Anne*, derived from a popular fiddle tune of the southern uplands, was performed by the De Paur Chorus with Leonard de Paur conducting, and recorded on Columbia Records (now CBS). *Blow, Ye Winds in the Morning*, which was not recorded, is a narrative of the whalers' life adapted by Joanna Colcord. Both were commissioned by the JCPenney Bicentennial Music Project. Other works commissioned for the project were composed by David N. Baker, William Billings, Emma Lou Diemer, Walter Ehret, Ernest Bloch, Norman Dello Joio, Jester Hairston, Roger Nixon, and Dorothy Klotzman.[56]

Western Paradise, commissioned by the National Symphony Orchestra, was written for narrator and orchestra. It was premiered in October 1976 with Antal Dorati, conductor, and William Conrad, narrator. Based on a text by Donald Dorr, it "focused on the break between the colonies and the British as seen from the British point of view."[57]

Epigrams and Hymn was commissioned by the Princeton Theological Seminary and the Bryn Mawr and Brick Presbyterian Churches. It was written for mixed chorus and organ using the texts of John Greenleaf Whittier, Reverend John Murray, and Samuel Longfellow.

Despite the exhaustive demands of his fifth opera, *Frederick Douglass*, and his teaching load, Kay composed seven works from 1976 to 1988. *Jersey Hours* (1978), another work with text by Donald Dorr, was written for voice and three harps. It was performed initially, January 7, 1979, on a series entitled, "Teaneck Artists Perform." *Chariots*, also written in 1978, was commissioned by the Saratoga Performing Arts Center. It was premiered in 1979 at Saratoga Springs, with Ulysses Kay as guest conductor of the Philadelphia Orchestra. Kay envisioned the "chariots," explains Steven Stucky, as "symbolic of a person's aspirations and being." Further, Stucky predicts that the work, based on the spiritual, "Swing Low, Sweet Chariot," will be performed often because "it is demonstrative 'about' something listeners can quickly apprehend."[58]

Festival Psalms (1978), for solo baritone, mixed chorus and piano, took two years to complete. It was commissioned and performed by the Holland Community Chorale in Holland, Michigan, on March 13, 1984. *Tromba* (1983) was commissioned by Fred Irby III. The three-movement work—"Prologue," "Nocturne," "Mobile"—was given its premiere by Irby, trumpet, and Ronald Tymus, piano, at the Baird Auditorium of the Smithsonian Institution in Washington, DC, May 24, 1985.

Five Winds (1984), for woodwind quintet—a four-movement work—was written for the 1984 Tidewater Music Festival. However, only the first three movements were premiered there on July 5. The final movement was completed on or about July 21. Kay attended the festival at the invitation of the festival faculty and stayed four or five days. He concluded that the "Tidewater Music Festival is a very nice summer camp for high school students, although not as extensive as Brevard or Tanglewood. The setting is beautiful, and they do very good work."[59]

Pantomime and *Two Impromptus* were both written in 1986. The first is a fantasy for solo clarinet. The second work, commissioned by Affiliate Artists, Inc. of New York, was premiered by Marcantonio Barone, pianist, on February 8, 1987, in Weill Recital Hall, New York City.

Throughout his career, Kay has addressed often-neglected areas of composition and has encouraged, enlightened, and inspired others. He composes not only for the professional musician, but for the amateur and school musician as well. He has lectured, conducted, adjudicated competitions, and served as composer-in-residence throughout the United States and in Yugoslavia, Italy, France, and England. He has served with his peers on corporate boards and has been elected to membership in auspicious organizations. Among these are the American Academy and National Institute of Arts and Letters, the Black Music Center at Indiana University, the American Symphony Orchestra League, the Executive Board of the National Black Music Colloquium and Competition, and the American Composers Alliance.

Ulysses Kay was elected a corporate member of the MacDowell Association (1961); was appointed Distinguished Professor of Music at Lehman College, New York, NY (1973); was the Hubert H. Humphrey Lecturer at Macalester College, St. Paul, Minnesota (1975); and was the second composer to fill the Mu Phi Epsilon Endowed Chair of Composition at the Brevard Music Center, Brevard, North Carolina (1979). Significant among the competitions he has adjudicated were the *Prix Italia* Competition in Trieste (1960) and the Kennedy Center-Rockefeller Foundation International Competition for Excellence in the Performance of American Piano Music, Washington, DC (1978).

Tributes have been extended him in varied forms, notable among which are the following: Kay was guest conductor of the American Music Symposium sponsored by the Rockefeller Foundation at Arizona State University (1967); served as composer-in-residence at the Bellagio Study and Conference Center in Bellagio, Italy (1982); and was selected to address the "Music of the Black Composer" Conference at the Smithsonian Institution (1985). He received the first award given by the New Jersey State Council on the Arts (1969); the Alumni Citation from the University of Rochester (1972); and the Alumni Achievement Award from the University of Arizona in 1980. Kay was also one of several composers featured during the Black American Music Symposium at the University of Michigan (1985) and during the American New Music Consortium's Fourth Annual Festival in New York (1985).

Singular among other tributes was his selection as one of the thirteen composers represented on the "Black Composer Series" released by Columbia Records (1974-79). The set, consisting of nine volumes which spanned two centuries of music, documents the richness and diversity of composition by black composers. A similar presentation occurred in 1977, when the New York Philharmonic Orchestra hosted "A Celebration of Black Composers" that included three orchestral concerts and two recitals at Lincoln Center Library and the Museum of the Performing Arts.

Kay has received a total of six honorary doctorates, the latest from the University of Missouri-Kansas City Conservatory (1981). Other honorary degrees have been received from the Dickinson College in Carlisle, Pennsylvania (1978), University of Arizona in Tucson (1969), Illinois Wesleyan in Bloomington (1969), Bucknell University in Lewisburg, Pennsylvania (1966), and Lincoln College in Lincoln, Illinois (1963).

Special "All-Ulysses Kay Concerts" and "Ulysses Kay Days" have been highlighted events at many colleges and universities through the years. It is only logical that what should follow would be a "Ulysses Kay Week!" This occurred in a 1988 "Share a Composer" project when Boston honored Kay in a "Ulysses Kay Week," March 9-14. Four area universities—the University of Massachusetts (Harbor campus), Tufts University, Northeastern University, and Harvard University—united to honor him with performances of his music. The aim of this project is to bring a composer's music and ideas to as large and diverse an audience as possible. Composers honored in the past include Henry Brant, Vincent Persichetti, and Karl Husa. During the week, Kay was featured in a discussion, "The Making of a Composer," and his *Five Portraits*, *Forever Free*, and *A New Song* were performed.

As this century draws to a close, Kay has retired from Lehman College, ending a twenty-year tenure. He continues to live with his family in Teaneck, New Jersey. A working composer still, Kay's latest offspring is *String Triptych*, which was commissioned by the Missouri Unit of the American String Teachers Association. It was premiered by the Missouri All-State High School String Orchestra, January 23, 1988, in Osage Beach, Missouri, with Paul Vermel conducting. He maintains his alliance with BMI through service on the Board of Advisors for the "BMI Award to Student Composers," and in 1987 was Presiding Judge.

Additional works performed in early 1988 include *Jersey Hours* (February 1) in Teaneck; *Forever Free* (March 25) in Durham, North Carolina; *Presidential Suite* (April 1) by the St. Joseph Symphony (Mo); and *Five Portraits* (April 21 and 22) by Robert Mann of the Juilliard Quartet at the Library of Congress. In 1989, performances of his works included *Of New Horizons* and excerpts from *Southern Harmony* by the Lancaster Symphony (Lancaster, PA) with Stephen Guzenhauser, conductor. The Chicago Sinfonietta (Chicago, IL), conducted by Paul Freeman, presented *Western Paradise* with William Warfield, narrator, and *String Quartet No. 2* was performed by the Charleston String Quartet at Haverford College (Haverford, PA) where Kay was guest composer.

More accolades followed in 1989 when Kay won the Lancaster Symphony Society Award in Lancaster. The composer was also featured on an all-Kay program at Lehman College. This program included three chamber works and a concert adaptation of the opera, *Jubilee*, with Julius P. Williams, music director.

In April, 1991, Kay's largest work, the opera, *Frederick Douglass*, received its world premiere in Newark, NJ. Performed by the New Jersey State Opera in Newark at the Symphony Hall, it was conducted by Alfredo Silipigni with Kevin Maynor in the role of Frederick Douglass.

Kay's contribution to America's cultural life and to its contemporary music scene is outstanding. His distinguished career, reflecting personal industry, discipline, and will, sets an encouraging, honorable, and inspiring example for all who follow. His message to aspiring composers strongly advocates continued study and growth in order to better express one's vision and individuality.[60]

Ulysses Kay's stature among our leading American composers is assured by the increasing performances of his compositions and preserved by the broadening research efforts of scholars throughout the world. Dissertations, analytical treatises, biographical essays, and comprehensive music studies strengthen the knowledge of the man and the perception of his work.

Musicologists in the coming century, will continue to classify American composers into schools and periods. History and theory texts will determine "common practice" and readdress the influence of the multi-integrated and cross-cultural interaction of America's resources. While today's discourse explores and exposes the contemporary trends among American composers, tomorrow's will assess, conclusively, the richness and diversity of America's music and define the role of the American composer in the musics of the world.

NOTES

1.   David N. Baker, Lida M. Belt, and Herman C. Hudson, *The Black Composer Speaks* (Metuchen, N.J.: Scarecrow Press, 1978), p. 141.

2. Nicolas Slonimsky, "Ulysses Kay," *The American Composers Alliance Bulletin* 7 (1958): 3.

3. Robert D. Herrema, "The Choral Works of Ulysses Kay," *The Choral Journal* 11 (December 1970): 5.

4. Interview with Ulysses Kay by Constance Hobson, April 12, 1986 in Teaneck, NJ.

5. *Ibid.*

6. *Ibid.*

7. *Ibid.*

8. *Ibid.*

9. *Ibid.*

10. Eileen Southern, "Kay, Ulysses Simpson," *Biographical Dictionary of Afro-American and African Musicians* (Westport, Connecticut/London, England: Greenwood Press, 1982), p. 226.

11. Verna Arvey, *In One Lifetime* (Fayetteville: University of Arkansas Press, 1984), pp. 103-4.

12. Herrema, p. 5.

13. Slonimsky, p. 4.

14. Kay to Hobson.

15. Slonimsky, p. 4.

16. Kay to Hobson.

17. Herrema, p. 6.

18. *Ibid.*

19. Richard Thomas Hadley, "The Published Choral Music of Ulysses Kay," reprinted in *The Choral Journal*, 15 (January 1975): 32.

20. Southern, p. 226.

21. Herrema, p. 9.

22. Baker, p. 146.

23. Kay to Hobson.

24. Baker, pp. 143-44.

25. Slonimsky, p. 3.

26. Ross Parmenter, "Music Composed by Negroes Heard," *New York Times*, May 22, 1950, p. 17.

27. Slonimsky, p.4.

28. Kay to Hobson.

29. Loren Jenkins, "Rome's Embassy of the Arts," *The Washington Post*, September 3, 1988, p. F1.

30. *Ibid.*, p. F6.

31. Oliver Daniel, "Ulysses Kay," *BMI*, composer brochure, 1976.

32. Lucius Wyatt, "Ulysses Kay's Fantasy Variations: An Analysis," *The Black Perspective in Music* 5 (Spring 1977): 75.

33. Kay to Hobson.

34. "Ulysses Kay," *The E. Azalia Hackley Memorial Collection of Negro Music, Dance and Drama*, The Detroit Public Library, Detroit, MI.

35. Ulysses Kay, "Thirty Days in Musical Russia," *Hi-Fi Review*, 2 (February 1959): 36.

36. *Ibid.*, pp. 36-37.

37. Ulysses Kay, "Impressions of the Soviet Musical Scene," *American Composers Alliance Bulletin*, 8 (1959): 17-18.

38. *Ibid.*, p. 18.

39. "The Odyssey of Ulysses," *Down Beat* 25 (October 2, 1958): 11.

40. Nat Hentoff, "Jazz in Print," *Jazz Review* 2 (April 1959): 37.

41. Sally MacDougall, "Music Scales the Iron Curtain," *World-Telegram and Sun Feature*, Magazine Section, January 10, 1959, no page number.

42. Kay, "Thirty Days," p. 53.

43. *Ibid.*, p. 53.

44. Hadley, pp. 48-49.

45. Hope Macleod, "Maker of Music," *New York Post*, June 13, 1968, magazine page three, 47.

46. Daniel, *BMI* brochure.

47. Catherine Dower, "Ulysses Kay: Distinguished American Composer," *Musart* 24 (January/February 1972): 10.

48. Kay to Hobson.

49. *Ibid.*

50. *Ibid.*

51. Daniel, *BMI* brochure.

52. Ann P. Basart, "Music Reviews," *MLA NOTES* 30 (September 1973): 152-53.

53. David Ewen, "Kay, Ulysses Simpson," *American Composers: A Biographical Dictionary* (New York: G.P. Putnam's Sons), 1982, p. 367.

54. Hildred Roach, *Black American Music: Past and Present, Volume II, Pan-African Composers Thenceforth and Now* (Malabar, FL: Robert E. Krieger Publishing Co.), 1985, p. 18.

55. Southern Harmony, "Kay Work Premiered in North Carolina," *Music Club Magazine*, 55 (Spring 1976): 15.

56. Information obtained from promotional materials for the JCPenney release, "A Bicentennial Celebration: 200 years of American Music."

57. Ewen, p. 367.

58. Stucky, Steven. "Orchestral Music," *MLA Notes*, (December 1985): 391.

59. Kay to Hobson.

60. Baker, p. 142.

Works and Performances, 1939–1988

"See" references, e.g., *See also*: B87 and D35, identify citations in the "Bibliography" and "Discography" sections.

- **1939** -

W1.　*SINFONIETTA FOR ORCHESTRA* (MSS only; withdrawn by composer; 14 min.)
　　2-2-2-2, 4-2-0-0, timp, hp, str.
　　See also: B372, B386

　　PREMIERE: 1939 Apr 19; Syracuse, NY; Rochester Civic Orchestra; Howard Hanson, cond.

　　OTHER SELECTED PERFORMANCE

　　W1a.　1941 Mar 4; Tucson, AZ; Tucson Symphony Orchestra; George C. Wilson, cond.

W2.　*SONATINE FOR VIOLA AND PIANO* (MSS withdrawn by composer; 6 min.)
　　In one movement.

W3.　*TEN PIECES FOR CHILDREN* (MSS only; 7 min.)
　　Solo piano.
　　1. "So gay"　2. "Tender thought"　3. "Sprite's dance"　4. "Little tune"　5. "Old lament"　6. "Make believe"　7. "Two voices"　8. "Playing, playing"　9. "Slumber song"　10. "March song."
　　Alternate title: *Ten Short Essays*; originally entitled *Thirteen Pieces for Children*; reduction and retitle by composer.

See also: W63; B204, B396

PREMIERE: 1940 May 27; Rochester, NY; Mary Beeson, piano.

OTHER SELECTED PERFORMANCES

W3a.   1958 May 4; Brooklyn, NY; Brooklyn Academy; Roy Eaton, piano.

W3b.   1963 Apr-May; Decatur, IL; Millikin University Music Department.

- 1940 -

W4.   *CONCERTO FOR OBOE AND ORCHESTRA* (MSS only; withdrawn by composer; 15 min.)
2(picc)-2(Eng hn)-2-2, 4-2-1-0, timp, str.
See also: B373, B386

PREMIERE: 1940 Apr 17; Rochester, NY; Rochester Civic Orchestra; Robert Sprenkle, oboe; Howard Hanson, cond.

W5.   *FIVE MOSAICS* (MSS only; withdrawn by composer; 8 min.)
Chamber orchestra; 1-1-1-1, 2-1-1-0, perc, cel, str.
See also: B372, B386

PREMIERE: 1940 Dec 28; Cleveland, OH; Cleveland Philharmonic Orchestra; F. Karl Grossman, cond.

W6.   *PIANO SONATA* (MSS only; withdrawn by composer; 12 min.)
1. "Allegretto" 2. "Andante" 3. "Allegro."
Won first prize in the Phi Mu Alpha Competition, 1940.

PREMIERE: 1940 Dec 29; Cleveland, OH; Thomas Nichols, piano.

OTHER SELECTED PERFORMANCE

W6a.   1942 Feb 15; New York, NY; League of Composers; Irma Wolpe, piano.

- 1941 -

W7.   *DANSE CALINDA* (MSS only; 25 min.)
Ballet in two scenes.
Theater orchestra; 2-2-2-1, 2-2-2-0, timp, perc, pf, str.

After a story by Ridgeley Torrence.
See also: W29; B386

PREMIERE: 1941 Apr 23; Rochester, NY; Rochester Civic Orchestra; Howard Hanson, cond.

OTHER SELECTED PERFORMANCE

> W7a.   1962 Nov 18; Worcester (MA) Symphony; Harry Levenson, cond.

W8.   *FOUR PIECES FOR MALE CHORUS* (MSS only; 9 min.)
Male Chorus (TTBB); a cappella.
1. "Between two hills" (Carl Sandburg) 2. "Song" (Shakespeare) 3. "With rue my heart is laden" (A. E. Houseman) 4. "Spanish Johnny" (Willa Cather).

PREMIERE: 1948; De Paur Infantry Chorus on tour; Leonard de Paur, cond.

- 1942 -

W9.   *SONATINA FOR VIOLIN AND PIANO* (MSS only; 9 min.)
1. "Allegro moderato" 2. "Andantino" 3. "Allegro."
See also: B168

PREMIERE: 1943 Jan 24; New York, NY; League of Composers; Stefan Frenkel, violin; Leonard Bernstein, piano.

W10.   *THREE FANFARES FOR FOUR TRUMPETS* (DUCH/LEEDS 1964; 4 min.)
Originally entitled *Trumpet Fanfares for Four Trumpets*.
See also: D19; B382

PREMIERE: 1947 Oct 25; New York City; Composer's Forum.

- 1943 -

W11.   *AS JOSEPH WAS A-WALKING* (MSS only; 3 min.)
Mixed chorus (SATB); a cappella.
Text: Anonymous.

W12.   *CHRISTMAS CAROL* (PEER/SO 1957; 3 min.) Women's chorus (SSA); a cappella.
Text: Sara Teasdale.

Private record pressing: University Treble Choir, Illinois State University; Donald Armstrong, cond.
See also: B120, B198, B388

W13.   *FLUTE QUINTET* (MSS only; 14 min.)
Flute and string orchestra.
1. "Allegro" 2. "Adagio" 3. "Allegro moderato."

PREMIERE: 1947 Feb; New York, NY; WNYC Music Festival; Arthur Lora, flute; CBS String Quartet.

W14.   *PRELUDE FOR UNACCOMPANIED FLUTE* (PEM/CF 1976; 2 min.)
Revised in 1975.
See also: D11; B76, B114, B116, B169, B214, B251, B390

PREMIERE: 1953 May 17; Orono, ME; University of Maine; Patricia Damour, flute.

W15.   *SUITE IN B* (MSS only; 12 min.)
Oboe and piano.
1. "Prelude" 2. "Recitative and air" 3. "Dance."

PREMIERE: 1949 Nov 29; American Academy in Rome; Pietro Accaroni, oboe; Gherardo Macarini, piano.

OTHER SELECTED PERFORMANCES

W15a. 1958 May 4; Brooklyn, NY; Brooklyn Academy; Alen Tormy, flute; Alan Booth, piano.

W15b.   1958 May 25; New York, NY; Five Spot Cafe; Antoinette Handy, flute; Robert Pritchard, piano.

W16.   *SUITE FOR BRASS CHOIR* (MSS only; withdrawn by composer; 9 min.)
4(trp)-4(hn)-3(trb-tuba).
1. "Fanfare and lyric" 2. "Chorale" 3. "Toccata."
See also: B370, B386

PREMIERE: 1947; Cincinnati, OH; Cincinnati Conservatory of Music.

OTHER SELECTED PERFORMANCES

W16a. 1958 Nov 3; Fort Meade, MD; Fort Meade Service Club; members of the US Army Field Band; Richard Pittman, dir.

W16b. 1962 May 17; Baltimore, MD; Peabody Conservatory of Music; Brass Ensemble; Armand Sarro, cond.

W17.   *DUO FOR FLUTE AND OBOE* (DUCH/MCA 1964; 5 min.)
1. "Allegretto" 2. "Andantino" 3. "Allegro."
Alternate title: *Suite for Flute and Oboe*.
See also: D18; B87, B88, B91, B120, B370, B382, B394

PREMIERE: 1947 Oct 25; New York, NY; Composer's Forum; Carleton Sprague Smith, flute; Antonio Estevez, oboe.

OTHER SELECTED PERFORMANCES

W17a. 1953 May 17; Orono, ME; University of Maine; Carole Shoemaker, flute; Beverly Pettengill, clarinet.

W17b. 1961 Jan 8; Summit, NJ; Chamber Music Circle; New York Chamber Soloist.

W17c. 1961 Feb 28; Teaneck, NJ; Chamber Music Circle.

W17d. 1964 Aug 30; Woodstock, NY; Maverick Concert Hall; John Solum, flute; Melvil Kaplan, oboe.

- 1944 -

W18.   *COME AWAY, COME AWAY DEATH* (PEER/SO 1954; 3 min.)
Male chorus (TTB); a cappella.
Text: Shakespeare.
See also: B120, B236

PREMIERE: 1948; De Paur Infantry Chorus on tour; Leonard de Paur, cond.

W19.   *EVOCATION* (MSS only; 10 min.)
Concert band; picc-2(f1)-2(ob)-Eng hn-1(E^b cl)-3(B^b cl)-bass cl-2(alto sax)-tenor sax-baritone sax-4(hn)-3(crnt)-bar hn-3(trb)-tuba, timp, perc.
See also: B372

PREMIERE: 1946 May 10; Detroit, MI; Wayne State University; Wayne State University Band; Graham T. Overgard, cond.

W20.   *OF NEW HORIZONS: OVERTURE* (CFP 1953; 8 min.)
Orchestra; 3(picc)-3-3-3, 4-3-3-1, timp, hp, pf(cel), str; PR.
Commissioned by Thor Johnson; awarded the American
Broadcasting Company Prize, 1946.
See also: D9; B4, B15, B39, B78, B80, B103, B117, B120, B158,
B180, B269, B271, B273, B393, B394, B395, B400

PREMIERE: 1944 Jul 29; New York, NY; Lewisohn Stadium; New
York Philharmonic; Thor Johnson, cond.

OTHER SELECTED PERFORMANCES

W20a. 1947 Mar 10; New York, NY; Carnegie Hall; Juilliard
School Orchestra; Thor Johnson, cond.

W20b.   1954 Feb 23; Tucson, AZ; Tucson Symphony
Orchestra; the composer, guest cond.

W20c. 1956 Feb 5; Madrid, Spain; Orquesta de Madrid at
Teatro Monumental; Everett Lee, cond.

W20d. 1956 Feb 7; Barcelona, Spain; Orquesta Filarmónica de
Barcelona at Palacio de la Música; Everett Lee, cond.

W20e. 1957 Nov 20; Malmo, Sweden; Konserthus Orchestra.

W20f. 1957 Nov; Denver Symphony; Saul Caston, cond.

W20g.   1958 Oct 15; Moscow, USSR; Tchaikovsky Hall;
Moscow State Radio Orchestra; Gennady Rozhdestvensky,
cond.

W20h. 1962 Mar 5; University of Arizona Symphony; Henry
Johnson, cond.

W20i. 1962 May 5; Hofstra Symphony; Elie Siegmeister, cond.

W20j.   1963 Oct 19; Villanova, PA; American Symphony
Orchestra; Leopold Stokowski, cond.

W20k. 1963 Oct 21; New York, NY; Carnegie Hall; American
Symphony Orchestra; Leopold Stokowski, cond.

W20l.   1964; Peru; Orquesta Sinfónica Nacional of Lima;
Rodolfo Barbacci, cond.

W20m.   1964 Aug 28; Brevard, NC; Brevard Festival
Orchestra; James Christian Pfohl, cond.

W20n.   1964 Nov 21; Portland, OR; Portland Junior Symphony Orchestra; Jacob Avshalomov, cond.

W20o.   1967 May 10; University of California at Santa Barbara; the composer, guest cond.

W20p.   1967 May 14; Long Beach, CA; Long Beach State College Orchestra; the composer, guest cond.

W20q.   1967 May 15; Seattle Youth Symphony; Vilem Sokol, cond.

W20r.   1969 Oct 23, 24, 27; Chicago Symphony; Irwin Hoffman, cond.

W20s.   1970 Mar 17, 23; three performances: St. Petersburg, FL; Florida Gulf Coast Symphony; Irwin Hoffman, cond.

W20t.   1971 Jun 30; Chicago, IL; Grant Park Symphony.

W20u.   1975 May 22; New York, NY; Inaugural Concert for the New York City Bicentennial Celebration; Symphony of the New World; Everett Lee, cond.

W20v.   1977 Jan 12, 15, 17; Chicago Symphony; Irwin Hoffman, cond.

W20w.   1977 Jan 22, 23, 27, 29; Feb 2,3; New Jersey Symphony; Irwin Hoffman, cond.

W20x.   1980 Jan 20; Buffalo, NY; Nov 16; New York, NY; Carnegie Hall; Buffalo Philharmonic; Julius Rudel, cond.

W20y.   1983 Feb 12; Bronx Symphony Orchestra; Joseph Dellicarri, cond.

- **1945** -

W21.   *SUITE FOR ORCHESTRA* (AMP; 19 min.)
           3-3-3-3, 4-3-3-1, timp, perc, pf, str.
           1. "Fanfare"   2. "Three-four"   3. "Scherzo"   4. "Olden tune: finale."
           See also: B35, B39, B72, B120, B193, B255, B263, B271, B317, B386, B393, B398

PREMIERE: 1950 May 21; New York, NY; Town Hall; American Youth Orchestra; Dean Dixon, cond. Won the BMI prize in 1947.

OTHER SELECTED PERFORMANCES

W21a.   1952 Jan 4; Turin, Italy; Italian National Network Broadcast; Torino Radio Orchestra; Dean Dixon, cond.

W21b.   1961 Jan; Sante Fe, NM; Rio Grande Symphony; John Hiersioux, cond.

W21c.   1962 May 20; Kansas City Civic Orchestra; Hugo Vianella, cond.

W21d.   1964 Sep 12, 13; New York, NY; Delacourte Theater; New York Orchestral Society; Joseph Eger, cond.

- 1946 -

W22.   *BRIEF ELEGY* (DUCH; 4 min.)
           Oboe and string orchestra.
           Alternate title: *Allegro for Oboe and Strings*; also arranged for oboe and piano.
           See also: B13, B120, B318, B386, B397

PREMIERE: 1948 May 9, Washington, DC; National Gallery of Art; National Gallery Orchestra; L. Shifrin, oboe; Richard Bales, cond.

OTHER SELECTED PERFORMANCES

W22a.   1956 Aug 18; Oyster Bay, Long Island, NY; Long Island Music Festival Concert; Long Island Little Orchestra; Clara Burling Roesch, cond.

W22b.   1962 Nov 18; Worcester (MA) Symphony; Harry Levenson, cond.

W22c.   1963 Apr-May; Decatur, IL; Millikin University Music Department.

W23.   *DEDICATION* (MSS only; withdrawn by composer; 8 min.)
           Mixed chorus (SATB); a cappella.
           Text by the composer.

W24.   *EIGHT INVENTIONS* (MSS; 8 min.)
       Solo piano.
       Revised and retitled *Four Inventions*.
       See also: W25; B73

       WASHINGTON, DC PREMIERE: 1952 Jun 8; Washington, DC;
       National Gallery of Art; Thomas H. Kerr, piano; *Five
       Inventions* performed.

W25.   *FOUR INVENTIONS* (DUCH/MCA; 5 min.)
       Solo piano.
       Originally entitled *Eight Inventions*; revision by composer.
       See also: W24; D6; B7, B34, B40, B175, B233, B271, B339, B396

       PREMIERE: 1947 Sep 29; New York, NY; Town Hall; Lucy
       Brown, piano.

       OTHER SELECTED PERFORMANCES

       W25a. 1977 Apr 26; Washington, DC; Catholic University of
       America; Ruth Norman, piano.

       W25b. 1980 Jan 15; Washington, DC; Kennedy Center;
       National Black Music Colloquium and Competition; Sharon
       Barron, piano.

       W25c. 1980 Feb 15; Washington, DC; National Gallery of Art;
       Raymond Jackson, piano.

       W25d. 1988 Feb 10; Hampton, VA; Ogden Hall; Hampton
       University; Nina Kennedy, piano.

W26.   *THE ROPE* (MSS only; 12 min.)
       Solo dancer and piano.
       Commissioned by Eleanore Goff; revised and retitled *Ancient Saga*
       by composer; 1947.

       PREMIERE: 1947 Jan 12; New York, NY; Kaufman Auditorium;
       92nd Street YMHA; Eleanore Goff, dancer.

W27.   *A SHORT OVERTURE* (DUCH/MCA 1973; 7 min.)
       Orchestra; 2(picc)-2-2-2, 2-2-2-0, timp, perc, str; PR.
       Won the Third Annual George Gershwin Memorial Award in
       1947.
       See also: D15; B122, B189, B212, B245, B271, B298, B309, B386,
       B390, B394

       PREMIERE: 1947 Mar 31; Brooklyn, NY; Academy of Music; New
       York City Symphony Orchestra; Leonard Bernstein, cond.

OTHER SELECTED PERFORMANCES

W27a.   1970 Apr-May; eight performances; Oakland Youth Symphony; Robert Hughes, cond.

W27b.   1979 Jun 3; Washington, DC; Peoples Congregational United Church of Christ; Urban Philharmonic; Darrold Hunt, cond.

W27c.   1992 Sep 25; Washington, DC; St. Paul's Lutheran Church; Washington Philharmonic Orchestra; Darrold Hunt, cond.

- 1947 -

W28.   *ANCIENT SAGA* (PEM/CF; 8 min.)
         Solo piano and string orchestra.
         Revision of earlier work entitled *The Rope* (1946).
         See also: B386

W29.   *DANSE CALINDA SUITE* (PEM/CF; 14 min.)
         Orchestra; 2(picc)-1(Eng hn)-2-1, 2-2-2-0, timp, perc, pf, str.
         Alternate title: *Suite from the Ballet "Danse Calinda."*
         Won the Anna Bobbit Gardner Award; Boston, MA; 1947.
         See also: W7; B372, B386

         PREMIERE: 1947 May 23; New York, NY; National Orchestral Association; Leon Barzin, cond.

W30.   *SONG OF JEREMIAH* (PEM/CF; 19 min.)
         Cantata for bass-baritone solo, mixed chorus (SATB), and
             orchestra; 2(picc)-2(Eng hn)-2-2, 2-2-2-1, timp, perc, hp, pf, str.
         Text: Biblical.
         Revision of *Song of Jeremiah*; originally written in 1945 for
             baritone, women's chorus (SSA), and organ.
         See also: B35, B78, B195

         PREMIERE: 1954 Apr 23; Nashville, TN; Roy Petty, baritone; Fisk University Choir; Harry von Bergen, cond.

         OTHER SELECTED PERFORMANCE

         W30a. 1955 May 22; New York, NY; Town Hall; Eugene Brice baritone; Interracial Fellowship Chorus; Harold Aks, cond.

W31.   *SUITE FOR STRINGS* (CFP 1961; 14 min.)
         String orchestra.

1. "Andante sostenuto" 2. "Lento" 3. "Allegro."
Alternate title: *Little Suite for String Orchestra.*
See also: B72, B102, B120, B220, B263, B264, B400

PREMIERE: 1949 Apr 18; Baltimore, MD; Baltimore Chamber Orchestra; the composer, guest conductor.

OTHER SELECTED PERFORMANCES

W31a. 1952 Jan 15; Italian Third Program from Naples; Allessandro Scarlatti Orchestra; Dean Dixon, cond.

W31b. 1952 Oct 26; New York, NY; Museum of Modern Art; Chamber Orchestra; Leopold Stokowski, cond.

W31c. 1954 May 16; Orono, ME; University of Maine.

W31d. 1962 May 29; Dortmund (Germany) Chamber Orchestra.

W31e. 1963 Sep-Oct; tour of the USSR; Clarion Orchestra; Newell Jenkins, cond.

- 1948 -

W32.   *CONCERTO FOR ORCHESTRA* (PEM/CF; 18 min.)
          2(picc)-2-2-2, 4-3-3-1, timp, perc, str.
          1. "Toccata" 2. "Arioso" 3. "Passacaglia."
          See also: D3; B18, B37, B104, B190, B195, B298

          PREMIERE: 1953; Venice, Italy; Teatro La Fenice Orchestra; Jonel Perlea, cond.

          OTHER SELECTED PERFORMANCES

          W32a. 1954 Feb; New York, NY; Cooper Union; David Broekman, cond.

          W32b. 1970; Rochester, NY; Eastman Philharmonic; Jonathan Sternberg, cond.

W33.   *PORTRAIT SUITE* (PEM/CF; 18 min.)
          Orchestra; 3-2-2-2, 4-3-3-1, timp, str.
          1. "Prologue"   2. "Asymetric"   3. "Reclining figure"
          4. "Blossoming" 5. "Epilogue."
          Won the Phoenix Symphony Orchestra Award for the best composition by a native Arizonan, 1948.   Movement 2

suggested by two sculptures by Wilhelm Lehmbruch: *Kneeling Woman* and *Rising Youth*; movement 3 suggested by Henry Moore's *Reclining Figure*; movement 4 suggested by the sculpture, *Blossoming*, by Jacques Lipchitz.
See also: B70, B372, B386

PREMIERE: 1964 Apr 24; Erie, PA; Erie Philharmonic; James Sample, cond.

W34.   *THE QUIET ONE* (PEM/CF; 50 min.)
Film score (16 mm).
A Film Documents, Inc. Production; James Agee, commentary and Richard Bagley, photography.
See also: W35; B39

W35.   *SUITE FROM "THE QUIET ONE"* (PEM/CF; 16 min.)
Orchestra; 1(picc)-1-1-1, 1-1-1-0, timp, perc, pf (cel), vib, str.
1. "Joys and fears"   2. "Street wanderings"   3. "Interlude"   4. "Crisis."
Alternate title: *"The Quiet One" Suite*.
See also: W34; B372

PREMIERE: 1948 Nov 19; New York, NY; Times Hall; New York Little Symphony; the composer, guest cond.

OTHER SELECTED PERFORMANCE

W35a.   1949 Sep; Saratoga Springs, NY; Yaddo Music Group Chamber Orchestra; Dean Dixon, cond.

- 1949 -

W36.   *PIANO QUINTET* (PEM/CF; 25 min.)
Piano and string quartet.
1. "Allegretto"   2. "Adagio"   3. "Allegro."
Alternate title: *Quintet for Piano and Strings*.
See also: B78, B168

PREMIERE: 1949 Nov 29; American Academy in Rome; Gherardo Macarini, piano; Quartetto della Radio di Roma.

OTHER SELECTED PERFORMANCES

W36a.   1954 Apr 18; Washington, DC; National Gallery of Art; Evelyn Swarthout, piano; American University String Quartet.

W36b. 1956 May 8-11; Bloomington, IL; Illinois Wesleyan
University; Second Annual Contemporary Arts Festival;
Dwight Drexler, piano; faculty quartet.

W36c. 1958 May 1; Rochester, NY; 28th Annual Eastman
School Festival.

W37. *STRING QUARTET NO. 1* (MSS only; withdrawn by composer;
26 min.)
1. "Allegro" 2. "Andante" 3. "Allegro scherzando" 4. "Allegro
moderato."
See also: B194

PREMIERE: 1953 May 24; Washington, DC; National Gallery of
Art; American University String Quartet.

OTHER SELECTED PERFORMANCE

W37a. 1956 Apr 29; Community Church, NY; Cumbo String
Quartet.

W38. *SOLEMN PRELUDE* (AMP 1950; 5 min.)
Concert band; 3-3-6-2, 4(sax), 4-3(cor)-2(trp)-4(bar)-1, timp, perc.
Commissioned by the Baylor University Band.
See also: B29

PREMIERE: 1950 Feb 16; Waco, TX; Baylor University; Baylor
University Golden Wave Band; Donald I. Moore, cond.

OTHER SELECTED PERFORMANCES

W38a. 1952 May 7; Rochester, NY; Eastman Theater;
Eastman School Symphony Band; Frederick Fennell, cond.

W38b. 1963 Apr-May; Decatur, IL; Millikin University Music
Department.

- 1950 -

W39. *BRASS QUARTET* (PEER/SO; 10 min.)
Two trumpets and two trombones.
1. "Fantasia" 2. "Arioso" 3. "Toccata."
Alternate title: *Quartet for 2 Trumpets, Tenor and Bass
Trombones*.
See also: D1; B75, B120, B256, B270, B395, B397

PREMIERE: 1952 Oct 12, Brooklyn, NY; Brooklyn Museum; Third Street Music School Quartet (Gotham Brass Ensemble).

OTHER SELECTED PERFORMANCES

W39a.   1956 May 8-11; Bloomington, IL; Illinois Wesleyan University student quartet.

W39b.   1958 Dec 18; Champaign-Urbana, IL; University of Illinois; Richard Tolley and John Stettler, trumpets; Thomas Wright and William Gallo, trombones.

W39c.   1962 Mar 3; New York, NY; Judson Hall; American Brass Ensemble.

W40.   *FUGITIVE SONGS* (PEM/CF; 18 min.)
Medium voice and piano.
1. "Song is old" (Herman Hagedorn) 2. "That day you came" (Lizette Reese) 3. "When the wind is low" (Carl Young Rice) 4. "Even song" (Ridgeley Torrence) 5. "The Fugitives" (Florence Wilkerson) 6. "The Mystic" (Wittner Bynner) 7. "Sentence" (Wittner Bynner) 8. "When I am dead" (Elsa Baxter).
See also: B80, B197, B199

PREMIERE: 1956 May 10; Bloomington, IL; Illinois Wesleyan University; Ann Rothschild, soprano; Barbara Cobb, piano (three songs).

OTHER SELECTED PERFORMANCES

W40a.   1958 Sep 28; New York, NY; Town Hall; Eugene Brice, baritone; Jonathan Brice, piano (first complete performance).

W40b.   1979 Nov 5; Champaign-Urbana, IL; University of Illinois; Carol McDougall, mezzo-soprano; Eric Dalheim, piano.

W41.   *PARTITA IN A* (PEM/CF 1979; 15 min.)
Violin and piano.
1. "Prelude" 2. "Burlesca" 3. "Interlude" 4. "Echo."
See also: B6, B168, B196, B396

PREMIERE: 1952 Apr 15; American Academy in Rome; Vittorio Emanuele, violin; R. Josi, piano.

OTHER SELECTED PERFORMANCES

W41a. 1954 Apr 25; New York, NY; Eastman Alumni Concert; Dorothy Happel, violin; Darrell Peter, piano.

W41b. 1955 Oct 5; New York, NY; Town Hall; Anahid Ajemian, violin; David Garvey, piano.

W41c. 1955 Nov; Houston TX; Anahid Ajemian (Sigma Alpha Iota Honorary Member).

W41d. 1979 Nov 5; Champaign-Urbana, IL; University of Illinois; Paul Rolland, violin; Stanley Fletcher, piano.

W41e. 1980 Jan 15; Washington, DC; Kennedy Center; National Black Music Colloquium and Competition; John McLaughlin Williams, violin.

W42. *PIETÀ* (PEM/CF 1978; 7 min.)
English horn and string orchestra.
Reduction by composer, for English horn and piano available.
See also: B12, B79, B184, B218, B261, B396

PREMIERE: 1958 Feb 12; New York, NY; Town Hall; 19th Annual Festival of American Music; Doris Goltzer, English horn; Knickerbocker Chamber Orchestra; Herman Neumann, cond.

OTHER SELECTED PERFORMANCES

W42a. 1985 Mar 19; New York, NY; American Composers Orchestra.

W42b. 1988 Feb 8; Hoboken, NY; Hoboken Chamber Orchestra; Gary Schneider, cond.

W43. *SHORT SUITE* (AMP; 7 min.)
Concert band; 3-3-6-2, 4(sax), 4-3(cor)-2(trp)-4(bar)-1, str bass, timp, perc.
1. "Fanfare" 2. "March" 3. "Interlude" 4. "Lyric" 5. "Finale."
To be played without pause.
Alternate title: *Short Suite for Band*.
See also: B29, B135, B196, B197, B199

PREMIERE: 1951 May 8; Waco, TX; Baylor University; Baylor University Golden Wave Band; Donald I. Moore, cond.

OTHER SELECTED PERFORMANCES

W43a. 1958 Jul 25; New York, NY; Central Park; Goldman Band.

W43b. 1959 Jul 24; Brevard, NC; The Brevard Music Center; Transylvania Concert Band; James Christian Pfohl, cond.

W43c. 1963 Apr-May; Decatur, IL; Millikin University Music Department.

W44.   *SINFONIA IN E* (PEM/CF; 20 min.)
Orchestra; 2-2-2-2, 4-3-3-1, timp, str.
1. "Larghetto" 2. "Allegro pesante" 3. "Adagio" 4. "Allegro."
Alternate title: *Symphony in E*.
See also: D16; B78, B88, B132, B203, B214, B239, B386, B396

PREMIERE: 1951 May 2; Rochester, NY; Eastman-Rochester Symphony Orchestra; Howard Hanson, cond.

OTHER SELECTED PERFORMANCES

W44a. 1954 Apr 1, 3; Cleveland (OH) premiere; Cleveland Symphony Orchestra; George Szell, cond.

W44b. 1961 Feb 19; Charleston, WV; Charleston Symphony Orchestra; Geoffrey Hobday, cond.

W44c. 1962 May 1; Tucson Symphony Orchestra; the composer, guest cond.

W44d. 1962 Nov 18; Worcester (MA) Symphony; Harry Levenson, cond.

W44e. 1987; Savannah, GA; Savannah Symphony; Julius P. Williams, guest cond.

W45.   *SONG OF AHAB* (MSS only 20 min.)
Cantata for baritone and ten instruments; 1-0-1-0, 1-1-0-0, timp, perc, pf, str.
Commissioned by the Quincy Fine Arts Society.
See also: B125, B258, B289

PREMIERE: 1951 May 17; Quincy, IL; J. Leslie Pierce, baritone; Quincy Chamber Music Ensemble; George Irwin, cond.

W45a. 1958 June 8; New York, NY; Kaufmann Concert Hall; George Irving, bass-baritone; Milton Rosenstock, cond.

W45b. 1958 Oct 15; New York, NY; Lyric Chamber Theater; Milton Rosenstock, cond.

W46. *TWO MEDITATIONS* (HWG; 5 min.)
Organ.
Included in the *Contemporary Organ Series, #27*.
See also: B39, B75, B120, B219, B249, B265, B293, B398

PREMIERE: 1952 Nov 23; Nashville, TN; Fisk University; Arthur Crowley, organ.

OTHER SELECTED PERFORMANCES

W46a. 1953 Feb 1; CBS Network program; E. Power Biggs, organ (the first meditation).

W46b. 1955 April 25; Lemgo, Germany; Internationale Orget-Woche; David Pizarro, organ (first performance of entire work).

W46c. 1957 Oct 16; New York, NY; St. Paul's Chapel; Peter M. Fyfe, organ.

W46d. 1957 Nov 3; New York, NY; Corpus Christie Church; Leonard Raver, organ.

W46e. 1963 Apr-May; Decatur, IL; Millikin University Music Department.

W46f. 1964 Sep 20; Nashville, TN; Christ Episcopal Church.

W46g. 1988 Sep 13; Ann Arbor, MI; University of Michigan, Hill Auditorium; Brandon de Wilder Spence, A. Mus. D. candidate, organ.

- 1951 -

W47. *THE LION, THE GRIFFIN AND THE KANGAROO* (MSS only; 12 min.)
Film Score; fl-cl-bsn, hn-trp, 1 perc, str quartet.
Commissioned by Peter Hollander; Hollander-Tait Productions documentary film, made in Italy.
See also: B72

- 1952 -

W48.   *THREE PIECES AFTER BLAKE* (PEM/CF; 14 min.)
         Dramatic soprano and orchestra; 1-1-2-1, 2-2-1-0, timp, perc, str.
         Text: William Blake.
         1. "To the evening star" 2. "Mad song" 3. "Contemplation."
         Included in "Music in the Making" series.
         See also: W88; B3, B60, B101, B109, B128, B133, B188, B276,
             B395

         PREMIERE: 1955 Mar 27; New York, NY; Cooper Union; Shirlee
             Emmons, soprano; David Broekman, cond.

         OTHER SELECTED PERFORMANCE

             W48a. 1977 Aug 29-Sep 2; New York, NY; A Celebration of
                 Black Composers; New York Philharmonic Chamber
                 Orchestra; Irene Oliver, soprano; Paul Freeman and Leon
                 Thompson, conds.

- 1953 -

W49.   *A LINCOLN LETTER* (CFP 1958; 4:30 min.)
         Mixed chorus (SATB); bass soloist; a cappella.
         Text: "The Bixby Letter," supposedly by Abraham Lincoln.
         Dedicated to Carl Haverlin.
         See also: B120, B183, B194, B199, B220, B393, B394

         PREMIERE: 1953 Sep 1; Lincoln, IL; Bruce Foote, bass; College
             Choir of Lincoln College; William Tagg, cond.

         OTHER SELECTED PERFORMANCES

             W49a. 1954 Nov 21; San Francisco, CA; Schola Cantorum of
                 the University of San Francisco; Giovanni Camajani, cond.

             W49b. 1955 May 25; San Francisco, CA; the M. H. de Young
                 Memorial Museum; Vahan Toolajian, baritone; Schola
                 Cantorum of the University of San Francisco; Giovanni
                 Camajani, cond.

W50.   *TRIUMVIRATE* (PEER/SO 1954; 12 min.)
         Male chorus (TTBB); a cappella.
         1. "Music" (Ralph Waldo Emerson) 2. "Children's hour" (Henry
         Wadsworth Longfellow) 3. "Night March" (Herman Manville).

Commissioned by Leonard de Paur for the De Paur Infantry Chorus.
See also: B78, B120

PREMIERE: 1954 Oct 17, New York, NY; Hunter College; De Paur Infantry Chorus; Leonard de Paur, cond.

OTHER SELECTED PERFORMANCES

W50a. 1953-54; American tour; De Paur Infantry Chorus; Leonard de Paur, cond.

W50b. 1954 Jan/Feb; tour of Japan; De Paur Infantry Chorus; Leonard de Paur, cond.

W50c. 1955 Apr 10; New York, NY; Carnegie Hall; De Paur Infantry Chorus; Leonard de Paur, cond.

- 1954 -

W51. *HOW STANDS THE GLASS AROUND?* (AMP 1956; 3 min.)
Mixed Chorus (SSATB); a cappella.
Text: James Wolfe.
Commissioned by The Randolph Singers; originally part of work entitled, *Two Madrigals*.
See also: W54, W55; D20; B51, B94, B165, B197, B322

PREMIERE: 1955 Jul 24; Weston, VT; Weston Playhouse; The Randolph Singers; David Randolph, cond.

OTHER SELECTED PERFORMANCES

W51a. 1955 Sep 27; New York, NY; Carnegie Hall; The Randolph Singers; David Randolph, cond.

W51b. 1959 Mar 2; Moscow, ID; University of Idaho; Music Building, Recital Hall; Festival of Contemporary Music; student choral group; Glenn R. Lockery, cond.

W52. *SERENADE FOR ORCHESTRA* (AMP 1955; 18 min.)
2(picc)-2-2-2, 4-2-3-1, timp, str.
1. "Andante amabile" 2. "Presto" 3. "Elegy" 4. "Allegro."
Commissioned by the Louisville Philharmonic Society.
See also: D14; B106, B120, B167, B195, B232, B386, B395, B397

PREMIERE: 1954 Sep 18; Louisville, KY; Louisville Orchestra; Robert Whitney, cond.

> W52a. 1956 Feb 18; New York, NY; Carnegie Hall; NAACC [sic] Concert; Alfredo Antonini, cond.

> W52b. 1956 May 24; Berlin, Germany; Hochschule für Musik; West Berlin Radio Symphony Orchestra; Moritz Bomhard, cond.

> W52c. 1960 Sep 24; Toronto, Canada; Canadian Broadcasting Company Orchestra.

> W52d. 1966 Nov 3, 4, 6; Chicago Symphony; Jean Martinon, cond.

> W52e. 1971 Jan 23; New York Philharmonic; Young Peoples Concert; Dean Dixon, cond.

> W52f. 1971 Mar 9, 19; Detroit Symphony; Paul Freeman, cond.

W53.   *SIX DANCES FOR STRING ORCHESTRA* (DUCH 1965; 18 min.)
1. "Schottische" 2. "Waltz" 3. "Round dance" 4. "Polka"
5. "Promenade" 6. "Galop."
Alternate title: *American Dances.*
Included in the Leeds "Contemporary Classics for String Series," Alfred Antonini, cond. "Round Dance" and "Polka" often performed separately; recorded separately; alternate title: *Two Dances.*
See also: D12, D17; B78, B120, B194, B195, B266, B281

PREMIERE: 1953 May 10; excerpts performed on CBS Radio; "String Serenade;" Alfred Antonini, cond.

> W53a.   1962 Nov 18; Worcester (MA) Symphony; Harry Levenson, cond.

> W53b.   1963 Oct 31; Canadian Broadcasting Corporation; Vancouver Orchestra; Glen Morley, cond.

W54.   *TWO MADRIGALS* (7 min.)
Mixed Chorus (SSATB); a cappella.
Each part published separately.
1. "How stands the glass around?" (AMP 1956; 3 min.)
2. "What's in a name?" (DUCH/LEEDS 1956; 4 min.).
See also: W51, W55; D20; B51, B195, B320

W55. *WHAT'S IN A NAME?* (DUCH/LEEDS 1956; 4 min.)
      Mixed chorus (SSATB); a cappella.
      Text: Helen F. More.
      Inscription: "Before the battle of Lexington, William Dawes and
      Paul Revere were both despatch (sic) to rouse the county,
      Dawes starting first. . . ."   Dedicated to The Randolph
      Singers; originally part of work entitled *Two Madrigals*.
      Included in the "Leeds Masterwork Choral Series."
      See also: W51, W54; D20; B51, B197, B322

      PREMIERE: 1955; on tour; The Randolph Singers; David Randolph,
      cond.

W56. *A WREATH FOR WAITS* (AMP 1956; 7 min.)
      Mixed chorus (SATB); a cappella.
      Text: Anonymous.
      1. "Noel" (2 min.) 2. "Lully lullay" (3 min.) 3. "Welcome yule"
      (2 min.).
      Commissioned by the Cornell University A Cappella Chorus; each
      piece published separately.
      See also: B118, B195, B196, B390

      PREMIERE: 1954 Dec 28; Ann Arbor, MI; Cornell University A
      Cappella Chorus; Robert Hull, cond.

      OTHER SELECTED PERFORMANCES

          W56a. 1960; Bloomington, IL; Illinois Wesleyan University;
          "Welcome Yule" performed by the Collegiate Choir; Lewis
          E. Whikehart, cond.

          W56b. 1971 Jul 21; Nashville, TN; Fisk University; "Lully
          Lullay" performed by the BSIM Chorale (Black Studies in
          Music Chorale).

          W56c. 1976 Dec 5; Washington, DC; National Gallery of Art;
          "Welcome Yule" performed by the Evelyn White Chorale;
          Evelyn White, cond.

- **1955** -

W57. *THE BOOR* (PEM/CF; 40 min.)
      Opera in one-act.
      Soprano, tenor, baritone soli, orchestra; 1(picc)-1(Eng hn)-1-1,
      1-1-1-0, timp, perc, pf, str.
      Libretto: Anton Chekov; translation: Vladimir Ussachevsky;
      adapted by the composer.

Commissioned by the Koussevitsky Foundation of the Library of Congress; dedicated to the memory of Serge and Natalie Koussevitsky.
See also: B41, B356

PREMIERE: 1968 Apr 2; Lexington, KY; University of Kentucky; concert performance.

W58.   *GRACE TO YOU, AND PEACE* (HWG 1957; 5 min.)
Mixed chorus (SATB) and organ.
Text: Biblical (adaption by Theodore Melnechuk).
Awarded first prize in the Moravian Anthem Contest (1956).
See also: B144, B197, B198, B238, B387

PREMIERE: 1956 May 20; Bethlehem, PA; Sesquicentennial Service; Central Moravian Church Choir; Robert Hall Elmore, organist-choirmaster.

OTHER SELECTED PERFORMANCE

W58a.   1958 Oct 12; Bethelehem, PA; Central Moravian Church; Central Moravian Choir; Festival Service and Dedication of the Möller Organ; Robert Elmore, organist-choirmaster.

W59.   *A NEW SONG* (CFP 1961; 8:30 min.)
Mixed chorus (SATB); a cappella.
Text: Biblical.
1. "Sing unto the Lord" (3:30 min.) 2. "Like as a Father" (2:30 min.) 3. "O Praise the Lord" (2:30 min.).
Alternate title: *Three Psalms for Chorus*.
Commissioned by the Illinois Wesleyan University College Choir; each piece published separately.
See also: D8; B79, B99, B144, B196, B197, B202, B390

PREMIERE: 1956 May 8-11; Bloomington, IL; Illinois Wesleyan University; Annual Symposium on Contemporary American Music; Illinois Wesleyan College Choir; Lloyd Pfautch, cond.

OTHER SELECTED PERFORMANCES

W59a.   1958; tour; Illinois Wesleyan Collegiate Choir.

W59b.   1959 Oct 18, Nov 15; Boston, MA; "Like as a Father;" King's Chapel Choir; Daniel Pinkham, cond.

W59c.   1962 Jan 14; New York, NY; Master Institute Theater; Master Institute Chorus and Orchestra; David Labovitz, cond.

- 1956 -

W60. *THE JUGGLER OF OUR LADY* (PEM/CF; 50 min.)
Opera in one-act.
Fifteen solo voices (1 soprano, 1 boy soprano, 2 mezzo-sopranos, 1 contralto, 3 tenors, 4 baritones, 3 basses); mixed chorus (SATB); and orchestra; 1(picc)-1-2-1, 1-1-1-0, timp, perc, hp, str.
Libretto: Alexander King.
See also: B1, B19, B26, B41, B52, B53, B127, B157, B177, B274, B294, B328

PREMIERE: 1962 Feb 23, 25; New Orleans, LA; Xavier University Opera Workshop (under the sponsorship of Sister M. Elise); Richard Harrison, dir.; Alex McDonald, choir dir.; Patricia Euth, stage dir. and settings designer; Mervin Wallace, tenor.

OTHER SELECTED PERFORMANCES

W60a. 1972 Nov 17, 19; Jackson, MS; Municipal Auditorium; Opera/South; Mervin Wallace, Benjamin Matthews, Wilma Shakesnider, Clyde Walker, Cornel Richie, soloists; Hollis Pippins, Lina Cleveland, James Gordon, dancers; Donald Dorr, designer and director; Margaret Harris, cond.

W60b. 1979 Aug 11; Brevard, NC; Brevard Music Center Opera Workshop; John R. McCrae, producer.

W61. *STRING QUARTET NO.2* (PEM; 18 min.)
1. "Allegretto" 2. "Adagio" 3. "Allegro agitato" 4. "Larghetto."
See also: B84, B86

PREMIERE: 1959 Nov 6; Champaign-Urbana, IL; University of Illinois; The Walden String Quartet.

OTHER SELECTED PERFORMANCE

W61a. 1985 Aug 10; Ann Arbor, MI; University of Michigan; Black American Music Symposium; Heritage String Quartet.

- 1957 -

W62. *SERENADE NO. 2* (DUCH/LEEDS 1964; 12 min.)
Four F Horns.

1. "Prelude"   2. "Arietta"   3. "Toccata"   4. "Fantasy"
5. "Epilogue."
Alternate title: *Serenade for Four Horns.*
Included in the "Leeds Music for Wind Series" (1954).
See also: B397

PREMIERE: 1959 Nov 5; Champaign-Urbana, IL; University of
Illinois; Thomas Holden, Kathryn Dieterich, Jan Bach, and
Richard Ely, horns.

W63.   *TEN SHORT ESSAYS* (DUCH/MCA; 7 min.)
Solo piano.
1. "So gay"   2. "Tender thought"   3. "Sprite's dance"   4. "Little
tune"   5. "Old lament"   6. "Make believe"   7. "Two voices"
8. "Playing, playing"   9. "Slumber Song"   10. "March Song."
Alternate title: *Ten Pieces for Children*; reduction and retitle of
earlier work, *Thirteen Pieces for Children.*
See also: W3; B34, B175, B339, B395, B400

W64.   *TWO SHORT PIECES* (GR/FC; 5 min.)
Piano (4 hands).
1. "Prelude"   2. "Moto perpetuo."

WASHINGTON, DC PREMIERE: 1982 Jan 21; Howard University;
"Meet the Composer Series;" "Moto Perpetuo" performed by
the Hobson-Kerr Duo, (Constance T. Hobson and Hortense R.
Kerr, piano).

- 1958 -

W65.   *FDR: FROM THIRD TERM TO PEARL HARBOR* (MSS only;
16 min.)
Television score; 1-1-1-0, 2-2-2-0, perc, str.

PREMIERE: 1958 Apr 13; score for the episode, "FDR: From Third
Term to Pearl Harbor," from the television series, "The
Twentieth Century," CBS Network.

W66.   *NEW YORK: CITY OF MAGIC* (MSS only; 40 min.)
Television score.
Alternate title: *City of Magic.*
Commissioned and produced by WNET, New York City.
See also: B88

PREMIERE: 1961 Oct 10; New York, NY; Museum of Modern Art.

W67.   *ORGAN SUITE NO.1* (PEM/CF; 7 min.)
1. "Andante maestoso" 2. "Pastorale" 3. "Finale."
Alternate title: *First Suite for Organ*.
Commissioned by Marilyn Mason, organ.
See also: D10; B81

PREMIERE: 1958 Dec 20; New York, NY; St. Paul's Chapel; Trinity Parish; Marilyn Mason, organ.

OTHER SELECTED PERFORMANCES

W67a.   1959 Sep 9; Fonteinkerk to Voorburg, Holland; Leonard Raver, organ.

W67b.   1963 Mar 24; Champaign, IL; University Place Christian Church; Marilyn Mason, organ.

W67c. 1963 April-May; Decatur, IL; Millikin University Music Department.

W67d. 1985 Aug 11; Ann Arbor, MI; First Congregational Church; Herman Taylor, organ.

- 1959 -

W68.   *THE EPICURE* (DUCH/MCA; 4 min.)
Soprano and bass soli; mixed chorus (SATB); orchestra.
Text: Abraham Cowley.
Arrangement of "The Epicure" from *Phoebus Arise*; also arranged for mixed chorus (SATB); piano.
See also: W72

W69.   *THE FALL OF CHINA* (MSS only; 17 min.)
Television score; 2-2-0-0, 1-3-2-1, pf, perc, str.

PREMIERE: 1959 Nov 15; score for the episode "The Fall of China," from the television series, "The Twentieth Century."

W70.   *INCIDENTAL MUSIC TO "SCENE AND SONG"* (MSS only; 8 min.)
Orchestra; cl, hn, vln, perc, pf.
Commissioned by Vinnie Burrows.
See also: B394

W71.   *HYMN-ANTHEM ON THE TUNE "HANOVER"* (CFP 1960; 4 min.)
Mixed chorus (SATB); organ or piano.
Text: Sir Robert Grant.

Alternate title: *O Worship the King*.
See also: B87, B99, B144, B201

PREMIERE: 1961 (early); Lenox, MA; Berkshire Music Center;
Tanglewood Festival Chorus; Hugh Ross, cond.

OTHER SELECTED PERFORMANCE

W71a.   1961 Jul-Aug; Rochester, NY; Kilbourn Hall;
University of Rochester; Eastman School of Music Chorus;
David Felter, cond.

W72.   *PHOEBUS, ARISE* (DUCH; 30 min.)
Cantata for soprano and bass soli; mixed chorus (SATB); and
orchestra; 1(picc)-1-2-1, 2-2-1-0, timp, perc, pf/cel, str.
1. "Prelude" (composer; 4:30 min.) 2. "No!" (Thomas Hood;
4 min.) 3. "Tears, flow no more" (Lord Herbert of Cherbury;
4:30 min.)   4. "Phoebus, arise" (William Drummond;
3:30 min.) 5. "Song"   (Thomas Middleton and William
Rowley; 3:45 min.) 6. "The Epicure" (Abraham Cowley; 3:30
min.) 7. "Epilogue" (composer; 2:30 min.).
Commissioned by the International Music Council of New York
City.
See also: W68, W74; B83, B171, B187, B200

PREMIERE: 1959 May 17; New York, NY; Town Hall; Interracial
Fellowship Chorus; Harold Aks, cond.

OTHER SELECTED PERFORMANCE

W72a. 1963 April-May; Decatur, IL; Millikin University Music
Department.

W73.   *SUBMARINE!* (MSS only; 14 min.)
Television score; 1-1-1-1, 2-2-2-0, 2 perc, str.
See also: B162

PREMIERE: 1959 Apr 12; score for the episode "Submarine!," from
the television series "The Twentieth Century;" CBS Television
Network.

W74.   *TEARS, FLOW NO MORE* (DUCH/MCA; 4 min.)
Women's chorus (SSA); piano.
Text: Lord Herbert of Cherbury.
Arrangement of "Tears, Flow No More" from *Phoebus, Arise*; also
arranged for soprano, bass, mixed chorus (SATB), and
orchestra.
See also: W72

- 1960 -

W75.   *ADMIRAL BYRD* (MSS only; 25 min.)
Television score; 1-1-1-1, 2-2-2-0, 2 perc, hp, str.

PREMIERE: 1960 Dec 25; score for the episode, "Admiral Byrd," from the television series, "The Twentieth Century," CBS Television Network.

W76.   *THE SHAPE OF THINGS* (MSS only; 16 min.)
Television score; 1-0-1-0, 2-1-0-0, perc, hp, str.

PREMIERE: 1960 Mar 12; score for the NBC news program, "World Wide 60."

W77.   *THE THREE MUSKETEERS* (MSS only; 15 min.)
Television score; 1-0-1-1, 2-1-1-0, 1 perc, str.
Commissioned by David Susskind.

PREMIERE: 1960 Dec 1; score for a Talent Associates, Ltd. production.

- 1961 -

W78.   *FLOWERS IN THE VALLEY* (CFP 1962; 5 min.)
Mixed chorus (SATB); a cappella.
Text: Anonymous.
Dedicated to Sigma Alpha Iota; under sponsorship of Sigma Alpha Iota in the American Music Awards Series.
See also: B395

PREMIERE: 1962 Aug 20; Chicago, IL; Sigma Alpha Iota National Convention; Sigma Alpha Iota Chorus; Margaret Hillis, cond.

OTHER SELECTED PERFORMANCE

W78a.   1962; Illinois Wesleyan University Choir; Lloyd Pfautsch, cond.

W79.   *STRING QUARTET NO. 3* (PEM/CF; 15 min.)
1. "Allegretto" 2. "Adagio-Presto-Adagio" 3. "Finale."
Commissioned by the University of Michigan; dedicated to the Stanley Quartet.
See also: B202, B203, B382

PREMIERE: 1962 Feb 20-21, Apr 2; Ann Arbor, MI; University of Michigan School of Music; The Stanley Quartet.

OTHER SELECTED PERFORMANCES

W79a.   1962 Mar; Madison, WI; MTNA; Stanley Quartet.

W79b.   1962 Sep 17; Boston, MA; Afro-American String Quartet.

W79c.   1963 Dec; Urbana, IL; University of Illinois; The Walden String Quartet.

W80.   *TRIGON* (CFP; 12 min.)
Wind orchestra; 3-3-4-3, 4-3-3-1, timp, perc, hp.
1. "Prelude" 2. "Canticle" 3. "Toccata."
Commissioned by the American Wind Symphony.
See also: B88, B202, B299

PREMIERE: 1961 Jun 18; Pittsburgh, PA; First International Festival of Contemporary Music for Wind Symphony Orchestra; American Wind Symphony; Robert A. Boudreau, cond.

OTHER SELECTED PERFORMANCES

W80a.   1961 Jul 15; Marlow, England; Jul 16; Ray Island Gardens; Maidenhead, England; American Wind Symphony; Robert Boudreau, cond.

W80b.   1961 Summer; American Wind Symphony on tour of England; Robert Boudreau, cond.

W80c.   1962 Nov 30; Cambridge, MA; Harvard University Band; James A. Walker, dir.

- 1962 -

W81.   *ALLELUIA* (AMP 1967; 3:30 min.)
Mixed chorus (SATB); orchestra.
Arrangement of "Alleluia" from *Choral Triptych*; also arranged for mixed chorus (SATB); piano or organ.
See also: W82; D2; B146

OTHER SELECTED PERFORMANCE

W81a.　1976 Feb 22; Washington, DC premiere; Peoples Congregational United Church of Christ; Evelyn White Chorale; Evelyn White, cond.

W82.　*CHORAL TRIPTYCH* (AMP 1967; 13 min.)
Mixed chorus (SATB); string orchestra.
Text: Biblical.
1. "Give ear to my words, O Lord" (5:30 min.) 2. "How long wilt Thou forget me, O Lord?" (4:30 min.)　3. "Alleluia" (3:30 min.).
Commissioned by Daniel Pinkham under a Ford Foundation Grant; also arranged for mixed chorus (SATB) with piano or organ; each song published separately.
See also: W81; D2; B120, B165, B166, B322, B396, B397, B398

PREMIERE: 1963 Mar 21; New York, NY; Museum of Modern Art; King's Chapel Choir of Boston; Daniel Pinkham, cond.

OTHER SELECTED PERFORMANCES

W82a.　1964 May; New York City; Master Institute Chorus and Orchestra; David Labovitz, cond.

W82b.　1981 Oct 4; Oberlin, OH; Oberlin Conservatory Choir.

W83.　*FOREVER FREE* (AMP 1975; 12 min.)
Band; 3-2-6-2, 5(sax), 4-3-2(trp)-3(bar)-1, str bass, timp, perc.
1. "Prelude" 2. "Toccata" 3. "Proclamation."
Alternate title: *A Lincoln Chronicle*.
Commissioned by Broadcast Music Inc. for the U.S. Civil War Centennial Commission and the commemoration of the one hundredth anniversary of the issuance of the Emancipation Proclamation.
See also: B29, B50, B135, B215

PREMIERE: 1962 Sep 22; Washington, DC; Lincoln Memorial; U.S. Marine Band; Captain Dale Harpham, cond.

OTHER SELECTED PERFORMANCES

W83a.　1963 Jan 31; Washington, DC; Departmental Auditorium; U.S. Marine Band; Capt. Dale Harpham, cond.

W83b. 1963 April-May; Decatur, IL; Millikin University Music Department.

W83c.   1963 Dec 2; Trenton, NJ; Fort Dix Army Band.

W83d.   1967 Feb 17, 20; UCLA Band; the composer, cond.

W84.   *GOING HOME* (MSS only; 7 min.)
Film score; cl, hn, 1 perc, hp, bass.
Commissioned by and dedicated to Peter Hollander.
See also: B203

PREMIERE: 1962 Sep 29, Oct 10; United Nations Film Department production on the Congo.

W85.   *THE LAND* (MSS only)
Television score.
Commissioned by Reuben Frank for an NBC news documentary.
See also: B316

PREMIERE: 1962 Mar 13; United Nations film featuring Chet Huntley.

W86.   *NOSOTROS* (MSS only)
Film score.
Commissioned by and dedicated to Peter Hollander for viewing in Latin America; United Nations Film Department production.
See also: B203

W87.   *TO LIGHT THAT SHINES* (DUCH/MCA 1964; 5 min.)
Mixed chorus (SAB); piano or organ.
Text: Samuel Johnson.
Commissioned by the New York Society for Ethical Culture.
See also: B99

PREMIERE: 1962 May 27; New York, NY; New York Ethical Culture Chorus and Organ.

W88.   *TRIPTYCH ON TEXTS OF BLAKE* (PEM/CF; 14 min.)
High voice, violin, violoncello; piano.
1. "To the evening star" 2. "Mad song" 3. "Contemplation."
Commissioned by Kermit Moore; reduction by composer of *Three Pieces After Blake* (1952).
See also: W48

PREMIERE: 1963 Feb 22; Winston-Salem, NC; Winston-Salem Teachers College; Clarmoor Quartet.

OTHER SELECTED PERFORMANCE

W88a.   1985 Mar 24; Montclair, NJ; Hoboken Chamber Ensemble; Lila Deis, soprano.

- 1963 -

W89.   *FANTASY VARIATIONS* (DUCH/MCA 1966; 15 min.)
         Orchestra; 2(picc)-2-2-2, 4-3-3-1, timp, perc, str.
         Introduction, theme, and 13 variations; PR.
         See also: D4; B33, B90, B106, B176, B336, B337, B343, B394

         PREMIERE: 1963 Nov 19; Portland, ME; Portland Symphony;
         Arthur Bennett Lipkin, cond.

         OTHER SELECTED PERFORMANCES

             W89a. 1963 Dec 2; New York, NY; Lincoln Center; Brooklyn
             Philharmonic; Siegfried Landau, cond.

             W89b. 1978 Feb 28, Mar 1; New Orleans Philharmonic; Denis
             DeCoteau, cond.

             W89c. 1982 Oct 10; Cleveland Orchestra; Eric Leinsdorf, cond.

             W89d.   1986 Feb 7; Oakland, CA; Oakland Symphony
             Orchestra.

W90.   *INSCRIPTIONS FROM WHITMAN* (PEM/CF; 25 min.)
         Mixed chorus (SATB); orchestra; 2-2-2-2, 4-3-3-1, timp, perc, hp,
         str.
         Text: Walt Whitman.
         Two movements.
         Commissioned by the Tercentary Commission of the State of New
         Jersey and the New Jersey Symphony Orchestra for the New
         Jersey Tercentary.
         See also: B205, B321

         PREMIERE: 1964 Apr 26; Atlantic City, NJ; Coorhees Chapel
         Choir; New Jersey Oratorio Society Male Chorus; New Jersey
         Symphony Orchestra; Kenneth Schermerhorn, cond.

         OTHER SELECTED PERFORMANCE

             W90a. 1964 Apr 27; Camden, NJ; Apr 28; Englewood, NJ;
             Apr 29; Newark, NJ; May 2; Brunswick, NJ; Coorhees
             Chapel Choir; New Jersey Oratorio Society Male Chorus;
             New Jersey Symphony Orchestra; Kenneth Schermerhorn,
             cond.

W91.   *UMBRIAN SCENE* (DUCH/MCA 1965; 12 min.)
           Orchestra; 2-2-2-2, 4-3-3-1, timp, perc, hp, str; PR.
           Commissioned by Edward B. Benjamin.
           See also: D21; B1, B11, B90, B95, B120, B210, B395

           PREMIERE: 1964 Mar 31; New Orleans, LA; New Orleans
           Philharmonic Symphony; Werner Torkanowsky, cond.

           OTHER SELECTED PERFORMANCES

               W91a.   1964 Aug 16; New York, NY; Philharmonic Hall;
               Orchestra of America; Leonard de Paur, cond.

               W91b. 1966 Nov 10; Rochester Philharmonic; Laszlo Somogyi,
               cond.

               W91c.   1967 Mar 5; Kansas City Philharmonic; Hans
               Schweiger, cond.

               W91d. 1969 Sept 14, 24; Oct 3, 6, 12; Buffalo Philharmonic;
               Lukas Foss, cond.

               W91e.   1971 Nov 18; Birmingham, AL; Birmingham
               Symphony; the composer, guest cond.

               W91f. 1985 Mar 12; New York, NY; Carnegie Hall; National
               Orchestra of New York; Alvaro Cassuto, cond.

                              - 1964 -

W92.   *EMILY DICKINSON SET* (DUCH 1965; 6 min.)
           Women's chorus (SSA); piano.
           Text: Emily Dickinson.
           1. "Elysium is as far" 2. "Indian summer" 3. "Ample make this
           bed."
           Commissioned by Burton A. Cleaves; dedicated to the Simmons
           College Glee Club; included in the Leeds "Masterwork Choral
           Series."
           See also: B389

           PREMIERE: 1965; Boston, MA; Simmons College Glee Club; Burton
           A. Cleaves, cond.

W93.   *ESSAY ON DEATH* (MSS only)
           Television score.
           A Leo Hurwitz Production on John F. Kennedy for WNET, New
           York, NY.

W94.   *REVERIE AND RONDO* (PEM/CF 1977; 7 min.)
       Orchestra; 3-2-2-2, 4-3-3-1, timp, perc, str, or 3-2-2-2, 2-2-2-1,
          timp, perc, str.
       Alternate title: *Two Pieces for Orchestra.*
       See also: B252, B319

       PREMIERE: 1968 Oct 11; Flint, MI; Flint Symphony Orchestra;
       William Byrd, cond.

       OTHER SELECTED PERFORMANCE

          W94a.   1982 Feb 26, 27; Williamstown, MA; Berkshire
          Symphony Orchestra; Julius Hegyi, cond.

                          - 1965 -

W95.   *CONCERT SKETCHES* (PEM/CF; 10 min.)
       Band; 3-3-7-2, 4(sax), 4-3(cor)-2(trp)-3(bar)-1, str bass, timp, perc.
       1. "Prologue"   2. "Parade"   3. "Promenade"   4. "Carnival"
          5. "Holiday"   6. "Epilogue."
       Written for the Ostwald Band Composition Award Competition,
          sponsored by the American Bandmasters Association; a semi-
          finalist entry.
       See also: W130; B135

W96.   *FOUR HYMN-ANTHEMS* (DUCH/MCA 1965; 8 min.)
       Mixed chorus (SATB); organ.
       1. "God, the Lord" (John Keble; paraphrased from Psalms of
          David; 2 min.)   2. "Lo, the earth" (Henry Wadsworth
          Longfellow; 2 min.) 3. "Love Divine" (Charles Wesley; 2 min.)
          4. "O come Emmanuel" (Veni, Veni, Emmanuel; 2 min.).
       Each anthem published separately.
       See also: B144

W97.   *PRESIDENTIAL SUITE* (PEM/CF 1977; 12 min.)
       Orchestra; 3-2-2-2, 4-3-3-1, timp, perc, str.
       Commissioned by the Greater Boston Youth Symphony.
       See also: B206

       PREMIERE: 1966 Mar 13; Boston, MA; Symphony Hall; Greater
       Boston Youth Symphony; the composer, guest cond.

       OTHER SELECTED PERFORMANCES

          W97a.   1970 Apr; Mt. Vernon, NY; Philharmonic Society of
          Westchester; John Barnett, cond.

W97b. 1984 May 19; Haddonfield, NJ; Haddonfield Symphony Orchestra.

W98.   *TWO DUNBAR LYRICS* (DUCH/MCA 1966; 5 min.)
Mixed chorus (SATB); a cappella.
Text: Paul Laurence Dunbar.
1. "A Starry night" 2. "Madrigal."
Commissioned for the seventy-fifth anniversary of West Virginia State College; included in the "Masterwork Choral Series."
See also: B32, B207

PREMIERE: 1966 Mar 18; Institute, WV; West Virginia State College.

OTHER SELECTED PERFORMANCE

W98a. 1985 Aug. 11; Ann Arbor, MI; First Congregational Church; The Brazeal Dennard Chorale; Brazeal Dennard, cond.

- 1966 -

W99.   *THE BIRDS* (DUCH/MCA 1969; 14 min.)
Women's chorus (SA); piano.
1. "The Great black crow" (P. J. Bailey) 2. "The Skylark" (J. Hogg) 3. "The Peacock" (W. Cowper); SSA; piano 4. "The Throstle" (Alfred Lord Tennyson) 5. "Answer to a child's question" (S. C. Taylor).
Commissioned by Burton A. Cleaves.
See also: B397

PREMIERE: 1967 Dec 3; Boston, MA; Simmons College Glee Club; Burton A. Cleaves, cond.

W100.   *MARKINGS* (DUCH/MCA 1968; 21 min.)
Orchestra; 3-3-3-3, 4-3-3-1, timp, perc, str; PR.
Commissioned by the Meadow Brook Festival, Oakland University; written in memory of Dag Hammarskjöld and dedicated to Oliver Daniel.
Front cover: Annual UNESCO-International Issue, *Pan Pipes*; Mar 1971.
See also: D7; B1, B18, B54, B100, B120, B121, B134, B210, B211, B275

PREMIERE: 1966 Aug 18; Rochester, MN; Oakland University; Meadow Brook Festival; Detroit Symphony; Sixten Ehrling, cond.

OTHER SELECTED PERFORMANCES

W100a. 1967 Mar 2, 3, 4, 5; Cleveland Orchestra; Sixten Ehrling, cond.

W100b. 1967 May 7; Tempe, AZ; Phoenix Symphony; Guy Taylor, cond.

W100c. 1969 Oct 19; Birmingham Symphony; Paul Freeman, cond.

W100d. 1969 Dec 1; New York, NY; Lincoln Center; Philharmonic Hall; Symphony of the New World; Paul Freeman, cond.

W100e. 1970 Jan 29; Dallas Symphony; Paul Freeman, cond.

W100f. 1970 Aug 5; Grant Park Symphony; Paul Freeman, cond.

W100g. 1970; Buffalo (NY) Philharmonic; Paul Freeman, cond.

W100h. 1971 Nov 16; Aalborg, Denmark; radio broadcast of the Danish State Radio Orchestra; Paul Freeman, cond.

W100i. 1976 Dec; 1977 Jan; Pittsburgh Symphony; Donald Johanos, cond.

W100j. 1977 Sep; Latin American Tour; New York Philharmonic; Zubin Mehta, cond.

W100k. 1978 Sep 28, 29, 30; Oct 1; New York, NY; Avery Fisher Hall; New York Philharmonic; Zubin Mehta, cond.

W100l. 1981 Dec 11, 12; Columbia (OH) Symphony Orchestra; Evan Whallon, cond.

W100m. 1980 Sep 28; New York City, Lehman College; New York Philharmonic; Zubin Mehta, cond.

W101.   *A THING OF BEAUTY* (MSS only; 15 min.)
Film score; chorus (SATB); some percussion.
Commissioned by and dedicated to Fisk University; a Trafco production.

W102.   *TWO SONGS FOR CHILDREN* (1970; 2 min.)
Voice and piano.
1. "Where the boats go" (Robert Louis Stevenson; CAN) 2. "The Little elf-man" (John Kendrick Bangs; DUCH).

Commissioned by the Juilliard School of Music; written for the Juilliard Repertory Project; each song published separately.

- 1967 -

W103.   *AULOS* (PEM/CF 1980; 14 min.)
Solo flute, 2 horns, string orchestra, percussion.
Commissioned by and dedicated to John Solum; also arranged for solo flute and piano.
See also: B8, B120, B396

PREMIERE: 1971 Feb 21; Bloomington, IN; Indiana University; Indiana University Chamber Orchestra; John Solum, flute; Wolfgang Vaccano, cond.

OTHER SELECTED PERFORMANCE

W103a. 1985 Aug 14; Ann Arbor, MI; University of Michigan; Black American Music Symposium; Harold Jones, flute; Kermit Moore, cond.

W104.   *STEPHEN CRANE SET* (DUCH/MCA 1972; 16 min.)
Cantata for mixed chorus (SATB); instrumental ensemble of 13 players; 1-1(Eng hn)-1(bc1)-1, 2-2-2-0, perc; PR.
Text: Stephen Crane.
1. "Black riders" 2. "Mystic shadow" 3. "A Spirit" 4. "War is kind."
Commissioned by the Chicago Musical College of Roosevelt University in honor of its one hundredth anniversary.
See also: B305, B393, B394, B396, B397

PREMIERE: 1968 Feb 4; Chicago, IL; Chicago Musical College; David S. Larson, cond.

W105.   *SYMPHONY* (PEM/CF 1977; 24 min.)
Orchestra; 3-3-3-3, 4-3-3-1, timp, perc, str.
Four movements.
Alternate title: *Symphony No. 1.*
Commissioned by the Illinois Sesquicentennial Commission.
See also: B213, B308

PREMIERE: 1968 Mar 28; Macomb, IL; Chicago Symphony Orchestra; Jean Martinon, cond.

OTHER SELECTED PERFORMANCE

W105a.   1974 Mar 9; New York, NY;   Juilliard Theatre
Orchestra; James Conlon, cond.

- 1968 -

W106.   *BLEEKER STREET SUITE* (MSS only; withdrawn by composer;
7 min.)
Elementary orchestra with recorders, etc.; piano sketch only.
1. "Entrata" 2. "Lullaby" 3. "Novelette" 4. "Ostinata."

W107.   *HERALDS I* (PEM/CF 1978; 1 min.)
Brass octet; 4(trp), 4(trb).
Alternate title: *Fanfares for Four Trumpets and Four Trombones*.
Dedicated to Oliver Daniel.

PREMIERE: 1968 Sep 9; New York, NY; International Music
Congress.

W108.   *SCHERZI MUSICALI* (DUCH/MCA 1971; 17 min.)
Chamber orchestra; 1-1-1-1, 1-0-0-0, str; PR.
Commissioned by the Chamber Music Society of Detroit for its
twenty-fifth anniversary.
See also: B30, B396

PREMIERE: 1969 Feb 13; Detroit, MI; Princeton Chamber
Orchestra; Interlochen Arts Woodwind Quintet; Nicholas
Harsanyi, cond.

OTHER SELECTED PERFORMANCES

W108a.   1981 Mar 24; Brooklyn Philharmonic Chamber
Orchestra; Tania León, cond.

W108b. 1971 May; St. Paul (MN) Chamber Orchestra.

W109.   *THEATER SET* (DUCH/MCA 1971; 15 min.)
Orchestra; 3-3-3-2, 4-3-3-1, timp, perc, str.
1. "Overture" 2. "Ballad-chase music" 3. "Finale."
Commissioned by the Junior League of Atlanta for Robert Shaw
and the Atlanta Symphony Orchestra; dedicated to Robert
Shaw.
See also: B106, B208, B257

PREMIERE: 1968 Sep 26; Atlanta, GA; Atlanta Symphony
Orchestra; Robert Shaw, cond.

OTHER SELECTED PERFORMANCE

W109a. 1970 August; Washington, DC; National Symphony
Orchestra; Leon Thompson, cond.

- 1969 -

W110.   *THE CAPITOLINE VENUS* (PEM/CF; 45 min.)
Opera in one-act.
Soli: soprano, 2 tenors, 3 baritones, 2 basses; orchestra: 1-1-2-1,
1-1-1-0, timp, perc, hp, str.
Libretto: Judith Dvorkin after Mark Twain.
Commissioned by the Quincy Society of Fine Arts.
See also: B41, B45

PREMIERE: 1971 Mar 12; Champaign-Urbana, IL; University of
Illinois; Krannert Center for the Performing Arts; University
of Illinois Opera Group; Richard Aslanian, cond.; David
Barron, dir.; Laura Zirner, des.

W111.   *ONCE THERE WAS A MAN* (PEM/CF; 18 min.)
Narrator; mixed chorus (SATB); orchestra; 3-2-3-2, 4-3-3-1, timp,
perc, hp, str.
Text: Randall Caudill.
Alternate title: *A Covenant for Our Time*.
Commissioned by the 1969 Worcester (MA) Music Festival.
See also: B42, B303

PREMIERE: 1969 Sep 18; Detroit, MI; Detroit Symphony; Sixten
Ehrling, cond.; William Warfield, narr.

W112.   *PARABLES* (DUCH/MCA 1970; 12 min.)
Mixed chorus (SATB); chamber orchestra; 1-1-1-1, 1-1-1-0, perc,
cb; PR.
Text: Anonymous.
1. "The Old armchair" 2. "The Hell-bound train."
Commissioned by the American Choral Directors Association.
See also: B209, B393, B395, B397

PREMIERE: 1971 Mar 6; Kansas City, MO; First Annual
Convention of the American Choral Directors Association;
Kansas State University Concert Chorale; Rod Walker, cond.;
Kansas State University Chamber Orchestra; Paul Roby, cond.

OTHER SELECTED PERFORMANCE

W112a. 1971 Jul 1; Denton, TX; North Texas State University
Chorus and Chamber Orchestra.

- 1971 -

W113.   *FACETS* (PEM/CF; 12 min.)
Piano and woodwind quintet.
Commissioned by the Eastman School of Music for its fiftieth
anniversary; dedicated to W. Hendl.
See also: B210, B306

PREMIERE: 1971 Oct 19; Rochester, NY; Eastman School of Music
Faculty, "Musica Nova;" W Hendl, cond.

OTHER SELECTED PERFORMANCES

W113a. 1986 Oct 5; Turin, Italy; Ensemble Antidogma.

W113b. 1987 Mar 19, 20; Meet the Moderns; Lukas Foss, cond.

W114.   *TRIPLE SET* (MCA/BEL 1972; 9 min.)
Male chorus (TTBB); a cappella.
1. "Ode: to the cuckoo" (Michael Bruce) 2. "Had I a heart" (R. B.
Sheridan) 3. "A Toast" (R. B. Sheridan).
See also: B396, B397

- 1972 -

W115.   *FIVE PORTRAITS* (PEM/CF 1979; 15 min.)
Violin and piano.
Commissioned by the McKim Fund of the Library of Congress;
private record pressing: Washington, DC; Juilliard String
Quartet (NY).
See also: D5; B6, B212, B399

PREMIERE: 1974 Feb 22; Washington, DC; Library of Congress;
Ruggiero Ricci, violin; Leon Pommers, piano.

W116.   *FOUR SILHOUETTES* (DUCH/MCA 1973; 3:30 min.)
Concert band; 2-1-5-2, 4(sax)-2-3(trp)-1(bar)-1, str, bass, timp,
perc.
Suitable for junior high or high school bands.
See also: B29, B135

PREMIERE: 1973 Dec 8; New York, NY; Lehman College Band; J. Dellicarri, cond.

W117.   *PENTAGRAPH* (PEM/CF 1978; 17 min.)
Women's chorus; a cappella.
1. "The Miller's song" (Isaac Bickerstaffe); three-part chorus (SSA) 2. "King Arthur" (Anonymous); two-part chorus (SA) 3. "To be or not to be" (Anonymous); three-part chorus (SSA) 4. "The Flamingo" (Lewis Gaylor Clark); two-part chorus (SA) 5. "The Monkey's glue" (Goldwin Goldsmith); divided chorus (SSSAAA).
Available with piano accompaniment.
See also: B400

- 1973 -

W118.   *FIRST NOCTURNE* (MCA/BEL 1973; 5 min.)
Solo piano.
Commissioned by Mrs. Eric Stein; dedicated to James Dick.
See also: B7, B34, B212, B272, B393, B396, B397

PREMIERE: 1973 Jul 4; Round Top Piano Institute; James Dick, piano.

OTHER SELECTED PERFORMANCE

W118a.   1980 Jan 15; Washington, DC; Kennedy Center; National Black Music Colloquium and Competition; Theodore Hendricks, piano.

W119.   *GUITARRA* (PEM/CF 1985; 12 min.)
Solo guitar.
1. "Prelude" 2. "Arioso" 3. "Finale."
Alternate title: *Suite for Solo Guitar*.
Commissioned by and dedicated to Wilbur P. Cotton; revised in 1985.
See also: B12, B334, B391

PREMIERE: 1985 Dec 8; London, England; Wigmore Hall; Jorge Morel, guitar.

W120.   *HARLEM CHILDREN'S SUITE* (MSS only; withdrawn by composer; 9 min.)
Elementary orchestra.
1. "Prelude" 2. "Aria" 3. "Finale."

Commissioned by the Harlem School of the Arts; dedicated to
Dorothy Maynor.
See also: B58

PREMIERE: 1975 Mar; New York, NY; The Harlem School of the
Arts.

W121.   *SECOND NOCTURNE* (MSS only; withdrawn by composer; 5 min.)
Solo piano.

- 1974 -

W122.   *HERALDS II* (PEM/CF 1978; 1 min.)
Three trumpets; playable on C or B^b trumpets.
Alternate title: *Fanfare for Three Trumpets*.
Written for the Graduate Center of the City University of New
York.
See also: B242

PREMIERE: 1974 Oct 10; Brooklyn College Brass Ensemble.

- 1974-76 -

W123.   *JUBILEE* (PEM/CF; 2 hrs.)
Opera in three acts.
Libretto: Donald Dorr; based on a novel by Margaret Walker.
13 principals, (3 sopranos, 1 mezzo-soprano, 3 tenors, 2 baritones,
3 basses, 1 boy soprano); double chorus (SATB); orchestra;
3-2-3-2, 4-2-3-0, timp, perc, str.
See also: B1, B26, B31, B56, B107, B131, B228, B253

PREMIERE: 1976 Nov 20; Jackson, MS; Opera/South; Hilda Harris,
Marcia Baldwin, Vinson Cole, Clyde Walker, John West,
Raymond Bazemore, Adelaida Acevedo-Anderson, Richard
Mundt, Alfred Anderson; James DePriest, cond.

OTHER SELECTED PERFORMANCE

W123a.   1977 Nov 19; Jackson, MS; Opera/South; Francois
Clemmons, Adelaide Anderson, Norma Hirsch, Carl Nelson,
Jonathan Green, Cary Smith, Gregory Servant, Curtis
Rayam, James Pickens; Paul   Freeman, cond.; Ian
Strasfogel, stage dir.

W124.   *QUINTET CONCERTO* (PEM/CF; 17 min.)
Solo brass quintet; 2(trp), hn, 2(trb) or 1(trb), and tuba; orchestra; 3-2-3-2, 3-1-1-0, timp, perc, str.
Commissioned by the Juilliard School of Music.
See also: B31, B163, B213, B246

PREMIERE: 1975 Mar 14; New York, NY; Alice Tully Hall; Juilliard School of Music; Juilliard Orchestra; W Hendl, cond.

OTHER SELECTED PERFORMANCES

W124a.   1976 Mar; New York, NY; Lincoln Center; Celebration of Contemporary Music Festival.

W124b. 1980 Apr 15; Grambling, LA; Shreveport Symphony; John Shenaut, cond.

W125.   *VISIONS* (MSS only; 1:15 min.)
Solo piano.
Dedicated to William Grant Still; published in *The Black Perspective in Music* 3 (May 1975): 222-23.
See also: B294

- 1975 -

W126.   *EPIGRAMS AND HYMN* (PEM/CF; 6 min.)
Anthem for mixed chorus (SATB); organ.
Text: John Greenleaf Whittier; Reverend John Murray; Samuel Longfellow.
Commissioned by the Princeton Theological Seminary, and the Bryn Mawr and Brick Presbyterian Churches for the Bicentennial.
See also: B396

PREMIERE: 1976 May 15; New York, NY; Brick Presbyterian Church Choir; T. Charles Lee, cond.

W127.   *SOUTHERN HARMONY* (PEM/CF; 20 min.)
Orchestra; 3-3-3-3, 4-3-3-1, timp, perc, str.
1. "Prelude: lands of beginnings"   2. "Fife and drums" 3. "Variants"   4. "Elysium."
Commissioned by the Southeastern Regional Metropolitan Orchestra Managers Association; based on themes and motives from *The Southern Harmony* by William Walker (1809-1875), a.k.a. "Singin' Billy;" includes 6 public domain tunes.
See also: B31, B182, B268, B396, B400

PREMIERE: 1976 Feb 10; Wilmington, NC; University of North Carolina; Kenan Auditorium; North Carolina Symphony Orchestra; John Gosling, cond.

OTHER SELECTED PERFORMANCE

W127a. 1980 Apr 15; Grambling, LA; Shreveport Symphony Orchestra; John Shenaut, cond.

W128. *TWO FOLK SETTINGS* (JCP; 5 min.)
Mixed chorus (SATB); a cappella.
1. "Sally Anne" (2 min.) 2. "Blow, ye winds in the morning" (3 min.).
Commissioned by the JCPenney Bicentennial Music Project, 1975; published by arrangement with Carl Fischer, Inc.
See also: D13; B322

W129. *THE WESTERN PARADISE* (PEM/CF; 16 min.)
Narrator and orchestra; 3-3-3-3, 4-3-3-1, timp, perc, hp, str.
Text: Donald Dorr; originally for female narrator.
Five movements.
Commissioned by the National Symphony Orchestra for the Bicentennial.
See also: B31, B222

PREMIERE: 1976 Oct 12; Washington, DC; National Symphony Orchestra; Antal Dorati, cond.; William Conrad, narr.

- 1977 -

W130. *PROLOGUE AND PARADE* (PEM/CF 1978; 3 min.)
Concert band; 3-1-6-1, 4(sax), 2-3-3-(bar-tuba), str, bass, timp, perc.
A commissioned contemporary work for school bands. Separate publication of "Prologue" and "Parade" from *Concert Sketches*, 1965.
See also: W95; B329

- 1978 -

W131. *JERSEY HOURS* (PEM/CF 1980; 12 min.)
Voice and 3 harps.
Text: Donald Dorr.
Alternate title: *Triptych for Voice and Three Harps.*

Commissioned by Mrs. Paul R. Emmanuel; also arranged for voice
and harp; voice and piano.
See also: B217, B331

PREMIERE: 1979 Jan 7; Teaneck, NJ; The Emmanuel Harp Trio
and Singer on series titled, "Teaneck Artists Perform."

OTHER SELECTED PERFORMANCE

W131a.   1985 Sep 29; Baltimore, MD; Res Musica Baltimore,
Inc.; William Brown, tenor; Sara Schuster, harp.

W132.   *CHARIOTS* (PEM/CF 1982; 15 min.)
Orchestra; 3-3-3-3, 4-3-3-1, timp, perc, hp, str.
Commissioned by the Saratoga Performing Arts Center.
See also: B6, B62, B301

PREMIERE: 1979 Aug 8; Saratoga Springs, NY; Philadelphia
Orchestra; the composer, guest cond.

OTHER SELECTED PERFORMANCES

W132a.   1980 Apr 15; Grambling, LA; Shreveport Symphony;
John Shenaut, cond.

W132b.   1984 Sep 28, 29, Oct 1; New York, NY; New York
Philharmonic.

- 1979-85 -

W133.   *FREDERICK DOUGLASS* (PEM/CF; full evening).
Opera in three acts.
Libretto: Donald Dorr.
Five soli; four supporting parts; women's chorus (SSA); double
chorus (SATB); children's chorus (SA); orchestra; optional off-
stage band.
Orchestra; 2(picc)-2-2(bcl)-2, 4-3-3-0, 2 perc, hp, mandolin, str.
Off-stage band; 2nd picc, E^b cl, 4(trp)-4(trb) or 5(trb), 3rd perc.
See also: B14, B217, B333

PREMIERE: 1991 Apr. 14; Newark, NJ; Newark Symphony Hall;
New Jersey State Opera; Kevin Maynor in role of Frederick
Douglass; Louis Johnson, dir; Salvatore Tagliarino, des.;
Alfredo Silipigni, cond.

- **1983-84** -

W134.   *FESTIVAL PSALMS* (PEM/CF 1984; 10 min.)
          Solo baritone; mixed chorus (SATB); piano.
          Commissioned by the Holland Community Chorale, Inc.
          See also: B10, B333

          PREMIERE: 1984 Mar 13; Holland, MI; Holland Community
          Chorale.

- **1983** -

W135.   *TROMBA* (PEM/CF; 9 min.)
          Trumpet; piano.
          Alternate title: *Suite for B^b Trumpet and Piano*.
          Commissioned by Fred Irby III.
          See also: B11, B65, B173, B288, B333

          PREMIERE: 1986 May 24; Washington, DC; Smithsonian
          Institution; Baird Auditorium; Fred Irby III, trumpet; Ronald
          Tymus, piano.

- **1984** -

W136.   *FIVE WINDS* (PEM/CF; 12 min.)
          Woodwind quintet; fl, ob, cl, hn, bsn.
          See also: B10, B334

          PREMIERE: 1985 Jul 5; St. Mary's, MD; Tidewater Music Festival;
          Tidewater Festival Quintet.

          OTHER SELECTED PERFORMANCE

          W136a. 1986 Jun 17; Brooklyn, NY; Woodhill Players.

- **1985** -

Continuing work on *Frederick Douglass*, opera.

- 1986 -

W137.   *PANTOMIME* (PEM/CF 1986; 5:30 min.)
Fantasy for solo clarinet.
See also: B12

W138.   *TWO IMPROMPTUS FOR PIANO* (MSS; 8 min.)
Solo piano.
Commissioned by Affiliated Artists, Inc.
See also: B13

PREMIERE: 1987 Feb 8; New York, NY; Weill Recital Hall; Marcantonio Barone, piano.

- 1987 -

W139.   *STRING TRIPTYCH* (CF; 7 min.)
String orchestra.
Commissioned by the Missouri Unit of the American String Teachers Association.

PREMIERE: 1988, Jan 23; Osage Beach, MO; Missouri All-State High School String Orchestra; Paul Vermel; cond.

Discography

This list includes all commercially produced discs, whether or not currently available. All are 33 1/3 rpm unless otherwise noted. The "See" references, e.g., *See also*: B115, and *See also*: W110, identify citations in the "Bibliography" and "Works and Performances" sections. The date following the entry title is the date of composition; the record title is enclosed in parentheses; and the date of record release is indicated by the word, "released." Further information appearing in discographic citations includes the performers and works of additional composers on the recordings.

D1.   *BRASS QUARTET* (1950)

    Folkways Records FM 3651. mono. released 1965; duration 8:32;
        (*Music for Brass Quintet*).
    American Brass Quintet.
    With works by Josquin des Prés, *et al*.
    See also: W39; B51, B126, B251, B256, B335

D2.   *CHORAL TRIPTYCH* (1962)

    Cambridge Records CRS 1416. stereo/CRM 416. mono. released
        1963; duration 12:53; (*Four Contemporary Choral Works*).
    King's Chapel Choir of Boston; Cambridge Festival Strings;
        Daniel Pinkham, cond.
    With works by Ned Rorem, *et al*.
    See also: W82; B126, B204, B251, B256, B335

D3.   *CONCERTO FOR ORCHESTRA* (1948)

    a.   Remington Musirama R 199-173. mono. released 1954;
            duration 12:43.

Teatro La Fenice Symphony; Jonel Perlea, cond.
With works by Norman Lockwood.

b. Varese Sarabande VC-81047. mono. released 1979; duration 12:43.
Berlin Radio Orchestra; Jonel Perlea, cond.
With works by Henry Brant.
See also: W32; B104, B126, B190, B251, B256, B298

D4. FANTASY VARIATIONS (1963)

Composers Recordings Inc. CRI SD-209 mono/stereo. released 1966; duration 15:40.
Oslo Philharmonic Orchestra; Arthur Bennett Lipkin, cond.
With works by Nicolai Berezowsky, *et al*.
See also: W89; B51, B126, B251, B256, B298, B335, B393

D5. *FIVE PORTRAITS FOR VIOLIN AND PIANO* (1972)

Grenadilla Productions 1056 (cassette tape). stereo. released 1986; duration 17:05.
Ruggiero Ricci, violin; Michael Andrews, piano.
With work by David Baker.
See also: W115; B399

HOW STANDS THE GLASS AROUND? *See: Two Madrigals*

D6. *INVENTION NUMBER III* (1964)

Opus One, Number Thirty-Five. stereo. released 1978; duration 2:12; recorded April 26, 1977. (*Contemporary Music On Records*).
Ruth Norman, piano.
From *Four Inventions*; with works by Ruth Norman, Mark Fax, *et al*.
See also: W25; B251

D7. *MARKINGS* (1966)

Columbia Records Col. M-32783. stereo. released 1974; duration 19:05; (*Black Composer Series, Vol. 3*).
London Symphony Orchestra; Paul Freeman, cond.
With work by George Walker.
See also: W100; B51, B55, B100, B115, B121, B134, B142, B143, B251

D8.   *A NEW SONG: 3 PSALMS FOR CHORUS* (1961)

> Gothic Records, Inc. G 78932. compact disc. GC 78932. cassette.
> released 1989; duration, app. 8:15; (*Music from Trinity
> Church, vol. 1: Choral Music by Twentieth Century American
> Composers*).
> Trinity Church Choir; James A. Simms, associate and principal
> cond; Larry King, music dir.
> "Sing unto the Lord" 3:02; "Like as a Father" 2:18; "O Praise the
> Lord" 2:49.
> With works by Daniel Pinkham, *et al.*
> *See also*: W59

D9.   *OF NEW HORIZONS* (1944)

> Century Record Company V-14599-2. stereo. released 1962;
> duration, app. 8-10 min.; (Recording of music composed by
> University of Arizona graduates for the one hundredth
> anniversary of the land grant colleges in the university
> system—1862-1962).
> University of Arizona Symphony Orchestra; Henry Johnson, cond.
> With works by Robert Backsa and Robert McBride.
> *See also*: W20; B203

D10.   *ORGAN SUITE NO. 1* (1959)

> Orion ORS-76255. stereo. released 1977; duration 8:35 (*American
> Organ Music of Three Centuries*)
> Thomas Harmon, organ.
> With works by Samuel Barber, *et al.*
> *See also*: W67; B51, B216, B251

D11.   *PRELUDE FOR FLUTE* (1975)

> Eastern ERS-513. stereo. (2 discs), released 1973; duration, app.
> 3:00; (*Contemporary Black Images for Flute*).
> D. Antoinette Handy, flute.
> With works by Arthur Cunningham, Noel Da Costa, John Duncan,
> Robert L. Holmes, Joseph Kennedy, Hale Smith, Undine Smith
> Moore, and Frederick Tillis.
> *See also*: W14; B116, B169, B251

D12.   *ROUND DANCE AND POLKA* (1954)

> a.   London LL-1213. mono. released 1955/56; duration, app. 5:40;
>   (*Modern American Composers, Vol. 1*).
>   New Symphony Chamber Orchestra; Camarata, cond.
>   "Round Dance" 3:00; "Polka" 2:34.

From *Six Dances for String Orchestra*; with works by Robert McBride, *et al.*

b.   Composers Recordings Inc. CRI-119. mono. released 1958; duration, app. 5:40; (*Teen Scenes for String Orchestra*).
The New Symphony Orchestra of London; Camarata, cond.
"Round Dance" 3:00; "Polka" 2:34.
From *Six Dances for String Orchestra*; with works by Avery Claflin, *et al.*
See also: W53; D17; B126, B251, B256, B298, B335, B384

D13.   *SALLY ANNE* (1975)

Columbia Records/CBS Inc. M 33838. JCP. released 1975; duration 1:38; (*A Bicentennial Celebration: 200 Years of American Music*).
Leonard de Paur Chorus; Leonard de Paur, cond.
From *Two Folk Settings*; with arrangements by Wendell Whalum, Jester Hairston, and Alice Parker.
See also: W128; B215

D14.   *SERENADE FOR ORCHESTRA* (1954)

Louisville First Edition Records Lou-545-8 (XTV 22207). mono. released 1958/59; duration 17:58.
Louisville Orchestra; Robert Whitney, cond.; Jorge Mester, music dir.
With works by Luigi Dallapiccola, *et al.*
See also: W52; B103, B126, B196, B251, B256, B335, B365

D15.   *A SHORT OVERTURE* (1947)

Desto Records DC 7107. stereo. released 1970; duration 6:31; (*The Black Composer in America*).
Oakland Youth Orchestra; Robert Hughes, cond.
With works by George Walker, William Grant Still, Arthur Cunningham, William L. Dawson, Stephen Chambers, and William Fischer.
See also: W27; B5, B51, B122, B189, B245, B251, B298, B351, B393

D16.   *SINFONIA IN E* (1950)

Composers Recordings Inc. CRI-139. mono. released 1960; duration 17:56.
Oslo Philharmonic Orchestra; George Barati, cond.
With work by Norman Binkerd.
See also: W44; B51, B126, B201, B251, B256, B298, B335, B384, B397

D17.   *SIX DANCES FOR STRING ORCHESTRA* (1954)

Turnabout TVS 34536. stereo. released 1974; duration 19:40; (*The Contemporary Black Composer in the USA*).
Westphalian Symphony Orchestra, Recklinghausen; Paul Freeman, cond.
With works by William Grant Still.
See also: W53; D12; B51, B115, B213, B251, B298, B351, B397

D18.   *SUITE FOR FLUTE AND OBOE* (1943)

Composers Recordings Inc. CRI CD-561. compact disc. released 1988; duration 5:22 (*A Tribute to Otto Luening*).
New York Flute Club.
With works by Roger Goeb, *et al*.
See also: W17

D19.   *THREE FANFARES* [for four trumpets] (1964)

Crystal S230. stereo. released 1981; duration 1:35; (*Dallas Trumpets*).
Dallas Symphony Orchestra trumpet section (Richard Giangiulio, Bert Truax, Thomas Booth, and Glen Bell).
With works by Benjamin Britten, *et al*.
See also: W10

D20.   *TWO MADRIGALS* (1954)

Composers Recordings Inc. CRI-102. mono/stereo. released 1956; duration, app. 7:15; (*Lament for April 15th and Other Modern Madrigals*).
Randolph Singers; David Randolph, cond.
"How stands the glass around?" 3:29; "What's in a name?" 3:39.
With works by Avery Claflin, *et al*.
See also: W51, W54, W55; B51, B197, B251, B256, B335, B384

D21.   *UMBRIAN SCENE* (1963)

Louisville First Edition Records Lou-651 (XTV 96254). mono. released 1965; duration 9:25. (*The Louisville Orchestra*).
Louisville Orchestra; Robert Whitney, cond.; Jorge Mester, mus. dir.
With works by Charles Ives, *et al*.
See also: W91; B51, B126, B251, B256

WHAT'S IN A NAME? (1954) *See: Two Madrigals*

Bibliography by Kay

The bibliography is divided into two sections. The first, "Bibliography by Kay" (items prefixed by "K"), identifies articles that were written by the composer. The second section, "Bibliography about Kay and His Music" (items prefixed by "B"), contains articles related to the composer and his compositions. "See" references refer to individual works and particular performances as described in the "Works and Performances" section (e.g., *See*: W22) and in the "Discography" (e.g., *See*: D15). Additional citations (e.g., *See*: B6 and *See*: K6) refer to articles in the bibliographic sections, "Bibliography about Kay and His Music" and "Bibliography by Kay."

K1.　　"An American Composer Reports on Russian Musical Life." *National Music Council Bulletin* 19 (Winter 1959): 13-14.

Kay recounts visit to the Soviet Union with Roy Harris, Peter Mennin, and Roger Sessions, "arranged by the U.S. State Department under an agreement for cultural, technical and educational exchanges between the USSR and the U.S. The trip marked the first visit of a delegation of American composers to the Soviet Union by official invitation." Kay reveals that "the four American composers . . . were offered an opportunity to select the places they would like to visit and the people and things they would like to see. The choice . . . was narrowed down to Moscow, Leningrad, Tiflis and Kiev. These cities were chosen because of the variety of their musical life."

K2.　　"Ah, Roma!" *American Composers Alliance Bulletin* 3, no. 3 (1953): 16-17.

Narrative of Kay's lengthy visits to Perugia, Rome, and Naples (1950-51) to pursue his interest in the liturgical music of Italy. Other cities visited were Genoa, Torino, Firenze, and Arrezzo. "Knowing as we do the rich heritage of Italian liturgical music, one might think, as I did, that music in Italian churches is of high quality today. If the reader is of this opinion, let him disabuse himself of the idea, for nothing is further from the truth!" Kay described his experiences in the various regions with particular emphasis on performance, chorus participants, problems, and literature.

K3.   "I Hear Ya Talkin'." *American Composers Alliance Bulletin* 5, no. 2 (1955): 9.
         Kay reviews "Hear Me Talkin' to Ya," a chronicle on jazz, edited by Nat Shapiro and Nat Hentoff, and published by Rinehart. "[A] musical development . . . a way of life . . . is honestly and provokingly surveyed for those who are interested and would read. An excellent selection of long-playing records related to the group chapter headings and a detailed index make this book a most useful one."

K4.   "Impressions of the Soviet Musical Scene." *American Composers Alliance Bulletin* 8, no. 3 (1959): 17-18.
         Kay recounts his impressions of the music and musicians in Soviet Russia.

K5.   "The Roman Seasons." *American Composers Alliance Bulletin* 2, no. 3 (1952): 21-22.
         Impressions of the Italian musical scene based on Kay's observations during his three years at the American Academy in Rome as a Fellow and as a Fulbright student. "Possibly the most important factor is that policy in Italian musical life is based *primarily* on matters musical. True, audience and economic factors enter in, but only after musical considerations. And this occurs with no loss of public support and interest! Perhaps this state of affairs obtains because the Italian composers are in the forefront with the impressarios in all matters of policy, projects, and programming for concert, opera, and radio. And considering the scene as a whole, one senses a high general level of achievement with admirable direction, variety, continuity, and integration of materials, means, methods, and individuals."

K6.   "Stimulus for Talent." *American Composers Alliance Bulletin* 3, no. 1 (1953): 13, 16, 17.
         Kay reports on a long-range program, entitled "Student Radio Awards Competition," undertaken by BMI and radio broadcasters to encourage young American composers. Initiated in 1951, the activity has been aided by "those groups . . . responsible for the creation of concert music in the United States—music educators, publishers, performers, and the organizations through which these persons make themselves felt."

K7.   "Thirty Days in Musical Russia." *HiFi Review* 2 (February 1959): 35-38, 53.
         A diary of Kay's trip to Russia with Roy Harris, Roger Sessions, and Peter Mennin from September 17 to October 17, 1958. The daily account logs concerts, interviews, reviews, social gatherings, composer

interaction, and sight-seeing tours through the arts and political centers of Russia.

K8.   "Where Is Music Going?" *Music Journal* 20, no.1 (1962): 48, 99.
        Article reflects Kay's views on twentieth-century music, particularly noting "stylistic blending in . . . contemporary compositions." He concludes that "we are presently living in a musical period of great flux with a great deal being done creatively in a multitude of different styles of composition. Our decade will watch these styles and experiments, as they become more widely accepted by others, evolve and it remains for a very talented composer or others of perception and intelligence to utilize these factors and to mold them into a striking and comprehensive approach to composition."

Bibliography about Kay and
His Music

"See" references refer to related sources in the various sections of the volume: "W" to "Works and Performances," "D" to "Discography," "K" to "Bibliography by Kay," and "B" to "Bibliography about Kay and His Music."

B1.   Abdul, Raoul. *Blacks in Classical Music: A Personal History*. New York: Dodd, Mead, 1977, pp. 39-40, 57-58, 153, 197, 206, 212.
        A brief but colorful biographical sketch of Kay in which the author refers to Kay as "the most consistently played Black American composer.   One reason may be that he works within the broad European tradition . . . his output is so varied that there is a piece for every occasion."   Included also are brief notes of some of the performances of *Jubilee, Markings, Umbrian Scene,* and *Juggler of Our Lady. See*: W60, W91, W100, W123

B2.   ____. "The Current Scene." In *The Negro in Music and Art*, comp. and ed. by Lindsay Patterson. International Library of Negro Life and History. New York: Publishers Co., 1967, p. 187.
        In this source from the International Library of Negro Life and History, compiled under the auspices of the Association for the Study of Negro Life and History, Kay is briefly mentioned as a Negro composer whose works are often performed.

B3.   ____. "Reading the Score: Panorama of Symphonic Music." *Amsterdam News* (New York, NY), September 24, 1977, p. D6.
        Review of final concert in the New York Philharmonic's "Celebration of Black Composers" series featuring *Danse Nègre* (Samuel Coleridge-Taylor); *Danzas de Panama* (William Grant Still); *Concerto for Cello and Chamber Orchestra* (David Baker) with Eugene Moye, cellist; *Innerflexions* (Hale Smith); and *Three Pieces After Blake* (Ulysses Kay) with Irene Oliver, soprano. Abdul affirms that "the music of Ulysses Kay . . . lies firmly planted in the American main-

stream and, therefore, has a classic quality about it." *See*: W48a, B101

B4.   Alexander, Roy. "Music." *Time* (March 8, 1954): 71.
            Review of *Of New Horizons* conducted by Kay for the twenty-fifth anniversary of the Tucson Symphony in Arizona. *"Of New Horizons* started and ended with plenty of brass, but in the middle . . . made appealing use of melodic interweaving in the strings. And though composer Kay's melody kept getting interrupted by conflicting ideas, it also kept coming back. When the nine-minute work was over, the crowd gave the hometown composer the biggest hand of the evening." *See*: W20b; B103, B158, B269

B5.   Allen, William Duncan. "Musings of a Music Columnist." *Black Perspective in Music* 1 (Fall 1973): 107-14.
            Historical overview of blacks in the music profession. Mentions Kay as one of the composers represented on a program entitled, *The Black Composer in America*, given by the Youth Chamber Orchestra of Oakland, CA, under the direction of Robert Hughes. Selections from the program were recorded for Desto Records, *The Black Composer in America* (Stereo DC 7107). *See*: D15

B6.   "American Composer Update." *Pan Pipes of Sigma Alpha Iota* 72 (Winter 1980): 32-33.
            Compilation of premieres, performances, publications, and other information concerning Kay's works for the 1979-80 season. Of note is the premiere of *Chariots*, an orchestral rhapsody. *Five Portraits* and *Partita in A* (both composed for violin and piano) were published that year. *See*: W41, W115, W132

B7.   _____. *Pan Pipes of Sigma Alpha Iota* 73 (Winter 1981): 34.
            Compilation of performances, publications, and other news for 1980. Includes performances of *Four Inventions* and *First Nocturne* at the National Black Music Colloquium and Competition held at Kennedy Center (Washington, DC). Also cites performances of *Chariots*, *Southern Harmony*, and *Quintet Concerto* by the Shreveport Symphony in Grambling, LA, as well as performances of *Markings* by the New York Philharmonic and *Of New Horizons* by the Buffalo Philharmonic. Kay was the recipient of the University of Arizona's Alumni Achievement Award for 1980 and was visiting composer at Grambling State University.   Additionally, he was the resident Institute Fellow in the Humanities at Pennsylvania State University, April 3-May 4. *See*: W20x, W25b, W100m, W118a, W124b, W127a, W132a

B8.   _____. *Pan Pipes of Sigma Alpha Iota* 74 (Winter 1982): 32-33.
            Compilation of performances, publications, and other information for 1981. Among compositions performed were *Scherzi Musicali* and *Choral Triptych*. Kay was visiting composer at the University of

Missouri-Kansas City Conservatory of Music, November 2-6. *Aulos* won the Fifth Annual National Flute Association Competition. During February 1982, Kay was guest composer at Williams College (Williamstown, MA). *See:* W82, W103, W108

B9. _____. *Pan Pipes of Sigma Alpha Iota* 75 (Winter 1983): 32.
Compilation of performances, publications, awards, and appearances of Kay from 1981 through 1983. Mentions that Kay received an honorary Doctorate of Humanities degree from the University of Missouri on November 6, 1982. He was also guest composer at Howard University (Department of Music) for its "Meet the Composer Series," January 21-22, 1982.

B10. _____. *Pan Pipes of Sigma Alpha Iota* 77 (Winter 1985): 33.
Compilation of premieres, performances, and publications for 1984-85. Of note is the performance of *Festival Psalms* by the Holland Community Chorale on March 13, 1984. *Five Winds* received its premiere at the Tidewater Music Festival in July 1984. *See:* W134, W136

B11. _____. *Pan Pipes of Sigma Alpha Iota* 78 (Winter 1986): 28-29.
Compilation of premieres, performances, recordings, and appearances for 1985-86. Of special interest is the mention of an all-Kay program performed by the Kansas City Symphony Orchestra in February and the premiere performances of *Tromba* and *Umbrian Scene* during May and March, respectively. *See:* W91f, W135

B12. _____. *Pan Pipes of Sigma Alpha Iota* 79 (Winter 1987): 30.
Compilation of premieres, performances, and publications for 1985-87. *Guitarra* received its premiere in London, England; other works performed during this period included *Jersey Hours, Five Winds, Facets,* and *Pietà. Facets* is scheduled to be performed in New York City on March 19 and 20, 1987, on "Meet the Moderns," with Lukas Foss, conductor. A new work, *Pantomime,* has been written for solo clarinet and is published by Carl Fischer. *See:* W42, W113b, W119, W131, W136, W137

B13. _____. *Pan Pipes of Sigma Alpha Iota* 80 (Winter 1988): 30.
A summary of premieres, performances, and publications for 1987-88 includes the first performance of *Two Impromptus for Piano* (published by Pembroke/Fischer), played by Marcantonio Barone, pianist, on February 8, 1987, in the Weill Recital Hall, New York City. Other compositions performed that year were *Sinfonia in E* in Savannah, GA, by the Savannah Symphony, Julius P. Williams, guest conductor; *A Short Overture, Brief Elegy, Ancient Saga,* and *Reverie and Rondo* by the Rensselaer Polytechnic Symphony, Angelo Frascarelli, conductor in Troy, NY; and *Pietà* in New Jersey by the Garden State Chamber Orchestra, Frederick Storfer, conductor. Of special interest is the participation of Harvard University and three

other schools in the Boston area in a celebration, "Ulysses Kay Week," March 10-14, 1988. *See*: W22, W27, W28, W42, W44e, W94, W138

B14.   ____. *Pan Pipes of Sigma Alpha Iota* 84 (Winter 1992): 32.
            Notes the premiere of Kay's opera, *Frederick Douglass*, April 14, 1991, performed by the New Jersey State Opera Company with Alfredo Silipigni, conductor. Cites also librettist, Donald Dorr; director, Louis Johnson; and designer, Salvatore Tagliarino. *See*: W133

B15.   "American Composers Return from First Soviet Visit." *Musical America* 78 (December 1, 1958): 3, 33.
            Reflections of returning American composers, Ulysses Kay, Roy Harris, Peter Mennin, and Roger Sessions, who visited Russia under the auspices of the U.S. State Department in 1958. In a discussion of music life in the United States and in the Soviet Union, Kay explained that "the idea of the summer musical school, such as Aspen or Tanglewood, seemed completely new to Russian musicologists." He notes further that the high point of this tour was a concert of their own works in Moscow, which included Harris's *Fifth Symphony*, Kay's *Of New Horizons*, Mennin's *Sixth Symphony*, and Sessions's *Suite from "The Black Maskers."* "The concert was well publicized, the house sold out, and the program was exceptionally well received in Tchaikovsky Hall on Oct. 15. Sessions received an ovation, and the audience greatly appreciated and honestly enjoyed all the other music." *See*: W20g

B16.   "Amusements: Kay Wins Music Prize." *New York Times*, May 20, 1947, p. 33.
            Composer Kay receives fellowship to the American Academy in Rome. The grant is worth approximately three thousand dollars and covers the period from October 1, 1949 to September 30, 1950.

B17.   Anderson, Thomas Jefferson. "Black Composers and the Avant-Garde." In *Readings in Black American Music*, comp. and ed. by Eileen Southern. New York: W. W. Norton, 1972, p. 281.
            Discusses the influence the black composer is having upon the more recent facets of composition. Includes Kay and his relationship to the avant-garde movement in an excerpt from the article which first appeared in *Black Music In Our Culture*, edited by Dominique-René de Lerma (Kent, Ohio, 1970), pp. 63-67. *See*: B112

B18.   Ardoin, John. "A Black Composer's Concert." *American Musical Digest* 1, no. 5 (1970): 5-6 (Reprint from the *Dallas Morning News*, January 31, 1970).
            Reprint of review of concert of music by "American Negro Composers" performed by the Dallas Symphony with Paul Freeman, conductor. Includes performances of music by William Grant Still,

Ulysses Kay, George Walker and Stephen Chambers, a.k.a. Talib Rasul Hakim. "If a bond can be said to exist today between black and white composers, it is the common one of groping for a voice with which to communicate and to speak what each feels and must express through music. . . . But a man like Kay holds out the same sort of hope to black music that a man like Gunther Schuller does for the white composer. And Kay does so because of the obvious strength he has garnered between a mechanical work . . . the *Toccata* [from the *Concerto for Orchestra*, 1948] . . . and the stirring . . . *Markings* of 1966. . . . Kay has left the starting post: men like Chambers, Hale Smith and George Walker are still there. Whether they will sprint forward as Kay has done remains to be seen. At least there is someone to be followed." Photo of Kay and photo of Freeman included. *See*: W32, W100e

B19.   Ardoyno, Dolores. "Opera/South: How Do You Start an Opera Company for Blacks? Ask a White Sister." *Opera News* 37 (January 6, 1973): 10-13.
          Historical review of Opera/South, founded by Sister M. Elise, S.B.S. (1898-1982). Kay's *Juggler of Our Lady* and Still's *Highway 1, U.S.A.* were its first professional stagings. "A free matinee of the Kay and Still works pushed audience development to its logical source: schools. Students were bused in from surrounding counties that do not have easy access to opera. . . . Campus production work and the student matinee were heavily publicized. . . . But the real catalyst was the addition of one of the most exciting black conductors in the country, Broadway's Margaret Harris." *See*: W60a

B20.   Armstrong, Donald Jan. "A Study of Some Important Twentieth Century Secular Compositions for Women's Chorus with a Preliminary Discussion of Secular Choral Music from a Historical and Philosophical Viewpoint." D.M.A. dissertation, University of Texas at Austin, 1968. Discusses contemporary works by American composers, Elliott Carter, David Diamond, Dorothy James, Ulysses Kay, Boris Koutzen, Vincent Persichetti, Daniel Pinkham, William Schuman, and Virgil Thomson.

B21.   "Arranger for Rhapsody in Black." *New York Times*, September 2, 1977, p. C9.
          Account of final program of the week-long celebration of black composers featuring works by William Grant Still, Ulysses Kay, David Baker, and Hale Smith. Leon Thompson, conductor, cited the diversity of black music written in the European tradition. *See*: W48a

B22.   "Arts Academy Will Induct 14 New Members, May 23." *New York Times*, April 5, 1979, p. C11.
          Kay is one of the persons to be inducted into membership in the Academy of Arts and Letters in New York City.

B23.   Arvey, Verna. "Symphonies In Black." *Music Journal* (April 1974): 28-29, 32-36.
An overview of African and African-American composers from the mid-eighteenth century to 1974. Among those mentioned are Fela Sowande and J. K. Nketia, prominent African composers. Ulysses Kay and Hale Smith are mentioned as established American composers.

B24.   Austin, William H. *Music in the 20th Century: From Debussy through Stravinsky.* New York: W.W. Norton & Co., 1966, pp. 407, 505-6.
Kay is reported as one of Hindemith's students in America. Others mentioned are Howard Boatwright, Norman Dello Joio, Alvin Etler, Lukas Foss, Easley Blackwood, Mel Powell, and Yehudi Wyner. Austin further discusses the "variegated individual qualities" of an American school of composers during the 1930s. Kay is included in this group of composers born during the period, 1906-26, a group which Austin considers, "'a worthy counterpart of the American poets and painters of the same generation.'"

B25.   "BMI Names Kay to Top Music Post." *Afro-American*, National Ed., April 4, 1953, p. 7.
Notes the appointment of Kay to the position of editorial advisor on contemporary concert music at Broadcast Music, Inc. Brief biographical sketch included.

B26.   Bailey, Ben E. "Opera/South: A Brief History." *Black Perspective in Music* 13 (Spring 1985): 55-57, 68-71.
Historical overview of Opera/South and its productions. Includes programs and flyers listing names of principals, conductors, and directors of Kay's *Juggler of Our Lady* and of *Jubilee*. *See*: W60a, W123a

B27.   Baker, David N., Lida M. Belt, and Herman C. Hudson, eds. *The Black Composer Speaks: A Project of the Afro-American Arts Institute, Indiana University.* Metuchen, NJ: Scarecrow Press, 1978, pp. 139-71.
Provides definitive biography with text of interview with the composer and a full catalog of his compositions to 1976.

B28.   Baker, Theodore. *Baker's Biographical Dictionary of Musicians.* 8th ed., completely revised by Nicolas Slonimsky. New York: Schirmer Books, 1992, p. 897.
Biographical sketch of Kay includes an abbreviated list of compositions and a short bibliography.

B29.   *Band Music Guide.* 7th ed. Evanston, IL: Instrumentalist Co., 1978, p. 292.
This update to the sixth edition (Instrumentalist, 1975, p. 285) is

an index providing an "alphabetical listing of titles and composers of all band music." In the previous edition, Kay's *Four Silhouettes*, *Short Suite for Concert Band*, and *Solemn Prelude* are included, with descriptive information by size, grade, publisher, and date. *Four Silhouettes* is graded "for those beyond the beginning stage," *Short Suite*, for "more advanced instrumentalists," and *Solemn Prelude*, "mostly for college players." The current edition adds Kay's *Forever Free: A Lincoln Chronicle* which is also graded "mostly for college players." *See*: W38, W43, W83, W116

B30.   Basart, Ann P., comp. and ed. "Music Reviews." In *Notes, The Quarterly Journal of the Music Library Association* 30 (September 1973): 152-53.
    "New music" section includes a review of *Scherzi Musicali*, written by Arthur Custer. *See*: W108

B31.   "Bicentennial Overview." *Black Perspective in Music* 5 (Fall 1977): 238-40.
    Review of bicentennial events that focused attention upon the music of black composers. Noted are the commissions received by Kay from JCPenney, one of the first business corporations to contribute to the bicentennial observances for a choral work; from the National Symphony for *Western Paradise*; from the Southeastern Metropolitan Orchestra Managers Association for *Southern Harmony*; and from Opera/South for *Jubilee*. Other special concerts included performances by the Harvard University Band in a salute to black composers of band music. Kay's *Quintet Concerto* was performed during the "Celebration of Contemporary Music," sponsored by the New York Philharmonic and the Fromm Foundation. Triad Presentations (NY) and the Rene Chamber Ensemble (Los Angeles Museum) also presented concerts of music by black composers. *Jubilee* received its world premiere by Opera/South with James DePriest, conductor. *See*: D13; W123, W124a, W127, W129

B32.   "Black American Music Symposium: The Program." *Black Perspective in Music* 14 (Winter 1986): 55, 59, 69, 71, 72.
    Includes programs, articles, and photos of the Symposium on Black American Music held at the University of Michigan, August 9-15, 1985, during which Kay served as panelist on the composers' forum. His compositions, *Aulos*, *String Quartet No. 2*, *Organ Suite*, and *Two Dunbar Lyrics* were performed during the week-long symposium. *See*: W61a, W67d, W98a, W103a

B33.   Brooks, Tilford Uthratese. *America's Black Musical Heritage*. Englewood Cliffs, NJ: Prentice-Hall, 1984, pp. 196, 231-36, 285-91, 306-7.
    An update of the 1972 Washington University doctoral dissertation by Brooks ("A Historical Study of Black Music and Selected Twentieth Century Black Composers...") gives an historical overview

of black American music. Includes biographical sketches of seventeen African American composers whose works come from the "European Tradition," with lists of their compositions and recordings in the appendices. Ulysses Kay appears among the biosketches of "The Eclectics." Also provides a brief discussion of his musical style and includes an analysis of *Fantasy Variations*, a catalog of compositions to 1977, musical examples, and photo. *See*: W89; B336, B337

B34.   Brown, Ernest James. "An Annotated Bibliography of Selected Solo Music Written for the Piano by Black Composers." D.M.A dissertation, University of Maryland, 1976.

A descriptive catalog of keyboard music written by selected black composers. Includes biographical data of Kay and others. Lists his piano works: *Four Inventions, Ten Short Essays*, and *First Nocturne*, with brief descriptive information by style, meter, rhythm, level of difficulty, harmony, etc. *See*: W25, W63, W118; B271, B272, B339

B35.   Brown, Rae Linda. *Music, Printed and Manuscript, in the James Weldon Johnson Memorial Collection of Negro Arts and Letters: An Annotated Catalog*. Critical Studies on Black Life and Culture, vol. 23. New York: Garland Publishing, 1982, pp. 20-21.

Includes a miniature score of *Suite for Orchestra* and manuscripts of *Suite for Orchestra*, inscribed by Kay "'to the J. W. Johnson [James Weldon Johnson] Collection, Dec. 2, 1948'" and of *Jeremiah* with the inscription "'to CVV'" (Carl Van Vechten), signed and dated, "'New York, June 29, 1946.'" These compositions are housed in the collection which was established by Carl Van Vechten in 1941 at Yale. This collection is "a major repository for manuscripts, writings and first editions by major Black literary figures . . . less well known . . . is the fact that the collection also contains a rich deposit of musical materials which parallels the achievements of the musicians' literary counterparts." *See*: W21, W30

B36.   Bull, Storm. *Index to Biographies of Contemporary Composers*. Vol. 3. Metuchen, NJ: Scarecrow Press, 1987, p. 387.

This concordance of reference sources relating to composers "either still alive or who were born in 1900 or later" updates volumes 1 (1964) and 2 (1974). It adds 5,900 new entries and cites Kay in 25 sources, including foreign dictionaries and encyclopedias.

B37.   Burbank, Richard. *Twentieth Century Music*. New York: Facts on File Publications, 1984, pp. 81, 261, 352, 361, 376, 399, 405.

This source, with an introduction by Nicolas Slonimsky, includes a chronological listing of musical events and pertinent information concerning twentieth century musicians. Recorded are the dates of Kay's birth and the premiere dates of *Symphony in E, Markings, Stephen Crane, Aulos, Concerto for Orchestra, Quintet*, and *Western Paradise*. *See*: W32, W44, W100, W103, W104, W124, W129

B38.   Burgett, Paul Joseph. "Aesthetics of the Music of Afro-Americans: A Critical Analysis of the Writings of Selected Black Scholars with Implications for Black Music Studies and for Music Education." Ph.D. dissertation, Eastman School of Music of the University of Rochester, 1976.
        Discusses the ideology and aesthetics of two scholars, Alain Locke and Imamu Baraka, as they relate to black music and the implications that their theories bring to the development of curricula for music education. Briefly mentions Kay as one of the younger black musicians who writes in the classical tradition. Also cites Kay in the discography.

B39.   Butcher, Margaret Just. *The Negro in American Culture.* 2nd ed. New York: Alfred A. Knopf, 1972, p. 90.
        This source, which is based on materials left by Alain Locke, briefly mentions Kay's music "in terms of what *Times's* music critic called 'listenable fashion'. . . . His background music of *The Quiet One* was quiet indeed, if not banal. His symphonic score *Of New Horizons* . . . is far more important and won him good critical notices." Further mention is made of *Suite for Orchestra, Sinfonia in E*, and *[Two] Meditations. See:* W20, W21, W34, W44, W46

B40.   Butler, Stanley. *Guide to the Best in Contemporary Piano Music: An Annotated List of Graded Solo Piano Music Published Since 1950.* Vol. 2; *Levels 6 through 8.* Metuchen, NJ: Scarecrow Press, 1973, p. 42.
        Analysis of Kay's *Four Inventions.* "Discerning neo-baroque works of distinct character. Lines are always musical before being pianistic; require resourceful fingering and short pedals for legato. Wide stretch helpful. Three works have subject imitation in two or three voices. Tonal, freely using all twelve tones. I is a lovely three-voice Andante moderato concentrating on a wide-ranging subject; has episode with syncopated rhythm. II is a delightful Scherzando in 5/8 with dynamic and articulation variety. Frequent lateral staccato shifts." *See:* W25

B41.   Caldwell, Hansonia LaVerne. "Black Idioms in the Works of Six Afro-American Composers." Ph.D. dissertation, University of Southern California, 1975. 285 pp.
        Examines the black idiom in opera and discusses the achievements of Afro-American composers in serious music. Selected for review are: Scott Joplin, Clarence Cameron White, Alonzo Levister, Mark Fax, Arthur Cunningham, and Ulysses Kay. Includes a biography of Kay and analyses of his one-act operas: *The Boor, The Juggler of Our Lady*, and *The Capitoline Venus. See:* W57, W60, W110

B42.   Carr, J. "Choral Performances." *American Choral Review* 12 (July 1970): 118.
        Review of the world premiere of *Once There Was a Man* at the

Worcester (MA) Festival performed by the Detroit Symphony and the Kenneth Jewell Chorale, with Sixten Ehrling, conducting. "Kay's work relies heavily on a narrator to advance the hopeful notion that this country has always produced the leader it needed when the need was most pressing. Narrator William Warfield cited Washington, Lincoln, Franklin D. Roosevelt, John and Robert Kennedy, and Martin Luther King, Jr. for their ability to elicit whatever was needed to preserve the nation. . . . As an editorial, the new work is admirably optimistic; as a musical statement, though, it seems pallid." *See*: W111

B43.   Carter, Madison H. *An Annotated Catalog of Composers of African Ancestry.* New York: Vantage Press, 1986, p. 69.

Includes subject index, lists of publishers, and libraries from which composers' music may be obtained. The entry, s. v., "Kay, Ulysses Simpson," indicates six publishing houses that distribute his compositions.

B44.   Carter, Warrick L. "Black Composers: Their Contribution to Serious Music." *Orchestra News* 11 (June 1972): 6, 10.

Discusses the lack of information pertaining to contemporary European-influenced black composers in current music studies. Mention of important nineteenth and twentieth century composers includes Kay, Ignatius Sancho, Newport Gardner, Thomas Kerr, Adolphus Hailstork, among others. The author concludes "that black composers should be included in any study of music, not only because they are black and historically have been selectively omitted from all previous study of serious music, but more important, because they are (were) great musicians and offer the student and/or performer a new and challenging source of literature and information."

B45.   *Central Opera Service Bulletin* 14 (Fall 1971): 2.

Notes premiere performance of *Capitoline Venus* at the University of Illinois in Urbana. *See*: W110

B46.   Chapin, Louis. "Ulysses Kay." *BMI, The Many Worlds of Music* (February 1970): 9.

Review of Kay's rise "as a representative, articulate American composer." Includes biographical information and a discussion of Kay's compositional style, with observations by the composer. Chapin concludes that "Ulysses Kay possesses keen musical draftsmanship, superb discipline and a steady concern. From the middle of his road, the view ahead over the countryside looks lively and promising." Photo.

B47.   "Charter Members of SAI Bureau Send Their Best Wishes." *Pan Pipes of Sigma Alpha Iota* 78 (Winter 1987): 5.

The fortieth Annual Contemporary American Music Issue is dedicated to the twenty-two charter members who are regularly represented in the "American Composer Update" section. Congratulatory messages from many of the outstanding composers include Kay's greeting: "'All praises be to SAI—for keeping the record straight and encouraging us composers lo these many years.'"

B48.   Chase, Gilbert. *America's Music: From the Pilgrims to the Present*. New York: McGraw-Hill, 1955, pp. 557-58.
        Includes brief biography of Kay and an extensive bibliography on American music. Mentions Kay's musical training; his significant prizes and awards; his service in the Navy; and the performance of *Of New Horizons* in Tucson, with Kay, conductor. *See*: W20b; B4

B49.   "Classical Composer to Tour Russia for State Dept." *Jet* 14 (July 17, 1958): 62.
        Notes that Kay is selected for a thirty-day tour with five other composers. *See*: K1, K7

B50.   Cody, Carlos Bernard. "A Study of Selected Band Compositions of Three Twentieth Century Composers: William Grant Still, Ulysses Kay, and Hale Smith." Ph. D. dissertation, University of Southern Mississippi, 1990.
        Includes a biography of Kay and an analysis of Kay's *Forever Free: A Lincoln Chronicle*. According to the author, "The primary purpose of [the] study was to demonstrate that selected band compositions...can provide awareness, knowledge, and understanding about compositional styles of Afro-American composers of wind literature....Each...composition was analyzed with regard to form, melody, harmony, rhythm, scoring and instrumentation." *See*: W83

B51.   Cohn, Arthur. *Recorded Classical Music: A Critical Guide to Compositions and Performances*. New York: Schirmer Books, 1981, pp. 964-65.
        Gives critical analysis from the listener's perspective of ten of Kay's recorded works: *Fantasy Variations, Markings, Sinfonia in E, Six Dances for String Orchestra, Organ Suite No. 1, Brass Quartet*, "How Stands the Glass Around?," "What's In a Name?," *Umbrian Scene*, and *Short Overture*. *See*: D1, D4, D7, D10, D15, D16, D17, D20, D21

B52.   "College and School News." *Crisis* 69 (April 1962): 249.
        Includes a review of *The Juggler of Our Lady* at Xavier University on February 23, 1962, with Mervin Wallace, college senior, in lead role. *See*: W60a

B53.   "Commentary." *Black Perspective in Music* 1 (Fall 1973): 202.
        Notes Opera/South's 1972 performance of *The Juggler Of Our Lady* and of *Highway No. 1, U.S.A.* (Still); "Voice of America" recorded the performances. "According to the critics, the operas were effectively staged with special credits going to both participants and

composers, whose works proved to possess unusual audience appeal."
This unpublished recording may be found in the Library of Congress
(Motion Picture, Broadcasting, and Recorded Sound Division). *See*:
W60a

B54.   ____. *Black Perspective in Music* 2 (Spring 1974): 104, 106-7.
Notes Kay's appearance as guest composer at the James Dick
Piano Institute (Round Top, TX), June 1973, and as guest composer-
conductor at Appalachian State University (Boone, NC), April 1973.
Includes memo from C. Edward Thomas, Executive Director of the
Afro-American Music Opportunities Association (AAMOA), who
indicates that Kay was among the composers present for the
Baltimore Symposium (September 23-30). Notes, also, that the first
records of the "Black Composers Series" will include Kay's *Markings*
as well as compositions by the Chevalier de Saint-Georges, Clarence
Cameron White, Samuel Coleridge-Taylor, William Grant Still, and
George Walker. Dominique-René de Lerma is chief consultant for the
project. *See*: W100; D7; B100

B55.   ____. *Black Perspective in Music* 2 (Fall 1974): 231.
Notes the release by Columbia Records of a series of "at least 12
recordings featuring the works of some 20 black composers." The
first release of four recordings in March 1974 included *Markings* in
vol. 3. *See*: W100; D7

B56.   ____. *Black Perspective in Music* 3 (Spring 1975): 121, 122-23.
Historical overview of black choral organizations with emphasis
upon "new black opera companies" and productions. Opera/South is
mentioned for its presentation of Kay's *The Juggler of Our Lady* and
for its commission to Kay to write *Jubilee*, based on a novel by poet-
writer Margaret Walker, a professor at Jackson State University in
Mississippi. Cites also that Dominique-René de Lerma, then Director
for Research and Publications of AAMOA, notes the initiation of
"AAMOA's Black Music Symposia," an annual series of conferences
to begin in 1973. Cooperating universities and organizations include
Morgan State College, Johns Hopkins University, Goucher College,
and the Baltimore Symphony Orchestra. The 1974 symposium was
sponsored by the Houston Symphony Orchestra in cooperation with
the Black Arts Center, the Houston Independent School District,
Prairie View A&M, Rice, Texas Southern, and Houston Universities.
Kay was present at each symposium and served on the Artistic
Committee with Eileen Southern, George Walker, and Olly Wilson.
See: W60a, W123

B57.   ____. *Black Perspective in Music* 3 (Fall 1975): 345-48.
Report of AAMOA's Black Music Symposium in Minneapolis, MN
(May 1975), during which orchestral and chamber music programs
featured works of Ulysses Kay, R. Nathaniel Dett, Howard Swanson,
David Baker, Coleridge-Taylor Perkinson, and others. At the

completion of the symposia, AAMOA, with the assistance of the
hosting cities, plans "to organize a coalition of concerned citizens who
will assist in furthering the cause of black music. . . ." Also includes
a reprint of Carla Bley's article, "Corrective New Distribution," from
Jazz Composer's Orchestra Association, Inc., (Winter 1974).   Bley
noted that " . . . musicians are becoming impatient with the crass
commercialism of the established recording companies and are
striking out on their own." Bley further notes that these composers'
companies, "loosely known as FIRMS (Friendly Independent Record
Makers) . . . range from the large collection of contemporary
American composers' works on CRI . . . to the one-person, one-record
operation."   Among the composers included are Roger Sessions,
Stephan Wolpe, T. J. Anderson, George Crumb, and Kay.

B58.   ____. *Black Perspective in Music* 4 (Spring 1976):   124-26.
            Notes first performance of *Harlem Children's Dance Suite* by the
Harlem School of the Arts (New York, NY) in March.   *Quintet
Concerto* was included in the "Celebration of Contemporary Music
Festival" at Lincoln Center. *See*:   W120, W124a

B59.   ____. *Black Perspective in Music* 5 (Fall 1977):   236-37.
            Overview of program initiated by Altoona Trent Johns and Undine
Moore entitled, "The Black Man in American Music" at Virginia State
University, which "brought to the University . . . and the surrounding
community a wide variety of musical events encompassing all aspects
of Black music."   Included in the project was a "Music of Ulysses
Kay" concert in 1970.   Further reference is made to a news release
from the New York Philharmonic announcing "A Celebration of Black
Composers" (August 29-September 2, 1977).   The concerts will
present works of Ulysses Kay, Adolphus Hailstork, Roque Cordero,
and others, and will be held at Avery Fisher Hall, at the Lincoln
Center Library Auditorium, and at the Museum of the Performing
Arts. The "Celebration" is sponsored by the New York Philharmonic
with supporting funds from the New York State Council on the Arts
and the National Endowment for the Arts.

B60.   ____. *Black Perspective in Music* 6 (Spring 1978):   110.
            Review of the week-long "Celebration of Black Composers," which
included a performance of Kay's *Three Pieces After Blake*. *See*: W48a

B61.   ____. *Black Perspective in Music* 7 (Fall 1979):   277.
            Notes that during 1978, Kay received an honorary doctorate from
Dickinson College (Carlisle, PA) and a grant from the National
Endowment for the Arts.

B62.   ____. *Black Perspective in Music* 8 (Spring 1980):   120.
            Notes that Kay received the BMI Commendation of Excellence
Award after the world premiere of *Chariots*. He was also elected to

the American Academy and Institute of Arts and Letters in 1979. *See*: W132

B63.   ____. *Black Perspective in Music* 10 (Fall 1982): 234.
Notes an honorary doctorate conferred upon Kay by the University of Missouri-Kansas City in November 1981.

B64.   ____. *Black Perspective in Music* 13 (Spring 1985): 127.
Notes an all-Kay, "Meet the Composer" concert by the Kansas City Symphony in February 1985, which was co-sponsored by the Conservatory of Music of the University of Missouri-Kansas. Also notes the New York City performances of *Chariots* and *Umbrian Scene*. *See*: W91f, W132b

B65.   ____. *Black Perspective in Music* 13 (Fall 1985): 246.
Notes the aforementioned "Meet the Composer" concert in which Kay appeared as guest conductor. In addition, a concert/symposium, "Music of the Black Composer," was sponsored by the National Museum of American History (Roger Kennedy, director) and the Smithsonian Program in Black American Culture (Bernice Johnson Reagon, director). Featured among the performers were Fred Irby and Ronald Tymus [premiering Kay's *Tromba*], Thomas Flagg, D. Antoinette Handy, Rawn Spearman, and others. Kay gave the closing address. *See*: W135

B66.   "Composer Ulysses Kay to Judge Italian Talent." *Afro-American*, National Ed., September 17, 1960, p. 8.
Relates that Kay will serve on the International Music Jury of the "Prix Italia" at a meeting in Trieste, from September 26-October 3, 1960. The jury determines the recipients of the "Prix Italia" award, which is presented for internationally outstanding achievement in radio and television in the categories of music, literature, and documentaries. Includes biographical sketch of Kay, noting his USSR tour and his BMI experience.

B67.   "Composer Named Professor at Hunter College." *Jet* 34 (May 30, 1968): 47.
Notes Kay's appointment to Hunter College (NY). Gives brief sketch of composer's life and includes photo.

B68.   "Composer Reports on Russian Visit." *Amsterdam News* (New York, NY), November 29, 1958, p. 13.
Kay recounts his impressions of Russian music and of his tour in the USSR. Article provides background information concerning the U.S. State Department tour and includes a brief biographical sketch. Photo. *See*: K1, K7

B69.   "Composers in Focus." *BMI* (Winter 1976): 24-25.
Profile on Kay with photo, notes his achievements and works.

"After working for 15 years as musical consultant for BMI—a post he still holds—Kay was appointed professor of music at Herbert H. Lehman College . . . in 1968. . . . In 1972, he became Distinguished Professor of Music at Lehman College."

B70.　"Composer's Corner." *Musical America* (January 15, 1949): 33.
　　　Notes that Kay's *Portrait Suite* won "the contest for best symphonic work by a native of Arizona." It will be performed by the Phoenix Symphony. *See:* W33

B71.　"Composer's TV Practice." *Jet* 13 (May 1, 1958): 62.
　　　Notes that Kay has written the background music for segment, entitled: *FDR: Third Term to Pearl Harbor* for CBS-TV's "Twentieth Century." Includes photo. *See:* W65

B72.　"Concert Hall." *American Composers Alliance Bulletin* 2, no. 2 (1952): 22.
　　　Notes performances of *The Lion, the Griffin and the Kangaroo* in Rome on December 1951; *Suite for Orchestra* in Rome on January 4; and *Song for Strings* [*Suite for Strings*] in Naples on January 8. *See:* W21, W31a, W47

B73.　_____. *American Composers Alliance Bulletin* 2, no. 3 (1952): 17.
　　　Notes performances of *Five Inventions* by Thomas H. Kerr, Jr. at the National Gallery (Washington, DC) and of *Solemn Prelude* by the Eastman School Symphony Band at the University of Rochester. *See:* W24a, W38a

B74.　_____. *American Composers Alliance Bulletin* 2, no. 4 (1952-1953): 22.
　　　Notes performance of *Suite for Strings* at the Museum of Modern Art with Leopold Stokowski, conductor. *See:* W31b

B75.　_____. *American Composers Alliance Bulletin* 3, no. 1 (1953): 25.
　　　Notes premiere performances of *Brass Quartet* at the Brooklyn Museum (NY) by the Third Street Music School Quartet and of *Second Meditation* for organ by Arthur Crowley at Fisk University (Nashville, TN). *See:* W39, W46

B76.　_____. *American Composers Alliance Bulletin* 3, no. 2 (1953): 23.
　　　Notes performances of *Prelude for Flute Alone, Duo for Flute and Clarinet* (University of Maine), and *String Quartet [No. 1]* (National Gallery, Washington, DC). *See:* W14, W17a, W37

B77.　_____. *American Composers Alliance Bulletin* 3, no. 4 (1953-54): 14.
　　　Notes performance of *A Lincoln Letter* at Lincoln College (Lincoln, IL), with Bruce Foote, soloist. *See:* W49

B78.   _____. *American Composers Alliance Bulletin* 4, no. 1 (1954): 22-23.
                Reprints of excerpts of reviews of *Symphony in E* by Elmore Bacon
                (*Cleveland News*) and by Herbert Ewell (*Cleveland Plain Dealer*),
                April 2, 1954; of *Piano Quintet* by Paul Hume (*Washington Post and
                Times Herald*), April 19, 1954; of *Two Dances* ["Round Dance" and
                "Polka"] in *Southgate, Rochester Democrat and Chronicle*, March 8;
                and of *Triumvirate, Of New Horizons*, and *Song of Jeremiah* by
                Sidney Dalton (*Nashville Banner*), April 24. Other performances
                noted in April and May are: *Partita in A* and *Little Suite for String
                Quartet. See*: W20, W30, W31c, W36a, W41a, W44a, W50, W53

B79.   _____. *American Composers Alliance Bulletin* 7, no. 4 (1958): 25.
                Notes premiere performance of *Pietà* and its review in the *New
                York Herald-Tribune*, February 13, 1958. Also lists eight
                performances of "Like As a Father" by the Illinois Wesleyan
                University Choir on tour. *See*: W42, W59b

B80.   _____. *American Composers Alliance Bulletin* 8, no. 2 (1959): 24.
                Notes premiere performance of "Fugitives" (Town Hall) and other
                performances of *Grace to You, and Peace* (Central Moravian Church),
                Of New Horizons (Moscow State Radio Orchestra), and *Suite for
                Brass Choir* (U.S. Army Field Band, Fort Meade, MD). Of special
                interest is the review of *Of New Horizons* by Yuri Shaporin in *Pravda*
                (Moscow, USSR). *See*: W16a, W20g, W40a, W58a; B260

B81.   _____. *American Composers Alliance Bulletin* 8, no. 3 (1959): 22.
                Notes performance of *Quartet for Two Trumpets, Tenor and Brass
                Trombones* (University of Illinois), December 18, 1958, and the
                premiere performance of *First Suite for Organ* (New York), December
                29, 1958. *See*: W39b, W67

B82.   _____. *American Composers Alliance Bulletin* 8, no. 4 (1959): 27.
                Notes performance in Idaho of "How Stands the Glass Around?."
                See: W51b

B83.   _____. *American Composers Alliance Bulletin* 9, no. 1 (1959): 22-23.
                Notes performance of *Phoebus, Arise* (Town Hall) and includes
                selected comments from reviews by Francis D. Perkins in *New York
                Herald Tribune* and by Ross Parmenter in *New York Times*, May 18,
                1959. *First Suite for Organ* was performed in the Netherlands. *See*:
                W67a, W72

B84.   _____. *American Composers Alliance Bulletin* 9, no. 2 (1960): 22.
                Notes performances of *Short Suite for Band* (Brevard, NC); "Like
                As a Father" (King's Chapel Choir, Boston, MA); and *Serenade No.
                2 for Four Horns, Partita in A, Fugitive Songs*, and *Second String
                Quartet* (University of Illinois). The latter concert of chamber music

by Kay was reviewed by Dorothy Hagan in the *Champaign-Urbana Courier* (Champaign, IL, November 6, 1959). *See*: W40b, W41d, W43b, W59b, W61, W62

B85.   _____. *American Composers Alliance Bulletin* 9, no. 3 (1960): 32.
Notes performance of *Organ Suite No. 1* (Rochester, NY), January 3, 1960. *See*: W67

B86.   _____. *American Composers Alliance Bulletin* 9, no. 4 (1961): 22, 25.
Notes performance of *String Quartet* (Washington, DC), May 1, 1960, and two performances of *Organ Suite No. 1* (Indiana University, April 24, 1960, and Grambling College, May 1, 1960). *See*: W37, W67

B87.   _____. *American Composers Alliance Bulletin* 10, no. 1 (1962): 24, 29.
The "chamber" section notes performance of *Duo for Flute and Oboe* (Summit, NJ), January 8, 1961. The "choral" section notes performance of "Welcome Yule" (Illinois Wesleyan University) during the 1960 season. Includes also the premiere performance of *Hymn-Anthem on the Tune "Hanover"* at the Berkshire Music Center in July, and at the University of Rochester in August. *See*: W17b, W56a, W71a

B88.   _____. *American Composers Alliance Bulletin* 10, no. 3 (1962): 19, 24, 34.
The "orchestral" section includes reprints of excerpts of reviews. Bayard Ennis, of the *Charleston Gazette*, reviews the February 19 performance of *Sinfonia in E* by the Charleston Symphony Orchestra in Charleston, WV. The premiere performance of *Trigon* is reviewed by Donald Steinfirst of the *Pittsburgh Post*. The "chamber" section notes performances of *Duo for Flute and Oboe* in Teaneck, NJ (February 28); *Suite for Brass Choir* at the Peabody Conservatory of Music, Baltimore, MD (May 27); and *Serenade No. 3* [String Quartet No. 3] in Boston (September 17). The "vocal" section notes the premiere performance of *City of Magic* in New York (October 10). *See*: W16b, W17c, W44b, W66, W79, W80; B132, B299

B89.   _____. *American Composers Alliance Bulletin* 11, nos. 2-4 (1963): 34-36.
The twenty-fifth Anniversary Issue notes 1962 performances of *Brass Quartet* (New York City); *Psalm [A New Song]* (New York City); *Sinfonia in E* (Tucson); *String Quartet No. 2* (University of Michigan School of Music); *Suite for Organ* (Champaign, IL); *A New Song* (New York City); *Of New Horizons*; *Forever Free*; and *The Juggler of Our Lady*. *See*: W20, W39c, W44c, W59c, W60, W61a, W67b, W83

B90.   _____. *American Composers Alliance Bulletin* 12, no. 1 (1964): 20.
           Includes reviews of the premiere performance of *Fantasy Variations*. Marshall F. Bryant in the *Portland* (ME) *Press Herald* (November 29, 1963) states that "Fantasy Variations is an important contribution to American music and should find its way into the general orchestral repertoire and be widely used.'" Harrison Born in the *Portland Evening Express* (November 30) describes the work as "'interesting . . . it is a pleasant work, conservative in style, rich in sound skillful in construction.'" Harriett Johnson's review in the *New York Post* (December 3) emphasizes the skill and imagination of Kay. "'There is a tugging heartbreak . . . as if Kay couldn't help expressing pent-up sorrow and agitation from an idea which seems, at its core, a spiritual. Even in its lighter moments, when it becomes a complicated waltz tune, there is melancholy and frustration.'" Other 1963-64 performances noted are "Like As a Father" (King's Chapel Choir, October 13), *Umbrian Scene*, and *Of New Horizons* (American Symphony Orchestra, October 21). The premiere of *Umbrian Scene* is reviewed by Frank Gagnard in *Times Picayune* (New Orleans, LA; April 1, 1964), who reveals that Kay "'sought to evoke . . . memories of a trip to the Italian district of Umbria, . . . that included visual as well as musical impressions.'" *See:* W20k, W59b, W89, W91

B91.   _____. *American Composers Alliance Bulletin* 13, no. 1 (1965): 27.
           Notes 1964 performances of *Duo for Flute and Oboe* (Woodstock, NJ; and New York); *Forever Free* (Trenton, NJ); *Of New Horizons* (three performances—Portland, OR; Lima, Peru; and Brevard, NC); *Prelude—Two Meditations* (Nashville, TN); "Sing Unto the Lord" (Cambridge, MA); *String Quartet No. 3* (Urbana, IL); *Suite for Orchestra* (New York City); and *Umbrian Scene* (New York premiere). *See:* W17d, W20l, W20m, W20n, W21d, W46f, W59, W79c, W83c, W91a

B92.   ". . . Courante." *American Composers Alliance Bulletin* 10, no. 1 (1962): 18.
           "New Music" lists Kay's *Trigon* in its "Chamber Works" section. *See:* W80

B93.   _____. *American Composers Alliance Bulletin* 10, no. 2 (1962): 26.
           The "Commissions and Awards" section notes commission to Kay from the Society for Ethical Culture for the choral composition, *To Light That Shines*. *See:* W87

B94.   Cowell, Henry. "Current Chronicle: United States." *Musical Quarterly* 41-45 (January 1955-60): 86-87, 89.
           Notes that a revival of madrigal writing among American composers may be attributed to an invitation by David Randolph and the Randolph Singers, to write madrigals "with good performance as

a bait." Of Kay's "How Stands the Glass Around?," Cowell mentions that "he employs a solid imitative counterpoint, exceptionally well written, in a manner based on the old, but with a most consistent handling of minor sevenths and major ninths, in the texture." Musical examples provided. *See*: W51

B95. Cox, Ainslee. "New Works." *Music Journal* 22 (October 1964): 65.
Review of the New York opening concert of the twenty-first convention of the National Association of Negro Musicians, during which Kay's *Umbrian Scene* was performed. Another highlight was the presentation of awards to Frederick O'Neal of Actors' Equity and to Edward Kennedy (Duke) Ellington. *See*: W91

B96. Crabtree, Phillip D. "Research Report." *Choral Journal* 15 (January 1955): 32.
Reprint of dissertation abstract of "The Published Choral Music of Ulysses Simpson Kay," by Richard Thomas Hadley, Ph.D., The University of Iowa, 1972. *See*: B156

B97. Cumbo, Clarrissa and Marion Cumbo, comps. "In Retrospect . . . The Symphony of the New World." *Black Perspective in Music* 3 (Fall 1975): 320.
Collection of pictures and clippings relating to programs of the Symphony of the New World. Includes program featuring Kay's *Markings*, Beethoven's *Triple Concerto*, and Brahms's *Symphony No. 1*, with Paul Freeman, conductor. *See*: W100d

B98. Cunningham, Carl. "How Black Is Black?" *High Fidelity/Musical America* (January 1975): MA24-26.
Review of "five-day symposium sponsored by the Afro-American Music Opportunities Association Inc. (AAMOA), in conjunction with Houston's Black Arts Center and various public schools and universities in and around the city." Composers Kay, Leslie Adams, David Baker, Roque Cordero, Primus Fountain III, Talib Rasul Hakim, Howard Harris, Coleridge-Taylor Perkinson, Hale Smith, and George Walker, were in attendance for reading rehearsals or performances of their works. In addressing the question of black music specialties, the author notes that "my ears could detect no special traits to set the music apart. It was either good music or less good music, composed in general conformity with the compositional trends that have flowered and cross-pollinated to form accepted international styles of modern times. In several cases, it was music that deserved attention on its own merits, not on any national or racial association."

B99. Cunningham, W. Patrick, ed. *The Music Locator*, 2nd ed. 1980-81. Saratoga, CA: A Resource Publication, 1980, p. 441.
Provides titles of compositions described as suitable music for each part of a formal Catholic liturgy: thematic music, hymns of praise

and thanksgiving, and music for confirmation or religious commitment. Includes Kay's "Like As a Father," "O Praise the Lord," *To Light That Shines*, "Sing Unto the Lord," and *O Worship the King*, with descriptive information by style, copyright, and suitability for use in worship. *See*: W59, W71, W87

B100.   Current, Gloster B. "Black Composers Series." *Crisis* 83 (March 1976): 105-6.
A favorable review of the recordings from the Columbia Records Masterworks' Black Composers Series in column, "Listening Post." Provides background information for the series citing responsible groups, CBS and AAMOA; and individuals, Dr. Paul Freeman, conductor and Dr. Dominique-René de Lerma, researcher and notes preparer. Released in 1974-75, the eight-volume set includes Kay's *Markings* and a biographical sketch. *See*: W100; D7

B101.   _____. "Celebration of Black Composers—Black Music at the Philharmonic." *Crisis* 85 (January 1978): 7, 13.
Provides background and overview of the festival, "Celebration of Black Composers" and reviews of each of the five programs. Members of the program committee were Hale Smith, George Walker, Dominique-René de Lerma, Paul Freeman, Leon Thompson, and Kay. *Three Pieces After Blake*, sung by Irene Oliver, a graduate of the Cincinnati Conservatory and a woman with a "powerful voice," appears on the program with Dave Baker's *Concerto for Cello* and Hale Smith's *Innerflexions*. Photos. *See*: W48a

B102.   Daniel, Oliver. "A Laurel Leaf for Stokowski." *American Composers Alliance Bulletin* 2, no. 4 (1952-53): 2-7.
Notes first New York performance of *Suite for Strings* on October 26, at the Museum of Modern Art, featuring works by Henry Cowell, Ulysses Kay, John Lessard, Wallingford Riegger, and Alan Hovhaness. Includes reprints of reviews by music critics. Olin Downes (*New York Times*, Monday, October 27, 1952) describes Kay's *Suite for Strings* as " . . . the piece, at least of a musician of unmistakable gifts, if derivative style. The first movement is sharply despondent, the last lively and gay." Virgil Thomson (*New York Herald Tribune*, Monday, October 27) calls it "a warm and appealing piece . . . it is lyrical and dramatic rather than picturesque. . . . The maturing of this young talent, now well under way, is welcome news. Mr. Kay has a personal imagination and a note of authority." Howard Taubman (*New York Times*, Wednesday, October 29) notes that "Kay, (who, to my knowledge, has never been an experimental composer), employs harmonies and rhythms borrowed from the experimenters in a work which is primarily thematic." Taubman also credits Stokowski as having "an honorable record of espousing the cause of the living composer." *See*: W31

B103.   _____. "The New Festival." *American Composers Alliance Bulletin* 5, no. 1 (1955): 15-16.

Reprint of excerpt of *Time* article (March 8, 1954) by Roy Alexander who reviewed *Of New Horizons* (Tucson Symphony). Notes the following recording releases: *Concerto for Orchestra,* "Round Dance" and "Polka," and *Serenade for Orchestra. See*: W20; D3, D12, D14; B4, B158, B269

B104.   _____. "New Recordings." *American Composers Alliance Bulletin* 4, no. 2 (1954): 15-16.

Notes release of *Concerto for Orchestra* with brief description; includes summary of Kay's achievements of 1950. Of special interest are the 1954 reviews of the concerto in *Argonaut* (San Francisco, May 21); *Democrat and Chronicle* (Rochester, NY, May 30); *The Norfolk Virginian-Pilot*, May 30; the *Jewish Advocate* (Boston, June 3); *Boston Globe*, June 6; and *Christian Science Monitor* (Boston). *See*: W32; D3

B105.   _____. *Ulysses Kay*. New York: Broadcast Music, Inc., 1976.

Composer's brochure includes catalog of works to 1976, with descriptive information by title, genre, instrumentation, duration, and publisher. Definitive biographical sketch written by Oliver Daniel reviews highlights of Kay's career and recounts significant quotations from other reviewers. Photo.

B106.   Daniels, David. *Orchestral Music: A Handbook*. 2nd ed. Metuchen, NJ: Scarecrow Press, 1982, p. 166.

Descriptive information of orchestral music includes instrumentation, duration, publishers, and source of performance material as an aid to the planning of orchestral programs. This source can be useful to orchestral conductors and managers, choral directors, and others interested in the study of music. Includes five works by Kay: *Fantasy Variations, Scherzi Musicali, Serenade for Orchestra, Theater Set,* and *Umbrian Scene. See*: W52, W89, W91, W108, W109

B107.   Davidson, Celia Elizabeth. "Operas by Afro-American Composers: A Critical Survey and Analyses of Selected Works." Ph.D. dissertation, The Catholic University of America, 1980.

Includes a biography of Kay, as well as historical and analytical discussions of *Jubilee*. Other composers represented are: Clarence Cameron White, William Grant Still, Mark Fax, Harry Lawrence Freeman, and Scott Joplin. *See*: W123

B108.   Davis, John P., ed. *The American Negro Reference Book*. Englewood Cliffs, NJ: Prentice-Hall, 1966, pp. 753-54.

Kay, Howard Swanson, and Julia Perry are cited as "the most outstanding contemporary Negro composers who do not consciously write 'Negro music.'" Each of these composers "'seeks an impression

. . . without the fetters of a 'school' or an 'ideology.'" Brief sketch provides highlights of Kay's life and works.

B109.   Davis, Peter G. "Stimulating Celebration of Music." *New York Times*, September 4, 1977, p. 41.

Review of the "Celebration of Black Composers" concerts held in Avery Fisher Hall from August 29 to September 2, 1977. The fifth performance featured works by David Baker, Hale Smith, Samuel Coleridge-Taylor, and Ulysses Kay, with Leon Thompson, conductor. Kay's *Three Pieces After Blake*, with Irene Oliver as soloist, received a favorable review, noting particularly, "a vocal line that knew precisely when to take off without restraint." *See*: W48

B110.   De Lerma, Dominique-René.   *Bibliography of Black Music*. Greenwood Encyclopedia of Black Music. Volume 2, *Afro-American Idioms*. Westport, CT: Greenwood Press, 1981. p. 83.

One of a set of four volumes intended to encourage research in areas of black music and give impetus to the compilation of more such tools in this field. Titles for volumes 1 - 4 follow respectively: "Reference Materials," "Afro-American Idioms," "Geographic Studies," and "Theory, Education, and Related Studies." The second volume lists bibliographic sources, both periodical and book, that relate to Afro-American idioms—Minstrelsy, Spirituals, Ragtime, Musical Theatre/Comedy, Concert Music, Band Music, Blues, Gospel, Popular Music, and Jazz. Included in the "Concert Music" section is an article by Kay, "The Roman Seasons," from *Choral Journal* 10 (January 1970): 15-17. *See*: K5

B111.   _____. *Bibliography of Black Music*. Greenwood Encyclopedia of Black Music. Volume 4, *Theory, Education and Related Studies*. Westport, CT: Greenwood Press, 1984. p. 154.

The last volume of this four-volume set is divided into sections that concentrate upon specific instrument groups, performance practices, theory, education, interdisciplinary studies, liturgy, and women's and children's studies. Kay's article, "Where Is Music Going?," which appears in *Music Journal*, is cited. An index of authors is provided. *See*: K8

B112.   _____. *Black Music In Our Culture: Curricular Ideas On the Subject, Materials and Problems*. Kent, OH: Kent State University Press, 1970, pp. 1, 23, 32, 37, 63, 86, 102, 115, 118, 176, 185, 197, 258.

Brief mention of Kay as a rising composer, as an acquaintance of William Grant Still, and as one whose works receive publication. His influence upon the black music scene is also discussed in an article by T. J. Anderson.   Includes Kay in selective lists of scores, books/articles, and recordings. *See*: B17

B113.   _____. "Kay, Ulysses Simpson." *In Die Musik in Geschichte und Gegenwart: Allgemeine Enzyklopädie der Musik.* Supplement, Band 16. Kassel: Bärenreiter, 1979, col. 926-27.
Definitive biography of Kay's life and career. Includes catalog of major works written during 1943-1971, and provides descriptive information by title, date, and publisher. In German.

B114.   _____. "Music Reviews." *Black Perspective in Music* 4 (Fall 1976): 339.
Reprint of review of *Prelude for Unaccompanied Flute* written by Richard Kirby of Morgan State University. Kirby reveals that "'it is a work suitable for the professional flutist, but should not be overlooked by the advanced high school musician.'" *See*: W14;

B115.   _____. "Recent Recordings." *Black Perspective in Music* 5 (Fall 1977): 226.
Report of recording releases: *Dances, string orchestra*, the Westphalian Symphony, Paul Freeman, conductor (Turnabout TVS-34546); *Markings*, London Symphony Orchestra, Paul Freeman, conductor (Columbia M-32783—The Black Composers Series, v. 3). *See*: W53, W100; D7, D17

B116.   _____. "Record Review." *Black Perspective in Music* 1 (Fall 1973): 191.
Includes review of *Prelude for Flute*, performed by D. Antoinette Handy, among other compositions recorded in *Contemporary Black Images in Music for the Flute*. De Lerma describes the Prelude as "meditative and improvisatory." Recording company information provided. *See*: W14; D11

B117.   _____. *Reflections On Afro-American Music.* Kent, OH: The Kent State University Press, 1973, pp. 1, 9, 10, 25, 66, 83, 179, 197, 204n, 257, 267.
Cites Kay as a young and versatile composer, who follows the earlier generation of black composers, e.g., William L. Dawson, R. Nathaniel Dett, Harry Burleigh, among others. The author notes that the frequent performances of *Of New Horizons* and Kay's membership on the Honorary Advisory Board (Black Music Center at Indiana University) are indications of his growing influence as an important black composer. Mentions, also, the premiere performance of *Aulos* at Indiana University. *See*: W20; W103

B118.   _____. "A Selective List of Choral Music by Black Composers." *Choral Journal* (April 1972): 5-6.
List includes Kay's *A Wreath for Waits, The Birds*, and *Choral Triptych*, with descriptive information by arrangement, number of movements, and publication. Unpublished titles are listed with the composer's name. *See*: W56, W82, W99

B119.   _____. "The Teacher's Guide to Recent Recordings of Music by Black Composers." *College Music Symposium* (Fall 1973): 114-15.
          Discography "restricted to 'concert' music by composers of African ancestry." Includes recently released recordings that are invaluable to teaching programs. These recordings "survey a wide range of styles: the electronic imaginations of Olly Wilson and Halim el-Dabh, the serial writing of Hale Smith, the cellular mosaics of T. J. Anderson, the quasi-delicacy of the Chevalier de Saint-Georges, the neo-classical strength of Ulysses Kay and George Walker."

B120.   De Lerma, Dominique-René, ed. *Explorations in Black Music: The Seminar Program.* Bloomington: Indiana University, The Black Music Center, 1971, pp. 10, 39, 42-43, 71-72, 85-86.
          Proceedings of the seminar held June 27 to July 2, 1971, at Indiana University, and sponsored by the Black Music Center, the Indiana State Arts Commission, Office of the Vice-Chancellor for Afro-American Affairs, and the Indiana University Summer Sessions Office. Includes aims and objectives of the center and publications by the staff. Among its holdings are several phonorecords and compositions by Kay, with descriptive information by publishing and recording companies, dates, etc. Among the compositions are: *A Short Overture*; *Brass Quartet*; *Christmas Carol*; *Come Away, Come Away Death*; *Triumvirate*; *Aulos*; *Brief Elegy*; *Choral Triptych*; *Six Dances*; *Fantasy Variations*; *A Lincoln Letter*; *Markings*; *[Two] Meditations*; *Of New Horizons*; *Quartet for Trumpets and Trombones*; *Serenade for Orchestra*; *Suite for Flute and Oboe*; *Suite for Orchestra*; *Suite for String Orchestra*; and *Umbrian Scene*. Kay is a member of the Honorary Advisory Committee of the Black Music Center. *See*: W12, W17, W18, W20, W21, W22, W27, W31, W39, W46, W49, W50, W52, W53, W82, W89, W91, W100, W103

B121.   Delaunoy, Didier. "Finally, Black Composers Get the Recognition They Deserve." *Soul* 9 (July 8, 1974): 17.
          Discusses CBS recording series, "The Black Composer." Kay's *Markings* is included among the reviews of the first four albums. Reference is made to Kay as "probably the best known" of the composers recorded in this series and to the paucity of music by black composers on record. *See*: W100; D7

B122.   "Desto to Release Boxes of Music by Black Composers." *Billboard* 62 (August 22, 1970): 63.
          Kay's *A Short Overture* is included in the two albums of music of black composers scheduled for release by Desto Records. *See*: D15

B123.   "Doctoral Dissertations (1970-72)." *Black Perspective in Music* 1 (Spring 1973): 96.
          Among dissertations that include Kay and discuss various aspects of his compositions are those by Hansonia Caldwell, Celia Davidson,

Richard Hadley, and Laurence Hayes, written during 1970-72. *See*: B41, B107, B156, B161

B124. Dower, Catherine. "Ulysses Kay: Distinguished American Composer." *Musart* (January-February 1972): 9-10, 16-17.
Includes biographical sketch through 1971 and a chronological review and analysis of music. According to author Dower, "Ulysses Kay stands as a principal figure in the field of contemporary music . . . [his] compositions . . . have enjoyed world-wide performance."

B125. Downes, Edward. "New Lyric Group Makes its Debut." *New York Times*, June 9, 1958, p. 26.
Review of performance of *Song of Ahab*, presented by the Lyric Chamber Theater at the 92nd Street Young Men's and Young Women's Hebrew Association (New York, NY). George S. Irving was the soloist. *See*: W45a

B126. Duncan, John. "Art Music by Negro Composers on Record." *Negro History Bulletin* 31 (April 1968): 6-9.
Ulysses Kay is referred to as "the most frequently heard Negro composer on records." Works listed are *Brass Quartet, Concerto for Orchestra, Choral Triptych*, "Round Dance" and "Polka," *Serenade for Orchestra, Sinfonia in E, Umbrian Scene*, and *Fantasy Variations*. Other composers included in the article are Julia Perry, Amadeo Roldán, William Grant Still, Fela Sowande, Samuel Coleridge-Taylor, Howard Swanson, Clarence Cameron White, Duke Ellington, J. J. Johnson, and John Lewis. Discography included. *See*: D1, D2, D3, D4, D12, D14, D16, D21

B127. Durrett, C. William. "Jackson." *Opera News* 37 (January 13, 1973): 23.
Review of Opera/South's production of Kay's *Juggler of Our Lady* and Still's *Highway 1, U.S.A.* "The two operas are studies in contrast, the one based on the fourteenth century legend, the other a grimly modern story of the abuses of love." Further, Durrett cautions that "the *Juggler* is a small, delicate piece that probably should be done only on the highest plane of professionalism." *See*: W60a

B128. Dyer, Richard. "Black Composers: Flawed Celebration." *Boston Globe*, September 11, 1977, pp. 48, 52.
Critical review expresses author's displeasure of a concert in celebration of black composers. Comments reveal that he feels the idea is patronizing and that, in his view, the music was not performed well, the orchestra unprepared, and that some of the music was not written well. However, the critic gives Kay's *Three Pieces After Blake* and the *Cello Concerto* by David Baker, positive reviews. Includes

photos of George Walker, Roque Cordero, William Grant Still, and Ulysses Kay. *See:* W48

B129. *The Ebony Handbook.* By the Editors of Ebony. Chicago: Johnson Publishing Co., 1974, p. 461.
Mentions Kay, along with other black composers—Howard Swanson, Julia Perry, Arthur Cunningham, Olly Wilson, and William Grant Still—as one composer who is "finding a long-denied audience."

B130. *The Ebony Success Library.* Vol. 1, *1000 Successful Blacks.* The Editors of Ebony. Chicago: Johnson Publishing Co., 1973, p. 188.
Biographical sketch highlights Kay's education and awards. Provides also the names of his wife and their three daughters; and mentions several major works, *Concerto for Orchestra, Sinfonia in E, A Short Overture, Serenade for Orchestra,* and *The Boor.* Includes photo. *See:* W27, W32, W44, W52, W57

B131. Eggler, Bruce. "Jackson, Miss." *Opera News* 41 (January 22, 1977): 30.
A review of Opera/South's premiere performance of Kay's *Jubilee,* "the story of the antebellum, Civil War and Reconstruction eras in Georgia as seen through the life of a young female slave." Further, Eggler writes that "the largest audience yet turned out for . . . the premiere . . . and it was rewarded with one of the (formerly black, now increasingly integrated) company's best efforts to date—a pleasing if flawed work, well cast and conducted, adequately mounted, bringing a high-minded message of racial brotherhood to this one-time bastion of segregation." *See:* W123

B132. Ennis, Bayard E. "Sinfonia in E." *Charleston Gazette,* February 20, 1962 (reprinted in the *ACA Bulletin* 10, no. 3 (1962): 19).
Review of the February 19 performance of *Sinfonia in E* by the Charleston Symphony Orchestra in Charleston, WV, with Geoffrey Hobday, conductor. Of the performance Ennis states, "it is lucidly expressive and indicative of a well-schooled mind. There are echoes of folk music amidst its ingenious design." *See:* W44b; B88

B133. Ericson, Raymond. "A Fanfare of Black Composers by the Philharmonic." *New York Times,* August 21, 1977, section II, p. D13.
Article addresses the upcoming festival, "Celebration of Black Composers," at Lincoln Center by the New York Philharmonic, with Leon Thompson and Paul Freeman, guest conductors. Kay's *Three Pieces After Blake* is scheduled for performance. Also notes that many of the composers received commissions as a result of exposure during this festival; Opera/South has commissioned Kay for a new work. Photo of Thompson included. *See:* W48a

B134.   Ernst, David. "Record Reviews." *Black Perspective in Music* 2 (Fall 1974): 220-21.

    Review of *Markings* (the "Black Composers Series, Vol. 3") by the London Symphony Orchestra, with Paul Freeman, conductor. "The intense opening of this work, which is a large tone poem, has an immediate impact upon the listener. He is taken by surprise and begins to wonder what *could* happen next. . . . As the music progresses, the listener actually senses a moving form (sound pattern) gradually expanding and contracting, moving slowly from one state to another." *See*: W100; D7

B135.   Everett, Thomas. "Concert Band Music by Black Composers." *Black Perspective in Music* 6 (Fall 1978): 143-50.

    Provides a selected list of band music by black composers. The author notes that "most of the works are playable by high school, as well as college bands, and their musical worth and content are certainly more substantial than the most of the music being programmed by school bands." Includes *Concert Sketches, Forever Free, Short Suite*, and *Four Silhouettes*, with descriptive information. *See*: W43, W83, W95, W116

B136.   Ewen, David. *American Composers: A Biographical Dictionary*. New York: G. P. Putnam's Sons, 1982, pp. 366-68.

    A complete and contemporary biography, including quotations, musical analysis, statement by composer, bibliography, and a list of principal works to 1979. Provides, also, an appendix, "Index of Programmatic Titles," in which Kay's works are included.

B137.   Finkelstein, Sydney. *Composer and Nation: The Folk Heritage in Music*. New York: International Publishers, 1960, p. 321.

    In the chapter, "Jazz as Folk and Art Music," the author states that the Negro people "have developed other powerful forms of music expression." Cites Ulysses Kay and William Grant Still as composers "striving to master the 'learned heritage' of music."

B138.   Fleming, G. James and Christian E. Burckel, eds. *Who's Who in Colored America*. 7th ed. Yonkers-on-Hudson, NY: Christian E. Burckel and Associates, 1950, p. 319.

    Biographical sketch includes information on education, awards, prizes, compositions, family members' names, and address.

B139.   Floyd, Samuel A., Jr. and Marsha J. Reisser. *Black Music In the United States: An Annotated Bibliography of Selected Reference and Research Materials*. Millwood, NY: Kraus International Publications, 1983, pp. 58-59, 69, 71-72, 129-30, 138-39, 168-69.

    An annotated bibliography in which the authors survey both general and specific sources with regard to black music research. Included are indices, guides, directories, research tools, bibliographies, dictionaries, encyclopedias, histories, topical studies, biographies, and anthologies.   Records and record collections are reviewed, and a survey of repositories, with information pertinent to the study of black music, is also included. Provides recommendations for the use of the source, presentation of material, special features, and reviews of books. Kay appears in the sections entitled, "Indexes of Printed and Recorded Music," "Dictionaries and Encyclopedias—Biographical," "Topical Studies—Concert and Recital Music," "Iconographies," and "Records and Record Collections—Concert Music."

B140.   "4 Composers Tell of Trip to Russia." *New York Times*, November 13, 1958, p. 38.
Narrative of tour by American composers who participated in the exchange program sponsored by the U.S. State Department. Describes the training, goals, and pressures of USSR composers. Russian composers in the program are to visit the U.S. during the winter of 1958-59. *See*: K1, K4, K5

B141.   "Four New American Operas." *American Composers Alliance Bulletin* 10, no. 1 (1962): 1.
Mentions the recent world premieres of four contemporary operas: Kay's *Juggler of Our Lady*, Lawrence Moss' *The Brute*, Peggy Glanville-Hicks's *Nausicaa*, and Robert Ward's *The Crucible*, citing the "unprecedented audience response and critical acclaim throughout the world," and the "news-making significance . . . in the scope of attention afforded these works from such divergent musical centers as London, Frankfurt, Athens, and New York." *See*: W60

B142.   Freeman, Paul.   "Black Symphonic Music Will Now Be Heard." *Symphony News* 24 (December 1973/January 1974): 7-10.
The author, conductor-in-residence of the Detroit Symphony Orchestra since 1970, provides insights and events leading to the decision by Columbia Records to record a series devoted to "works by international black composers, covering two centuries of creativity." Composers, the Chevalier de Saint-Georges, Roque Cordero, and George Walker, "unknown to many in the concert world, along with the better-known British-American [sic] Samuel Coleridge-Taylor and Afro-Americans, William Grant Still and Ulysses Kay, are represented on the first four recordings . . . to be released in February 1974. The recording project, which should do much to rectify the sad neglect of black composers, had its origins in 1967." *See*: D7

B143.   Furie, Kenneth.   "Columbia's Black Composers Series." *High Fidelity Magazine* (June 1974): 71-73.
"The four-disc initial release features a wide variety of worthwhile music, superbly performed and recorded." Includes compositions by the Chevalier de Saint-Georges, William Grant Still, Ulysses Kay, and Roque Cordero. "Everything here deserved to be recorded.

Everything here would provide a welcome change of pace on our concert programs." Photo. *See*: D7

B144.   Garcia, William Burres. "Church Music by Black Composers: A Bibliography of Choral Music." *Black Perspective in Music* 2 (Fall 1974): 151.
        Compilation of "selected choral compositions by black composers which are suitable for performance in both Protestant and Catholic worship." Lists *Grace to You, and Peace*; "Lo, the Earth;" "Love Divine;" *A New Song*; and *O Worship the King*, with descriptive information by text, publisher, parts, accompaniment, number of pages, and cost. *See*: W58, W59, W71, W96

B145.   Gardner, Effie Tyler. "An Analysis of the Techniques and Style of Selected Black-American Composers of Contemporary Choral Music." Ph.D. dissertation, Michigan State University, 1979.
        Includes biographical sketch, complete lists of works to 1979, analyses of five choral works, and conclusions as to the style and technique of each composer discussed. In addition to Kay, other composers included are George Walker, Ronald Roxbury, Hale Smith, and James Furman. Makes recommendations for the use of music in educating secondary and college students in choral and nonchoral settings.

B146.   Garland, Phyl. "The Negro in Music." In *The Negro Handbook*, compiled by the Editors of *Ebony*. Chicago: Johnson Publishing Co., 1966, pp. 366-67.
        In section entitled "Classical and Related Music," the author mentions "Kay as one of the most heralded of the new school of Negro composers" who has received much acclaim. Refers also to *Choral Triptych* as "evidence of [his] standing as 'a masterful composer.'" Of *Alleluia*, a *Saturday Review* article states that "'it may well become a classic.'" *See*: W81, W82

B147.   George, Nelson. "New York Philharmonic's First Major Celebration of Black Composers," *Amsterdam News* (New York, NY), August 13, 1977, p. D2.
        Addresses the New York Philharmonic's "Celebration of Black Composers," concentrating on black conductors, Leon Thompson and Paul Freeman. The author pays considerable attention to earlier composers, the Chevalier de Saint-Georges and José M. N. Garcia. Ulysses Kay, George Walker, Adolphus Hailstork, David Baker, and Roque Cordero are cited among the contemporary composers whose works are represented. William Grant Still is given acclaim as a "pioneer in mixing classical and jazz techniques." Notes premiere performance of Hale Smith's *Innerflexions*. Mentions that Kay was one of those responsible for the selection of the works performed during the festival, along with Dominique-René de Lerma, Hale Smith, and George Walker.

B148.   George, Zelma Watson. "Negro Music In American Life." In *The American Negro Reference Book*, edited by J. P. Davis. Englewood Cliffs, NJ: Prentice-Hall, 1966, p. 754.
        Brief discussion of Kay and his music in section on "Modern Negro Composers."

B149.   Gleason, Ralph J. "Russians Show Eager Interest in American Jazz, Says Composer." *Boston Sunday Globe*, December 14, 1958, p. A13.
        Summary of article noting increased interest in jazz by Russians as observed by Kay. Gleason emphasizes that "a situation . . . is being completely goofed by our State Department. At Brussels this year instead of presenting the cream of our jazz artists, we halfheartedly offered a spattering of concerts and an International Youth Band. We were heavily, and rightly, criticized."

B150.   ____. "This is the Moment to Get Jazz to Russia." *San Francisco Sunday Chronicle*, November 23, 1958, p. 19.
        Commentary by Ulysses Kay, upon his return from Russia, highlights increasing interest in American jazz. Further evidence is provided by letters to David Diamond of Radio Free Europe and by a successful tour of Poland by Dave Brubeck. Gleason suggests that the United States " . . . send over . . . all the top creative artists of jazz." *See*: B250

B151.   Goines, Leonard. "Contemporary Black Composers." *Allegro* 73 (July/August 1973): 8.
        Historical overview of the relationship of the black composer to American music. Discussion of efforts by composers and by musical organizations reveals increased promotion and opportunities to hear serious black music of all kinds. "Unlike the case of the Russian 'Five,' or the French, 'Les Six,' where you can aurally categorize a member of a respective school by his overall sound, you cannot take the whole caucus of black composers and identify their music in that manner. This is not speaking from the standpoint of quality, but from the standpoint of nationalism or centralized ideas. Many are working along these lines, however, and are hoping that the black composer might become similarly identified in the near future. Black composers think and work in different ways, and because they do, must be handled individually." Includes photo.

B152.   "Good News." *Crisis* 57 (February, 1950): 102.
        Notes that Kay won the coveted "Prix de Rome."

B153.   Gray, John, comp. *Blacks In Classical Music: A Bibliographic Guide to Composers, Performers and Ensembles*. Westport, CT: Greenwood Press, 1988, pp. 6, 9, 41-44, 243, 246, 252.
        A compendium of bibliographies divided into chapters entitled "General Section," "Composers," "Symphony and Concert Artists," "Concert and Opera Singers," "Reference Works," and "Research

Centers/Dictionary Catalogs." Two indices provided. Kay appears in the chapter on composers and in the sections "Opera Companies," "Reference Works," and "Research Centers/Dictionary Catalogs."

B154.   Green, Robert A. "Report From Bloomington: The Black Music Center at Indiana University." *Current Musicology* 18 (1974): 35-36.
Overview of the establishment of Indiana University's "Black Music Center" detailing its purpose, its holdings, and activities in order to provide information of black composers, performers, and music. "Few Black composers or musicians have received the thorough treatment given to very minor European musical figures, and not many musicologists can name even a handful of the more than 100 operas written by Black composers in the last century." In order to fill the gap, the Center's purpose "is to collect and organize materials dealing with all aspects of Black musical cultures 'without restrictions of genre, geography, or chronology as these relate to research, curricular innovations, and performance.'" Notes that the first director was Dominique-René de Lerma and that its Honorary Advisory Committee included Kay, Leonard Bernstein, Robert Shaw, and Eileen Southern, among others.

B155.   Hadley, Richard T. "The Life and Music of Ulysses Simpson Kay." *Negro Educational Review* 26 (January 1975): 42-51.
Biographical sketch of Kay's life to 1975. Author divides Kay's life into periods entitled: Early Years; Professional Preparation; Years of Promise; Travel and Study in Italy; Travel and Study in Russia; In the United States Again; Prolific Decade; and Professor of Music.

B156.   ____. "The Published Choral Music of Ulysses Simpson Kay." Ph.D. dissertation, The University of Iowa, 1972.
Contains a biographical essay, analyses of Kay's published choral works, a summary of his choral style, bibliography, and three appendices. Hadley affirms that "Kay is a Black composer whose writing includes but few of the characteristics normally associated with Afro-American music. Even though the influence of Hindemith . . . is evident, this has not precluded the development of a personal style. . . . The choral works of Ulysses Simpson Kay are a significant addition to choral literature. The extent of his contribution has been demonstrated by its wide acceptance as meaningful [sic], contemporary musical expression by audiences, conductors, performers, and critics."

B157.   Hains, Frank. "Opera/South All-Black and Hopeful." *High Fidelity/Musical America* 23 (May 1973): 23, MA28.
Review of Opera/South's productions includes *The Juggler of Our Lady*. A brief summary of the legend is provided, noting that "the tale could be a temptation to excessive musical sentimentality, which in the main Kay eschews. His approach is basically traditional,

tricked up by rhythmic contrivances in which two meters are sometimes set against each other." *See*: W60

B158.   Harmon, Carter. "Return of Ulysses." *American Composers Alliance Bulletin* 4, no. 1 (1954): 10. (Reprint of article in *Time*, March 8, 1954).

Account of Kay's return to Tucson to conduct *Of New Horizons*. *See*: W20b; B4, B103, B269

B159.   Harris, Carl Gordon, Jr. "A Study of Characteristic Stylistic Trends Found in the Choral Works of a Selected Group of Afro-American Composers and Arrangers." D.M.A. dissertation. University of Missouri, Kansas City, 1972.

Traces the development of choral music by selected Afro-American composers from the late nineteenth century to contemporary times. Discusses characteristic trends in the compositions of Harry T. Burleigh; John Wesley Work, Jr.; John Wesley Work III; Frederick Work; Hall Johnson; Frederick Hall; and William L. Dawson, among others. Identifies the composers as "Black Trailblazers," "Black Nationalists," or "Black Innovators." Kay is placed in the latter category with Margaret Bonds, Hale Smith and Undine Smith Moore, all described as being "among those . . . who have drawn freely from divergent sources and styles to create their own unique compositions." Includes a brief biography of each composer and a discussion of stylistic trends evolved and developed in the performance of Negro spirituals by black college and professional choral groups. Of particular interest is a list of selected choral works by black composers and arrangers.

B160.   _____. "Three Schools of Black Choral Composers and Arrangers 1900-1970." *Choral Journal* 14 (April 1974): 11-18.

Discusses notable black composers and arrangers. Includes Kay as a "Black Innovator" and provides a brief sketch of his life and career.

B161.   Hayes, Laurence Melton. "The Music of Ulysses Kay, 1939-1963." Ph.D. dissertation, The University of Wisconsin, 1971.

Provides a brief biography and discusses the composer through an analysis of compositions to 1963. Hayes emphasizes that the "study further reveals that the period studied can be separated . . . into two periods with crystallizing tendencies beginning to show with a third period. Although there are overlapping characteristics concomitant to each of the decades of the 1940's and the 1950's, the two ten-year periods represent the two divisions with the style crystallization beginning to emerge in the early 1960's." Further, the author maintains that "the most accurate style classification should be that of an 'eclectic modern'."

B162.   "He Put Sound of Submarine to Music." *Amsterdam News* (New York, NY), April 4, 1959, p. 24.
Notes that Kay creates original music score for *Submarine!*, a segment to be aired on "The Twentieth Century," Sunday, April 12, 1959 at 6:30 p.m. on CBS-TV. *See*: W73

B163.   Henahan, Donal. "Ehrling Leads 3 U.S. Works at Juilliard." *New York Times*, March 11, 1976, p. 44.
Review of all-American music concert on Tuesday, March 9, 1976, featuring George Crumb's *Variazioni* (1959), Kay's *Quintet Concerto* (1974), and William Schuman's *Symphony No. 7* (1960). *See*: W124a

B164.   Hentoff, Nat. "Jazz in Print." *Jazz Review* 2 (April 1959): 37.
Article cites periodicals in which one would find writings on or reviews of jazz. Kay's observations on jazz interest in the Soviet Union are requoted here. *See*: B149, B150, B250

B165.   Herrema, Robert D. "Choral Music by Black Composers for High School Choirs." *School Music News* 35 (October 1971): 30-31.
Annotated bibliography of choral music by Afro-American composers that is suitable for performance by high school choirs. Includes Kay's *Choral Triptych* and "How Stands the Glass Around?." Provides descriptive information by parts, duration, and publisher. *See*: W51, W82

B166.   ____. "The Choral Works of Ulysses Kay." *Choral Journal* 11 (December 1970): 5-9.
Narrative of Kay's life and career with quotations by Kay. Discusses style and techniques in his choral compositions; includes analysis of *Choral Triptych*. "Of the many outstanding black composers on the scene today, Ulysses Kay certainly ranks among the finest. It would not be presumptuous to say that this statement also would be true if the word 'black' were omitted. . . . It is sometimes easier to describe a composer's style by what it is not. It is not black. Kay believes that a composer is a product of his extraction and environment as well as his political and ethnic interests, but should not be limited by them." Photo. *See*: W82

B167.   Hill, Donna Jean, comp. "Concert Hall." *American Composers Alliance Bulletin* 7, no. 1 (1957): 21-22.
Notes New York performances of *Brief Elegy* (Long Island Music Festival), August 18, 1956, and *Serenade for Orchestra* for Negro Music History Week (Town Hall), February 14, Dmitri Mitropoulos, conductor. *See*: W22a, W52

B168.   Hinson, Maurice. *The Piano in Chamber Ensemble: An Annotated Guide*. Bloomington and London: Indiana University Press, 1978, pp. 52, 476.
Includes three of Kay's chamber works, with statement of stylistic

features and descriptive information by duration, publisher, and grade of difficulty. *Partita in A* and *Sonatine* were mentioned as "easy flowing, warm sentiment: M-D." Includes description of two movements of *Piano Quintet*: "First Movement: striking themes achieve a powerful climax; piano used contrapuntally. Second movement: slow; eloquent; derives its appeal from the slow rise of a beautiful melodic idea; resounding combination of instruments in vertical lines gives it life. M-D to D." *See*: W9, W36, W41

B169.   Horne, Aaron. "A Comprehensive Performance Project in Clarinet Literature With an Essay on Solo and Ensemble Chamber Music for Woodwinds by Black Composers Composed from 1893-1976." D.M.A. dissertation, University of Iowa, 1976.
          Provides Kay's biography to 1968 and a catalog of his works for woodwinds. Includes chart of "Black Composers of Woodwind Literature," and a discography cites Kay's *Prelude for Flute. See*: D11

B170.   Hunt, Joseph. "Conversations with Thomas J. Anderson: Blacks and the Classics." *Black Perspective in Music* 1 (Fall 1973): 157-65.
          Reprint of interview published in the *Real Paper* (Cambridge, MA), May 16, 1973, pp. 26-32. A conversation with T. J. Anderson highlights the absence of music of black composers in the mainstream of classical music. Anderson affirms the "diversity of style" present in the music of Kay, George Walker, David Baker and Olly Wilson. "'I would suspect that when we get further away from the period and can analyze it properly, we will find that freedom was the most important ingredient for black composers at a time when whites were organizing music around systems—like Babbitt, Schoenberg, Webern. The desire to be free gave the black composer far more diversity than his white counterpart.'"

B171.   "Interracial Chorus Doing Kay's Work." *Amsterdam News* (New York, NY), May 16, 1959, p. 15.
          Notes the forthcoming performance of *Phoebus, Arise* by the Interracial Fellowship Chorus on May 17, 1959, at Town Hall, under the direction of Harold Aks, conductor, and David Labovitz, associate conductor. The cantata, which was commissioned by the Interracial Music Council, is based upon Elizabethan poetry and is written for chorus, soli, and orchestra. *See*: W72

B172.   "Interracial Group of Composers to Visit Russia." *Jet* 14 (September 25, 1958): 62.
          Mentions the four composers to visit Russia on an exchange program sponsored by the U.S. State Department (Ulysses Kay, Roy Harris, Peter Mennin, and Roger Sessions). *See*: K1, K4, K7

B173.   "Irby Premiers 'Tromba' by Ulysses S. Kay." *International Trumpet Guild Journal* 10, no. 1 (1985): 10.

Notes premiere performance of *Tromba*, performed by Fred Irby III and Ronald Tymus, on program sponsored by the National Museum of American History's Program in Black American Culture, Baird Auditorium, Smithsonian Institution, Washington, DC, on May 24, 1985. *See*: W135; B288

B174.   Jablonski, Edward. *The Encyclopedia of American Music.* Garden City, NY: Doubleday, 1981, pp. 394, 580.

Biographical sketch notes information of Kay's naval and educational careers, study in Italy, and affiliations with BMI, Lehman College (NY), and other universities. Provides catalog of important works to 1976. In an appendix of "American Music on Records," Jablonski laments that "Columbia's excellent and highly commendable (but, alas, not too well supported) 'Black Composers Series' resulted in recordings of much American music all too rarely heard, much of it by younger composers—Adolphus Hailstork, Hale Smith, Olly Wilson, and David Baker as well as the men of an earlier generation such as William Grant Still, George Walker, and Ulysses Simpson Kay.   The series resulted in at least 9 volumes of well performed and recorded music, but it appears to have ended there and the records are going out of print." *See*: D7

B175.   Jackson, Raymond. "The Piano Music of Twentieth-Century Black Composers As Illustrated Mainly in the Works of Three Composers." D.M.A. dissertation, Juilliard School of Music, 1973.

Discussion and analyses of piano works of R. Nathaniel Dett, Howard Swanson, and George Walker. Includes catalog of piano compositions by Ulysses Kay—*First Nocturne*, *Ten Essays*, and *Four Inventions*—in appendix of piano compositions by other black composers. *See*: W25, W63, W118

B176.   James, Shalor Lorenzo. "Contributions of Four Selected Twentieth-Century Afro-American Classical Composers: William Grant Still, Howard Swanson, Ulysses Kay, and Olly Wilson." Ph.D. dissertation, The Florida State University, 1988.

Includes an in-depth biography of Kay, a descriptive analysis of his *Fantasy Variations*, a classified list of Kay's compositions to 1986, and a letter from the composer. According to the author, "the purpose of the study is twofold . . . to develop a sourcebook which explores the contributions of four selected twentieth century Afro-American composers . . . and . . . to provide a perspective through which scholars and educators may become more aware of orchestral compositions by these composers and explore musical and philosophical influences on the composers, especially those arising from ethnic heritage." *See*: W89; B336

B177.   "The Juggler of Our Lady: Ulysses Kay." *American Composers Alliance Bulletin* 10, no. 2 (1962): 11-12.
    Excerpts of reviews of Kay's opera by Frank Gagnard in the *New Orleans Times-Picayune* and by *The Xavier Herald* (Xavier University), February 24, 1962. Gagnard reveals that "the story, which also served Massenet in the early part of the century, is the well-known tale of the street entertainer who seeks lodging for the night at a monastery. In gratitude to the Virgin for Her protection, the juggler offers as thanks his most precious gift—a demonstration of his talent—and a statue of Our Lady bends in blessing over the humble man." *Xavier Herald* notes also that Kay "supervised the final week's rehearsals for the world premiere . . . performed by members of the Xavier University Opera Workshop before an enthusiastic capacity audience." Photos included. *See*: W60

B178.   Kallin, Anna and Nicolas Nabokov, eds.   *Twentieth Century Composers*. Vol. 1, *American Music Since 1910*. Edited by Virgil Thomson. New York: Holt, Rinehart and Winston, 1971, pp. 154-55.
    Kay is included among the biographies and critiques of 106 composers. Provides list of his major works. Thomson refers to Kay as "a composer of taste, notably gifted for ballet and films."

B179.   "Kay, Ulysses Simpson." In *Encyclopedia Americana*. International ed. Danbury, CT: Grolier, 1987, p. 337.
    Provides biographical sketch with identification of important works. A partial catalog of works to 1975 is included.

B180.   "Kay to Conduct Work in Tucson." *Down Beat* 21 (February 24, 1954): 17.
    Notes Kay's forthcoming appearance as conductor of Tucson Symphony in a performance of his *Of New Horizons*. "Composer Ulysses Kay, winner of the 'Prix de Rome' for music in 1949 and in 1951, as well as more than six other major musical awards and fellowships since 1946, will appear." *See*: W20

B181.   "Kay Wins $3,000 Prize in Composition." *Amsterdam News* (New York, NY), May 28, 1949, p. 4.
    Notes grant awarded to Kay by the American Academy in Rome for a year's residence (October 1, 1949 to September 30, 1950). Includes photo and a biographical sketch. Of special interest is a listing of orchestras that have performed his compositions. Background information on the Academy is also provided.

B182.   "Kay Work Premiered in North Carolina." *Music Clubs Magazine* 55 (Spring 1976): 15.
    Review of the world premiere of *Southern Harmony* performed by the North Carolina Symphony, John Gosling, conductor. "According to Kay, the composition is based on motives and themes drawn from 'The Southern Harmony' of William Walker (1809-1875), a white

itinerant singing teacher from Spartanburg, South Carolina. . . . 'I decided to celebrate and pay tribute to our musical heritage from those times.'" *See*: W127

B183.   "Kay's New Choral Work to be Aired, On CBS Radio." *Jet* 4 (September 3, 1953): 66.
Notes that *A Lincoln Letter* is to be premiered on CBS. Includes photo. *See*: W49

B184.   "Kay's Work Premieres at Festival." *Amsterdam News* (New York, NY), February 15, 1958, p. 14.
Notes that *Pietà*, a work for English horn and strings, will receive its premiere performance on February 12, 1958 at Town Hall, on the opening program of the Nineteenth Annual Festival of American Music. The program will be broadcast by WNYC, sponsor of the eleven-day festival. *See*: W42

B185.   Kehler, George, comp. and annot. *The Piano In Concert*. Vol. 1. Metuchen, NJ: Scarecrow Press, 1982, p. 176.
Source book including names of some two thousand pianists who have made outstanding contributions in the performance world. Provides for each a biographical citation for the review of sources for all performances. Kay's *Four Inventions* is included in the entry of pianist, Lucy Brown, as among the compositions she performed in Town Hall (NY), September 29, 1947. *See*: W25

B186.   Kennedy, Michael. *The Oxford Dictionary of Music*.   Oxford, England: Oxford University Press, 1985, p. 374.
Brief sketch includes current information regarding Kay's life and works. Mention is made of Kay's study in Italy and of his study with Howard Hanson and Bernard Rogers at the Eastman School of Music. A partial catalog of works is provided. *See*: K2, K5

B187.   Kerr, Russell. "New York Concert and Opera Beat." *Musical Courier* 160 (July 1959): 10.
Review of the premiere of *Phoebus, Arise* (May 17), performed by the Interracial Fellowship Chorus. "The work uses English poems by William Drummond, Thomas Hood, Abraham Cowley and Lord Herbert, which have in common the celebration of the delights of sporting and love. It proved a melodious and very agreeable score." *See*: W72

B188.   Kimball, Robert. "Premiere Ends Black Fete On High Note." *New York Post*, September 3, 1977, p. 37.
Kay's work, *Three Pieces After Blake*, was given a favorable review. The composition was performed by Irene Oliver on the last night of the "Celebration of Black Composers"—a five-day fête held in New York at Lincoln Center (August 29 to September 3, 1977). *See*: W48a

B189.   Klein, Howard. "Overdoing 'Benign Neglect.'" *New York Times*, March 7, 1971, pp. 1, 9.

Review of Desto Recordings' *The Black Composer in America*, which includes Kay's *Short Overture*. Also reviewed is the recording by Natalie Hinderas (*Natalie Hinderas Plays Music by Black Composers*). Klein calls the first recording inadequate, however, praises the second one. Other comments include social and color line concerns. The reviewer expressed surprise that there are other black composers of "serious music." *See*: D15

B190.   Kolodin, Irving. *Orchestral Music: The Guide to Long-Playing Records*. New York: Alfred A. Knopf, 1955, p. 110.

Includes Kay's *Concerto for Orchestra* (Remington 199-173). "The resonance of the recording tends to blur somewhat the lines of the complicated texture. Playing and direction are excellent." *See*: D3

B191.   Krummel, D. W., Jean Geil, Doris J. Dyen, and Deane L. Root. *Resources of American Music History: A Directory of Source Materials from Colonial Times to World War II*. Urbana: University of Illinois Press, 1981, pp. 58, 251, 371.

Includes an interview with Kay, a former student of Hindemith, as part of the Hindemith Project housed in the Oral History, American Music Collection of the School of Music, Stoeckel Hall, Yale University. Mentions the Carl Haverlin Collection/BMI Archives which holds recent letters and autograph manuscripts of American composers, Ulysses Kay, Milton Babbitt, Elliott Carter, Henry Cowell, and many others. Lists the Moldenhauer Archives which houses the major holograph manuscripts of outstanding twentieth century composers, including Kay, Martinu, Delius, Bartók, Tcherepnin, Varèse, Křenek, Ganz, Gershwin, and others, as well as several musical estates, shorter holograph music materials, and autograph letters of late nineteenth and twentieth century composers.

B192.   Kupferberg, Herbert. *Book of Classical Music Lists*. New York: Facts on File Publications, 1985, pp. 143, 151, 162.

A compilation of trivia and oddities. Kay is entered in sections: "Musicians' Real Names," "Musical Astrology," "Black Musicians," and "Musicians with Names of Three Letters or Less." Includes indices of composers and compositions.

B193.   Kyle, Marguerite Kelly. "AmerAllegro." *Pan Pipes of Sigma Alpha Iota* 45 (January 1953): 57.

A summary of Kay's activities during 1952 notes his return to New York after a three-year tenure as a Fellow of the American Academy in Rome. His article, "The Roman Seasons," was published in the *ACA Bulletin* (October 1952). Performances noted include several broadcasts in Italy of *Suite For Orchestra* and *Song for Strings*. New York was the site for performances of *Solemn Prelude, Brass Quartet,* and *Suite for Strings*. Photo included. *See*: W21a, W31a, W31b, W38a, W39; K5

B194. ____. "AmerAllegro." *Pan Pipes of Sigma Alpha Iota* 46 (January 1954): 47.

A summary of premiere performances includes *Two Dances, String Quartet No. 1*, and *A Lincoln Letter* during 1953. Other performances noted are *First Meditation for Organ* and *Duo for Flute and Clarinet*. Also notes that Remington Records has released a recording of *Concerto for Orchestra*. Kay was appointed music consultant for BMI, and his article on liturgical music, published in Italy, was reprinted in the *ACA Bulletin*. Recent commissioned compositions include *Triumvirate* and a work for the Louisville Orchestra. *See*: W32, W37, W49, W50, W53; D3; K2

B195. ____. "AmerAllegro." *Pan Pipes of Sigma Alpha Iota* 47 (January 1955): 51-52.

Several compositions received premiere performances in 1954: *Two Dances, Concerto for Orchestra, Serenade for Orchestra, Promenade and Galop, Song of Jeremiah, A Wreath for Waits*, and *Two Madrigals*. Among other compositions performed during the year were, *Of New Horizons, Symphony in E, Piano Quintet, Partita in A, Little Suite for String Quartet, A Lincoln Letter*, and *Triumvirate*. *See*: W20, W30, W32, W36, W37, W41, W44, W49, W50, W52, W53, W54, W56

B196. ____. "AmerAllegro." *Pan Pipes of Sigma Alpha Iota* 48 (January 1956): 56.

Compilation of premieres, performances, and recordings in 1955. Premiere performances include *Three Pieces After Blake, Two Madrigals*, "How Stands the Glass Around?," and *Partita in A*. Other compositions performed were *Triumvirate, Two Meditations, Song of Jeremiah*, and *A Lincoln Letter*. Of special note was the publication of two new works: *Short Suite for Band* and *A Wreath for Waits*; the recording of *Serenade for Orchestra* and *Two Dances*; and the completion of *The Boor* and *A New Song*. *See*: W30, W41, W43, W46, W48, W49, W50, W51, W54, W56, W57, W59; D12, D14

B197. ____. "AmerAllegro." *Pan Pipes of Sigma Alpha Iota* 49 (January 1957): 55.

Compilation of premieres in 1956 includes *A New Song, Short Suite for Concert Band*, three *Fugitive Songs*, and *Grace to You, and Peace*. Other performances mentioned are *Of New Horizons, Serenade for Orchestra, First String Quartet, Quintet for Piano and Strings*, and *Quartet for Brass*. Cited also are the following new publications by Associated Music Publishers: "How Stands the Glass Around?," *Short Suite for Concert Band*, and *A Wreath for Waits*. Of special note is the recording of "What's in a Name?" and "How Stands the Glass Around?" by the David Randolph Singers by

Composers Recordings, Inc. A summary of Kay's activities notes completion of *Second String Quartet* and his prize winning composition in the national Moravian Anthem Contest, *Grace to You, and Peace*. *See*: W20, W36, W37, W39, W40, W43, W51, W52, W56, W58, W59, W61; D20

B198.   ____. "AmerAllegro." *Pan Pipes of Sigma Alpha Iota* 50 (January 1958): 59.

Compilation of performances in 1957 includes *Of New Horizons, Brief Elegy*, and *Two Meditations*. Additionally noted are new publications, *Short Suite for Concert Band* (Associated Music Publishers); *Grace to You, and Peace* (H. W. Gray); and *Christmas Carol* (Peer International). Of particular note is the featured article on Kay and his music by Nicolas Slonimsky in the *American Composers Alliance* (fall issue). *See*: W12, W20, W22, W43, W46, W58; B286

B199.   ____. "AmerAllegro." *Pan Pipes of Sigma Alpha Iota* 51 (January 1959): 70.

A summary of premieres includes *Pietà, Short Suite for Concert Band*, and "The Fugitives". Other performances noted are "Like As a Father," *Quintet for Piano and Strings, Suite in B, Ten Pieces for Children, Of New Horizons, Song of Ahab*, and *Grace to You, and Peace*. Also cited is Kay's completion of *Serenade No. 2, Two Short Pieces, Organ Suite No. 1*, and the television film score, *FDR, from Third Term to Pearl Harbor*, as well as the publication of *A Lincoln Letter* by C. F. Peters Corp. He also presented a paper, "A View of the Soviet Musical Scene by an American Composer" to the Italo-American Association in Rome. *See*: W3, W15, W20, W36, W40, W42, W43, W45, W49, W58, W59, W62, W64, W65, W67

B200.   ____. "AmerAllegro." *Pan Pipes of Sigma Alpha Iota* 52 (January 1960): 56.

Compilation of premieres and performances during 1958 and 1959. Premiere performances include *Organ Suite No. 1; Phoebus, Arise; String Quartet No. 2*; and *Serenade No. 2 for Four Horns*. Other performances noted were the first European performance of *Organ Suite No. 1* in Holland by Leonard Raver; "Like As a Father" by the King's Chapel Choir (Daniel Pinkham, conductor); and *Fugitive Songs, Partita in A*, and *Brass Quartet* at the University of Illinois. Also noted were the following film scores: *New York: City of Magic, Submarine!*, and *The Fall of China*. In November, Kay was guest lecturer at the University of Illinois. *See*: W37, W39b, W40b, W41, W59b, W62, W66, W67, W67a, W69, W72, W73

B201.   ____. "AmerAllegro." *Pan Pipes of Sigma Alpha Iota* 53 (January 1961): 61-62.

Compilation of performances, publications, recordings, and activities during 1960. Premiered were *Serenade No. 3* [sic] and

Hymn-Anthem on the Tune "Hanover." Performances of *Organ Suite No. 1, String Quartet No. 2,* and *Serenade for Orchestra* were presented in Indiana, Louisiana, Washington, DC, and Toronto, Canada, respectively. A new recording of *Sinfonia in E* was issued by CRI. Kay appeared on NBC-TV as guest composer, conducting his own score for "World Wide 60." Additionally, he was guest composer at the American Symphony Orchestra League Workshop (Asilomar, CA); was speaker at the American Symphony Orchestra Convention (St. Louis); and was the U.S. judge at the "Prix Italia" competition in Trieste. *See:* W44, W52, W61, W62, W67, W71; D16; B66

B202.   ____. "AmerAllegro." *Pan Pipes of Sigma Alpha* Iota 54 (January 1962): 57.

A review of 1961 premieres, publications, and performances includes *Trigon* and *Sinfonia in E.* Of special interest was the American Wind Symphony's tour of England where it performed *Trigon* with Kay as guest conductor. *A New Song* was published by C. F. Peters, and Kay completed a newly commissioned work, *String Quartet No. 3.* He was also elected to the MacDowell Association as a corporate member. *See:* W44, W59, W79, W80, W80b

B203.   ____. "AmerAllegro." *Pan Pipes of Sigma Alpha Iota* 55 (January 1963): 56.

A summary of performances in 1962 includes premieres of *String Quartet No. 3, The Juggler of Our Lady, To Light That Shines, Flowers in the Valley,* and *Forever Free.* Other compositions performed were *Of New Horizons, Suite for Orchestra, Suite for Strings,* and *Trigon.* An all-Kay concert by the Worcester (MA) Symphony featured *Brief Elegy, Six Dances for String Orchestra, Sinfonia in E,* and the ballet suite *Danse Calinda.* Kay was guest conductor of the Tucson Symphony and guest speaker at West Virginia State College and for the American Association of University Women in New Jersey. He also conducted his film scores, *The Land* for NBC News and *Nosotros* and *Going Home* for United Nations films. New publications listed were *Flowers in the Valley* (C. F. Peters) and *Two Short Pieces for Piano* (G. Ricordi). *Of New Horizons* was recorded by the University Symphony Orchestra for University of Arizona Recordings. *See:* W7a, W20, W21, W22b, W31, W44d, W53a, W60, W64, W78, W79, W80, W83, W84, W85, W86, W87; D9

B204.   ____. "AmerAllegro." *Pan Pipes of Sigma Alpha Iota* 56 (January 1964): 64.

A review of 1963 performances includes premieres of *Choral Triptych, Fantasy Variations,* and the announcement of forthcoming premieres of *Inscriptions from Whitman* and *Portrait Suite.* Other compositions performed were: *Organ Suite, A New Song, Phoebus, Arise, Two Meditations, Ten Pieces for Children, Solemn Prelude, Short Suite for Band, Forever Free, Brief Elegy,* and *Suite for Strings.*

Kay was awarded the Doctor of Music degree by Lincoln College (Lincoln, IL) on May 26, and he received commissions from Arthur Bennett Lipkin, the New Jersey Symphony and the New Jersey Tercentary Commission. Cambridge Recordings released *Choral Triptych* performed by the King's Chapel Choir of Boston, Daniel Pinkham, conductor. *See*: W3, W22, W31, W33, W38, W43, W46, W59, W72, W82, W83, W89, W90; D2

B205.   ____. "AmerAllegro." *Pan Pipes of Sigma Alpha Iota* 57 (January 1965): 66.
A summary of 1964 performances includes premieres of *Umbrian Scene, Portraits*, and *Inscriptions from Whitman*. Other compositions performed were: *Of New Horizons* (two performances) and *Suite for Orchestra*. Publishing information lists Duchess Music Corporation as exclusive publisher of Kay's compositions. *See*: W20, W21, W90, W91, W115

B206.   ____. "AmerAllegro." *Pan Pipes of Sigma Alpha Iota* 59 (January 1967): 82.
A summary of Kay's activities in 1966 includes his receipt of an honorary Doctor of Music degree from Bucknell University (PA) on June 5, and his appointment as Visiting Professor of Music at UCLA (October 1, 1966 through June 15, 1967). Premiere performances include: *Presidential Suite* and *Markings*. Other compositions performed were *Umbrian Scene* and *Serenade for Orchestra*; new publications cited were *Fantasy Variations* (CRI) and *Four Hymn-Anthems* (MCA Music Corporation). *Fantasy Variations* was also recorded by CRI. *See*: W52, W89, W91, W96, W97, W100; D4

B207.   ____. "AmerAllegro." *Pan Pipes of Sigma Alpha Iota* 60 (January 1968): 78-79.
In 1967, Kay appeared as guest conductor and consultant at the American Music Symposium (Arizona State College); was guest lecturer at Southern Connecticut State College (New Haven, CT); and received commissions from John Solum, the Simmons College Glee Club, and the Chicago Musical College of Roosevelt University. New publications included *Fantasy Variations, Four Hymn-Anthems, Two Dunbar Lyrics* (MCA), and *Choral Triptych* (AMP). Other compositions performed were *Forever Free, Markings*, and *Of New Horizons*. *See*: W20, W82, W83, W89, W96, W98, W100

B208.   ____. "AmerAllegro." *Pan Pipes of Sigma Alpha Iota* 62 (January 1970): 46, 68.
Includes photo of Kay receiving the honorary Doctor of Humane Letters degree, May 1969, at Illinois Wesleyan University. He is pictured with Dr. Carl Neumeyer, director of the School of Music and Dr. Robert S. Eckley, president of the University. In addition, on June 1, he was awarded the honorary Doctor of Music degree from the University of Arizona in Tucson. Premiere performances noted

include *Scherzi Musicali, Once There Was a Man*, and *Theater Set*. *See*: W108, W109, W111

B209. ____. "AmerAllegro." *Pan Pipes of Sigma Alpha Iota* 63 (January 1971): 65.
A review of Kay's activities in 1969 and 1970 includes mention of the honorary degrees conferred in 1969. He was also the recipient of the first award presented by the New Jersey State Council on the Arts in Princeton, NJ. A summary of 1969 premieres is provided. Other compositions performed in 1970 were *Umbrian Scene, Markings*, and *Of New Horizons*. Two new publications by MCA are *The Birds* and *Parables*. *See*: W20, W91, W99, W100, W112

B210. ____. "AmerAllegro." *Pan Pipes of Sigma Alpha Iota* 64 (January 1972): 63.
A summary of 1971 premieres includes *Aulos, The Capitoline Venus*, and *Facets*. Other works presented during the 1970-71 season were: *Parables, Of New Horizons, Presidential Suite, Scherzi Musicali, Theater Set*, and *Markings*. Of special interest is the fact that Kay composed *Facets* for the fiftieth anniversary of the Eastman School of Music. He also appeared as guest conductor of the Birmingham Symphony in a performance of *Umbrian Scene*; lectured in the Center for Creative Study (the Albert Schweitzer Chair in the Humanities) at the Juilliard School of Music; and participated in a three-day Composers Symposium at Montclair State College (NJ). *See*: W20, W91e, W97, W100, W103, W108, W109, W110, W112, W113

B211. ____. "AmerAllegro." *Pan Pipes of Sigma Alpha Iota* 65 (January 1973): 59.
Compilation of performances, publications, and activities during 1972 includes the performance of *The Juggler of Our Lady* (Opera/South) and the availability of *Triple Set* and *Pentagraph* from MCA. Of special interest is Kay's election to the Board of the American Symphony Orchestra League; his appearance as guest conductor of an all-Kay concert (Indiana State University in Terre Haute); and his recent appointment as Distinguished Professor of Music at the Herbert H. Lehman College of the City University of New York. In addition, he was one of the featured composers in a television documentary on "The Black Composer," presented by the Public Broadcasting Service which highlighted *Markings*, performed by the Dallas Symphony, with Paul Freeman, conductor. *See*: W60, W100e, W114, W117

B212. ____. "AmerAllegro." *Pan Pipes of Sigma Alpha Iota* 66 (January 1974): 59.
Compilation of premieres, publications, and recordings in 1973. *Five Portraits* will receive its premiere performance at the Library of Congress, Washington, DC, performed by Roger Ricci. James Dick

premiered *First Nocturne* in Round Top, TX. *Four Silhouettes* and *A Short Overture* were published by MCA, and *Markings*, performed by the London Symphony, Paul Freeman, conductor, is to be released by Columbia Records. Kay appeared as guest composer-conductor at Appalachian State University in Boone, NC. *See*: W27, W100, W115, W116, W118; D7

B213.   _____. "AmerAllegro." *Pan Pipes of Sigma Alpha Iota* 67 (January 1975): 60.
        Compilation of premieres and recordings in 1974 includes first New York performance of *Symphony* (Juilliard Theater Orchestra, James Conlon, conductor) in New York City, and releases of *Markings* (Columbia Records) and *Six Dances for String Orchestra* (Desto Records) with Paul Freeman, conductor. Kay participated in the Symposium of Symphonic Music by Black Composers in Houston, TX, and was lecturer at Fairleigh Dickinson University, Rutherford, NJ. *Quintet Concerto*, commissioned by the Juilliard School, was recently completed. *See*: W105a, W124; D7, D17

B214.   _____. "AmerAllegro." *Pan Pipes of Sigma Alpha Iota* 68 (January 1976): 57.
        Compilation of premieres, performances, publications, and other news in 1975 includes the first performance of *Quintet Concerto* (Juilliard Orchestra, Walter Hendl, conductor). Recently published scores were *First Nocturne* (Belwin Mills), *Epigrams and Hymn, Prelude* (unaccompanied flute), *Sinfonia in E* (Carl Fischer) and *Two Folk Settings* (JCPenney Bicentennial Music Project). Of special note is the information that Kay was the Hubert H. Humphrey Lecturer at Macalester College (St. Paul, MN), and guest composer-lecturer at both Skidmore College (Saratoga, NY) and at Dickinson College (Carlisle, PA). *See*: W14, W44, W118, W124, W126, W128

B215.   _____. "AmerAllegro." *Pan Pipes of Sigma Alpha Iota* 69 (January 1977): 54.
        Compilation of premieres, performances, publications, and recordings in 1976 includes first performances of *Southern Harmony* (North Carolina Symphony, John Gosling, conductor); *Epigrams and Hymn* (the choirs of the Brick Presbyterian Church, NY, T. Charles Lee, director); *Western Paradise* (National Symphony Orchestra, Washington, DC, Antal Dorati, conductor); and *Jubilee* (Opera/South, Jackson, MS). *Forever Free* was published by AMP, and "Sally Anne" from *Two Folk Settings* (De Paur Chorus, Leonard de Paur, conductor) was released on Columbia Records. Kay appeared, also, as guest composer-lecturer at Florida Technological University (Orlando, FL). *See*: W83, W123, W126, W127, W128, W129; D13

B216.   _____. "AmerAllegro." *Pan Pipes of Sigma Alpha Iota* 70 (January 1978): 48.
        Compilation of performances, publications, recordings, and other

news in 1977 includes performances of *Markings* (Pittsburgh Symphony); *Of New Horizons* (Chicago Symphony Orchestra and New Jersey Symphony Orchestra); *Three Pieces After Blake* (New York Philharmonic); *Jubilee* (Opera/South); and *Fantasy Variations* (New Orleans Philharmonic). Carl Fischer, Inc. has published *Three Pieces After Blake* and *Triptych on Texts of Blake*; Orion Records has recorded *Organ Suite*, performed by Thomas Harmon. Kay's activities included service as judge for composition entries in the Ruth Lorraine Close Fellowship Competition (University of Oregon, Eugene, OR) and in the Mu Phi Epsilon composition competition. *See:* W20w, W48a, W67, W88, W89b, W100i, W123; D10

B217.   ____. "AmerAllegro." *Pan Pipes of Sigma Alpha Iota* 71 (Winter 1979): 36.
Compilation of premieres, performances, awards, and appearances of Kay for 1978-79 includes the premiere of *Jersey Hours* (Teaneck, NJ) and performances of *Markings* in Latin America and New York City by the New York Philharmonic, Zubin Mehta conducting. Of note is the grant received by Kay and Donald Dorr from the National Endowment for the Arts to collaborate on an opera concerning the life of Frederick Douglass. *See:* W100, W131, W133

B218.   Lee, Grant. "Nothing in the News." *Musical Courier* 167 (March 1958): 5.
Notes the world premiere of *Pietà* on February 12, 1958 during the nineteenth annual Festival of American Music sponsored by Station WNYC (New York City). *See:* W42

B219.   Lester, William. "New Music for the Organ." *Diapason* 43 (December 1, 1951):31.
Review of *Two Meditations for Organ* which is published by H.W. Gray Co. in its "Contemporary Organ Series." ". . . the composer has an idea of the instrument for which he is writing, and to that extent at least the music will be effective as sound. The player's job in this duo of pieces is not a difficult one, given an organ of sufficient coloring powers, the music can be made attractive for service use, or for padding service in concert lists." *See:* W46

B220.   "'Long Hair,' But Not Long Winded Fits BMI's Composer Ulysses Kay." *New York Age*, October 10, 1953, p. 7.
Biographical information highlights Kay's *Suite for Strings*; his commission by the Louisville Symphony; and his position at BMI. "Few listeners are aware . . . [of] the control and licensing of this music agency Broadcast Music, inc. [sic] (BMI) on Fifth ave. [sic] Fewer still are aware of the existence of a modest, talented composer, Ulysses Kay, consultant and adviser on contemporary music at BMI." Also notes the premiere of *A Lincoln Letter*, the completion of *Triumvirate*, and film scores, *The Quiet One* and *The Lion, the Griffin and the Kangaroo*. Provides list of conductors and orchestras who

have performed Kay's compositions in Europe. Photo of Kay included, as well as one of Kay with Oliver Daniel, CBS radio producer and director. *See*: W31, W34, W47, W49, W50

B221.   Low, W. Augustus and Virgil A. Clift, eds. *Encyclopedia of Black America*. New York: McGraw-Hill Book Co., 1981, pp. 483, 590.
          Includes short biographical sketch with mention of Kay's education, naval experience, and teaching career. Notes that Kay "rapidly became the most important Afro-American composer of classical music in the United States, and sustained that reputation throughout his career. . . ." Lists several of his more important works dating from 1940 to 1968. Of particular interest is the section, "Music: History and Development" by Eileen Southern, in which Kay is referred to as one of the composers who continued to produce during the middle years of the twentieth century.

B222.   Lowens, Irving. "Debuts and Appearances." *High Fidelity/Musical America* 27 (February 1977): 37.
          Review of the National Symphony Orchestra's bicentennial premiere of works by Gunther Schuller, Ulysses Kay, and Miklos Rozsa. Of Kay's *The Western Paradise*, Lowens writes that "although Kay conceived the work with the voice of Helen Hayes in mind, [William] Conrad's rotund bass did it no violence. The story about the break between the Colonies and the Mother Country, beautifully shaded by Kay's subtle orchestral background, was effective and moving." *See*: W129

B223.   MacDougall, Sally. "Music Scales the Iron Curtain." *World-Telegram and Sun Feature Magazine Section*, January 10, 1959, p. 14.
          Narrative of U.S. composers in Russia "reveals how Reds let down the political bars for our ambassadors of culture." Includes observations and comments by Kay "'For four weeks, . . . we lived in a world of music, ballet, opera and the theater while we and the Russians interpreted our work to each other. . . . We met only kindness—friendly curiosity and kindness—while seeing our hosts under special circumstances in a world of the performing arts.'" *See*: K1, K4, K7

B224.   Machlis, Joseph. *Introduction to Contemporary Music*. 2nd ed. New York: W.W. Norton, 1979, p. 560.
          Kay is included in the section, "Dictionary of Contemporary Composers and Their Recorded Works." Machlis refers to Kay as "one of our leading black composers. . . . [He] has turned out a varied list of works marked by appealing lyricism, spontaneity, and rhythmic verve. Behind these is a highly musical personality that has absorbed important aspects of contemporary musical thought but has steadfastly maintained a middle-of-the-road position."

B225. MacLeod, Hope. "Maker of Music." *New York Post*, June 13, 1968, p. 47.

A feature article highlighting Kay's appointment as music professor at the Herbert H. Lehman College "which will be the new name of Hunter College (Bronx). . . ." Includes a biographical sketch, and provides a close view of the composer's personality and thoughts relating to his music. Of his appointment, Kay confides that "'music, like painting and so many other things, is changing at a tremendous rate. Teaching is right in the thick of it, and young people are very vitally concerned and interested.'" MacLeod states further that the "trim, soft-spoken Kay has a down-to-earth way of discussing his talent. He once said a composer is basically 'just a person trying to express himself. . . .'"

B226. Maschal, Richard. "Black Composers and Their Music." *Charlotte Observer*, April 30, 1978, pp. 1F, 12F.

Mentions Kay as a composer whose work appears in the *Black Composer in Music* recordings (CBS). The reviewer affirms that Kay's work and career have been helped by the interest in black music that was initiated by a Black Music Symposium held in 1967 at Spelman College (Atlanta, GA), during which the Atlanta Symphony performed the works of several black composers. He maintains, further, that black American music received a boost during the seventies citing broadened research efforts, the *Black Composer Series*, and "Celebration of Black Composers" by the New York Philharmonic. Includes photo of Kay. *See*: D7; B3, B101

B227. Maultsby, Portia. "Selective Bibliography: U.S. Black Music." *Ethnomusicology* 19 (September 1975): 421-49.

Lists Richard Hadley's dissertation, then unpublished, "The Published Choral Music of Ulysses Simpson Kay, 1943-68," in the bibliography. *See*: B156

B228. McCue, George, ed. *Music in American Society 1776-1976: From Puritan Hymn to Synthesizer*. New Brunswick, NJ: Transaction Books, 1977, p. 94.

Mentions Kay and his opera, *Jubilee*, in chapter, "The Other Side of Black Music," which pertains to black music that does not employ spiritual or jazz idioms. The author speaks of secular folk tunes, secular jubilee songs, and the Black Renaissance (ca. 1905-1940). *Jubilee* is referred to as a "larger vocal extension of what was once called the spiritual." *See*: W123

B229. McPherson, James M., Lawrence B. Holland, James M. Banner, Jr., Nancy J. Weiss, and Michael D. Bell. *Blacks In America: Bibliographical Essays*. New York: Doubleday, 1971, pp. 290-93.

Part VIII, "Blacks In American Culture, 1900-1970," includes section highlighting "Blacks In Opera and Symphonic Music." Discusses the state of the Afro-American artist indicating that acceptance by the broad American audience has been limited, with concert artists unable to perform in many places (save the Metropolitan Opera House) and few composers recorded. Noted are William Grant Still, William L. Dawson, and Howard Swanson. Although Kay is not included in the article, mention is made of Desto's recording, *The Black Composer in America*, on which *Short Overture* is performed. *See*: D15

B230.   "Mixed N.Y. Choir Performs Ulysses Kay Cantata." *Jet* 16 (June 4, 1959): 59.
Notes performance of *Phoebus, Arise* by the Interracial Fellowship Chorus. *See*: W72

B231.   Mootz, William. "Chamber Music Society To Open Season Oct. 31; New Work by Ulysses Kay To Be Heard Saturday." *Courier-Journal* (Louisville, KY), September 12, 1954, section 5, p. 3.
Notes world premiere of *Serenade for Orchestra* by the Louisville Orchestra in Columbia Auditorium at a weekly matinee. Mentions that Kay is the "first Negro whose work will be played," and that Kay feels "'that the composition expresses the joy of music-making and to me, this is a truly fulfillment of my efforts at creative work.'" *See*: W52; B232

B232.   ____. "Musical Tour de Force Hold[s] Matinee Attention." *Courier-Journal* (Louisville, KY), September 19, 1954, section 1, p. 22.
Review of *Serenade for Orchestra* (Louisville Symphony, Robert Whitney, conductor) acclaims the composition as "the premiere of the afternoon." Other works presented were composed by David Epstein, Boris Blacher, and Vincent Persichetti. *See*: W52; B231

B233.   "Music Calendar." *PM Daily*, September 29, 1947, p. 17.
Includes photo of Ulysses Kay and Lucy Brown, young American pianist, who will play the first performance of *Four Inventions* on her Town Hall debut. *See*: W25

B234.   "Music Exchange Slated." *New York Times*, September 13, 1958, p. 11.
Article reports that four U.S. composers, Ulysses Kay, Peter Mennin, Roy Harris, and Roger Sessions, will spend three weeks in the Soviet Union under a new cultural exchange pact—the United States-Soviet Cultural Exchange Program. *See*: K1, K4, K7

B235.   "Music Exchanges with Reds Urged." *New York Times*, November 2, 1958, p. 124.
Includes observations by Roger Sessions upon his return from tour of the Soviet Union with fellow composers, Kay, Mennin, and Harris, emphasizing that free communication could avoid conflict. Brief description of tour provided. *See*: K1, K4, K7

B236.   "Music Reviews." *Notes, The Quarterly Journal of the Music Library Association* 13 (March 1956): 148.

Review of *Come Away, Come Away Death*, written for men's voices in three parts. ". . . it is effective writing and will probably make its own way with choruses of somewhat exacting standards." *See*: W18

B237.   Myers, Kurtz, comp. and ed. *Index to American Record Reviews*. Boston, MA: G. K. Hall, 1978, pp. 69, 70, 72, 75, 123, 154, 181, 220, 266, 268, 364, 374, 407, 450, 573.

Information in this four-volume set is based on material originally published in *Notes, The Quarterly Journal of the Music Library Association*, between 1949 and 1977. The set is arranged in two sections. The first is primarily a listing by composers; the second is entitled "Composite Releases." Contains works by several composers, arranged alphabetically under the manufacturer's name and numerically by record number. A complete discography of Kay's works is provided. A list of abbreviations for periodicals appearing in the set, and an index, are extremely beneficial to the reader.

B238.   "N.Y. Composer Ulysses Kay Wis [sic] Moravian Contest." *Diapason* 47 (May 1, 1956): 2.

Notes that the Moravian Contest First Prize was awarded to Kay for his *Grace to You, and Peace*. "Mr. Kay's anthem will be premiered in a musical service May 20, the actual date of the 150th anniversary . . ." of the dedication of the Central Moravian Church. *See*: W58.

B239.   Nairn, Norman. "21st American Festival at Eastman." *Musical Courier* 143 (June 1951): 16-17.

Notes four premieres of American composers performed by the Eastman-Rochester Symphony, with Howard Hanson conducting, on May 2. "Ulysses Kay's *Sinfonia in E* provided a stimulating opening, a work with a sense of direction." *See*: W44

B240.   "New Music (1970-72)." *Black Perspective in Music* 1 (Spring 1973): 97-99.

Notes publication and premiere information for *Facets* (chamber music); *Parables* and *Triple Set* (choral and vocal ensemble); and *The Capitoline Venus* (opera). *See*: W110, W112, W113, W114

B241.   "New Music." *Black Perspective in Music* 2 (Spring 1974): 101-2.

Notes publication of *Four Silhouettes* (band); *Five Portraits* (instrumental solo); and *Pentagraph* and *Triple Set* (choral and vocal ensemble). *See*: W114, W115, W116, W117

B242.   ____. *Black Perspective in Music* 3 (Spring 1975): 102-3.
             Lists new music by Kay: *Harlem Children's Suite* (orchestral);
             Heralds II (chamber); *Quintet Concerto* (concertos); and *Second*
             Nocturne and *Guitarra* (instrumental solos). *See*: W119, W120,
             W121, W122, W124

B243.   ____. *Black Perspective in Music* 4 (Spring 1976): 108-9.
             Notes publication and premiere information for *Quintet Concerto*,
             Southern Harmony, *Epigrams and Hymn*, and *Two Folk Settings*
             ("Sally Anne" and "Blow, Ye Winds in the Morning"). *See*: W124,
             W126, W127, W128

B244.   ____. *Black Perspective in Music* 5 (Spring 1977): 120-21.
             Notes commissions and premiere performances of *Southern*
             Harmony, The Western Paradise, and *Jubilee*. See: W123, W127,
             W129

B245.   "New Recordings (1970-72)." *Black Perspective in Music* 1 (Spring
             1973): 101.
             Notes release of recording, *The Black Composer in America*, which
             includes Kay's *Short Overture* (Desto 7107). See: W27; D15

B246.   "New York." *Music Journal* 33 (May 1975): 43.
             Review of the world premiere of *Quintet Concerto*, which was
             performed by the Juilliard Orchestra, with Walter Hendl conducting.
             "Kay's provocative work contains a bit of real music (themes, arching
             phrases), not only disjointed fragments. Slight tendency to rambling
             but basically engrossing writing with something consequential usually
             going on. An Andante movement to be proud of. This welcome work
             is virtuoso stuff, and drew a brilliant performance from all
             forces. . . ." *See*: W124

B247.   Newlin, Dika. "25 Years of ACA: Highlights and Recollections."
             American Composers Alliance Bulletin 11, nos. 2-4 (1963): 12-13.
             History of organization of ACA, detailing aims and objectives; early
             contractual decisions; mention of composers who are members; and
             outstanding committees. Photo of Kay included.

B248.   Newman, Richard, comp. *Black Access: A Bibliography of Afro-*
             American Bibliographies. Westport, CT: Greenwood Press, 1984,
             p. 81.
             Lists dissertation by Richard Hadley, "The Published Choral Music
             of Ulysses Kay—1943 to 1968," among its bibliographies. *See*: B156

B249.   Noss, Luther. "Ulysses Kay: *Two Meditations*." In "Music
             Reviews." *Notes, The Quarterly Journal of the Music Library*
             Association 9 (December 1951): 170.
             Review of *Two Meditations* by Luther Noss, who writes that
             "Ulysses Kay, a young American composer whose work for other

musical media has received considerable recognition, offers organists a sample of his writing . . . (both pieces together total little more than three minutes), and hardly serves as a fair exhibition of his talent. However, most organists are grateful for even small favors . . . they are prepared, too, to conceal the composer's lack of experience in writing for the instrument (as is the case here) by careful registration and even a little judicious editing. Each piece is more or less a prelude based on a single idea, commenting briefly and without emotional excitement. Neither is difficult, and none need shy from the mild dissonances used." *See*: W46

B250.   "The Odyssey of Ulysses." *Down Beat* 25 (October 2, 1958): 11.
    Report of Kay's departure to Russia for the cultural exchange, sponsored by the U.S. Department of State. "Particularly interested in gauging the impact, if any, of American jazz on Russia and its composers, Kay huddled with *Down Beat* on a list of records to take with him to play behind the Iron Curtain, and on observations to make of the scene there." Included among the records were compositions by Miles Davis-Gil Evans, Duke Ellington, W. C. Handy (played by Louis Armstrong), Thelonious Monk, and Johnny Richards. *See*: B149, B150

B251.   Oja, Carol. *American Music Recordings*. Brooklyn, NY: Institute for Studies in American Music/Brooklyn College City University of New York, 1982, p. 185.
    "Lists over 13,000 commercially distributed recordings of some 8,000 pieces by nearly 1,300 American composers from the generation of Ives and Ruggles to the present." Organized alphabetically by composer and title of composition. Includes descriptive information by recording date, different issues of the recording, record company name, disc number, speed of disc, number and size of discs, release date, and finally, date of deletion. Provides bibliography and a list of abbreviations. Cites *Choral Triptych, Concerto for Orchestra, Six Dances for String Orchestra*, "Round Dance" and "Polka," *Fantasy Variations*, "How Stands the Glass Around?," *Invention No. 3, Markings, Prelude for Flute, Brass Quartet, Serenade, A Short Overture, Sinfonia in E, Organ Suite No. 1, Umbrian Scene*, and "What's In a Name?." *See*: D1, D2, D3, D4, D6, D7, D10, D11, D12, D14, D15, D16, D17, D20, D21

B252.   "Onstage." *Symphony Magazine* 33 (June/July 1982): 130.
    Notes premiere of *Reverie and Rondo* by the Berkshire Symphony Orchestra, Julius Hegyi, conductor, February 26, 1982. *See*: W94

B253.   "Opera Everywhere." *High Fidelity/Musical America* 27 (February 1977): 18-19.
    Article includes photos of the principal soloists in Opera/South's production of *Jubilee*, noting that the bicentennial production represented "a fitting . . . gift to the nation and centennial gift to . . .

Jackson State University. . . . And, no finer gift could have been found for author, cast, or sell-out audience at the November 20 world premiere of the two-and-a-half year effort." *See*: W123

B254.   "Orchestra List: Part II." *American Composers Alliance Bulletin* 10, no. 4 (1962): 21-22.
        Includes catalog of Kay's orchestral works to 1962, with descriptive information by instrumentation, publisher, and duration.

B255.   Parmenter, Ross. "Music Composed By Negroes Heard." *New York Times*, May 22, 1950, p. 17.
        Review of *Suite for Orchestra*, performed at Town Hall by the New York Chamber Orchestra, with Dean Dixon conducting. The reviewer notes that this program, sponsored by the African Aid Committee, and chaired by W. E. B. DuBois, featured the music of six black composers from five countries—Samuel Coleridge-Taylor, England; Amadeo Roldán, Cuba; Michael Moerane, Union of South Africa; Ingram Fox, British Guiana; and William Grant Still/Ulysses Kay, United States. *See*: W21

B256.   Pavlakis, Christopher. *The American Music Handbook*. New York: The Free Press, 1974, pp. 338, 448, 599.
        Includes biographical information, available records, and publishers of Kay's works: *Brass Quartet, Sinfonia in E*, "What's In a Name?," "How Stands the Glass Around?," "Round Dance" and "Polka," *Serenade for Orchestra, Fantasy Variations, Choral Triptych*, and *Umbrian Scene*.   Indicates that *Concerto for Orchestra* (Remington Records) is out-of-print. Kay's work as a judge for the "SAI Inter-American Awards" is noted. Of special interest is mention of a 90-minute program on PBS WNET/13, June 1972, which featured Kay on its "Special of the Week" segment, entitled "The Black Composer." *See*: D1, D2, D3, D4, D12, D14, D16, D20, D21

B257.   Phillips, Burrill. "New Music." *Notes, The Quarterly Journal of the Music Library Association* 29 (June 1973): 811.
        Theater Set for Orchestra is reviewed. *See*: W109

B258.   "Play New Works." *Symphony* 5 (June 1951): 14.
        Notes world premiere of *Song of Ahab* by the Quincy (IL) Chamber Music Ensemble. This composition, commissioned by the Quincy Society of Fine Arts, is a cantata for baritone voice and chamber orchestra with text from Herman Melville's "Moby Dick." *See*: W45

B259.   Ploski, Harry A., and Warren Marr II. *The Negro Almanac: A Reference Work on the AfroAmerican*. 3rd ed. New York: Bellwether Co., 1976, pp. 857-58.
        Brief biographical sketch with photo. "Ulysses Simpson Kay is a traditionally trained classical composer and the creator of eloquent symphonic music. . . . He is regularly performed and recorded

throughout the United States and Europe." Among works cited are: *Choral Triptych, Six Dances, Fantasy Variations, Sinfonia in E,* and *The Boor. See:* W44, W53, W57, W82, W89

B260.   "Pravda Hails U.S. Music." *New York Times,* October 18, 1958, p. 17.
          Review of works of the visiting American composers, Kay, Harris, Mennin, and Sessions in *Pravda,* the Soviet Union's leading newspaper. The reviewer, Yuri Shaporin, spoke favorably of the American compositions and cited, particularly, their originality. *See:* W20g; K7

B261.   "Premiere Musical Work of Ulysses Kay on Festival." *New York Age,* February 15, 1958, p. 17.
          Narrative of opening of WNYC's nineteenth annual festival identifies soloists, orchestra, and conductor who will perform Kay's *Pietà* and works of other composers. *See:* W42

B262.   "Radio." *American Composers Alliance Bulletin* 2, no. 1 (1952): 11.
          Notes performance of *Two Meditations* by E. Power Biggs on November 18. *See:* W46a

B263.   ____. *American Composers Alliance Bulletin* 2, no. 2 (1952): 18.
          Lists radio performance of Kay's *Suite for Orchestra* (January 4), with Dean Dixon conducting the Turino Radio Orchestra on Program Nazionale Network for Italy. Notes also the performance of *Song for Strings* (January 15) for the Italian Third Program, with Dean Dixon conducting the Allessandro Scarlatti Orchestra. *See:* W21a; W31b

B264.   ____. *American Composers Alliance Bulletin* 2, no. 4 (1952-53): 18.
          Notes broadcast of *Suite for Strings* on WNYC with Leopold Stokowski, conductor, on November 2. *See:* W31a

B265.   ____. *American Composers Alliance Bulletin* 3, no. 1 (1953): 19-20.
          Notes performance of *First Meditation* (February 1), by E. Power Biggs on CBS Network and a performance of *Quartet for Brass* (February 15), by the Brass Ensemble of the Third Street Settlement on WNYC. *See:* W39; W46a

B266.   ____. *American Composers Alliance Bulletin* 3, no. 2 (1953): 27.
          Notes broadcast of *Two Dances* (May 10) on CBS Network, with Alfred Antonini, conductor, and performances of *Suite for Strings* (May 19 and June 16) on WNYC, Leopold Stokowski, conductor. *See:* W31; W53

B267.   Reis, Claire R. *Composers in America: Biographical Sketches of Contemporary Composers with a Record of Their Works.* New York: Da Capo Press, 1977. pp. 203-4.
          This reprint of the 1947 MacMilllan publication includes biographical sketch and catalog of Kay's works from 1939 to 1946

divided by genre: "Orchestral Works," "Chamber Orchestra," "Band Music," "Choral Works," "Chamber Music," and "Stage Works." Descriptive information by title, duration, publisher/manuscript, and date is provided.

B268.   "Reports from Member Organizations." *National Music Council Bulletin* 36 (Spring 1977): 19.

A report from BMI notes the world premiere of *Southern Harmony*, which was commissioned by the Southeastern Regional Metropolitan Orchestra Managers Association and the National Endowment for the Arts. *See*: W127

B269.   "Return of Composer to Native Tucson, AZ to Conduct 'Of New Horizons,' April 1954." *Negro History Bulletin* 17 (May 1954): 181.

Reprint of an article in *Time* (March 8, 1954, p. 71), entitled "Return of Ulysses." Reviews the performance in Tucson of *Of New Horizons* with Kay, conductor, for the twenty-fifth anniversary of the Tucson Symphony. Mentions that Kay attended school on the GI Bill. *See*: W20b; B4, B103, B158

B270.   "Reviews." *Brass Quarterly* 2 (December 1958): 85-86.

Review of *Brass Quartet*, with detailed analysis of the music and its performance demands. The reviewer notes that it "is a serious, rather ambitious work for two trumpets, tenor and bass trombones. . . . More than anything else the work demands tone—vast, substantial tone. Ulysses Kay's *Brass Quartet* is not a piece for cowards, but neither is it a piece for the insensitive." *See*: W39; D1

B271.   Roach, Hildred. *Black American Music: Past and Present*. Boston: Crescendo Publishing Co., 1973, pp. 120-24, 149.

Contains short biographies of selected composers, list of readings and recordings, music terms, chronology, publishers, repositories, and index.   A summary of Kay's work to 1972 is provided.   Notes compositions that have been cited for awards: *Suite for Orchestra, A Short Overture*, and *Of New Horizons*. Roach includes a detailed analysis of *Four Inventions* (piano) with musical examples. In a discussion of musical style, she suggests that "Kay is significant for linking the Modern Period with the Space Age in his forward use of contemporary techniques, much as did Beethoven who bridged the [C]lassical and Romantic periods. Kay is one who produces quality works, and his courageous approach of maintaining a traditional principle amidst irregular, or contemporary methods, is unique." Photo included. *See*: W20, W21, W25, W27

B272.   _____. *Black American Music: Past and Present*. 2 vols. Malabar, FL: Robert E. Krieger Publishing Co., 1985, pp. 7, 17-19.

A two-volume set, which provides a history of black American music to the 1980s. Volume 1 is a revision and reprint of the 1973 publication. Volume 2, *Pan-African Composers Thenceforth and Now*, is an update. In it are highlights of Kay's life and career from 1973 to 1983 including performances, commissions, recording releases, and publications. Also included is an analytical outline of his *Nocturne for Piano*. *See*: W118; B271

B273.   "Russians Hear Music by 4 U.S. Composers." *New York Times*, October 16, 1958, p. 46.
Account of Radio Moscow's performances of Kay's *Of New Horizons* and works by fellow American composers, Mennin, Sessions and Harris. *See*: W20g; K1, K4, K7; B260

B274.   Ryder, Georgia. "Another Look At Some American Cantatas." *Black Perspective in Music* 3 (May 1975): 135-40.
Notes impact of Kay's *Juggler of Our Lady* and Still's *Highway No. 1, U.S.A.* upon the public-at-large. "This public acclaim given to the brilliant artists and scholars who produced these works undoubtedly attributed to the kindling of an avid interest in and receptivity to such music among Americans, black and white, who had 'discovered' Afro-American music during and immediately after the civil strife of the 1960s." *See*: W60; B19

B275.   Saal, Hubert. "Music—Black Composers." *Newsweek*, April 15, 1974, p.82.
Kay is mentioned as one whose work is included in Columbia Masterworks' "Black Composers Series." He is described as a "solidly trained classical composer." Of his *Markings*, the author states that it is "a powerful and expressive tone poem." Continuing, he maintains that "what this series of records documents is both the richness and the diversity of black composition. It also confronts the question of whether such a thing as black music exists . . . there are almost no overt signs of the 'black experience' in the music of . . . Kay, Walker and Anderson. They've been attacked by more militant blacks for composing 'white man's music.' Kay, sensitive to the criticism, insists that 'my experience as a black man is inevitably reflected in my music. But I don't know how to demonstrate that.'" Further Kay maintains "'that Tchaikovsky and Bartók had roots they could identify with and draw upon. Maybe that's what these young black composers are looking for.'" *See*: W100; D7

B276.   Sabin, Robert. "New Music." *Musical America* (April 1955): 26.
Notes first performance of *Three Pieces After Blake* on "Music in the Making" series at Cooper Union (NY), March 27. *See*: W48

B277.   "Saluting Negro Composers." *Tones and Overtones* 1 (Spring 1954): 79-80.
This University of Alabama (Montgomery) publication, edited by John Duncan, includes a short biography and a catalog of Kay's works to 1954.

B278.   "Scholarships in Composition for Students at Brevard Music Center."
Triangle of Mu Phi Epsilon 73 (1979): 4.
Notes establishment of summer scholarships for two composition
students by ASCAP. "These students will have the opportunity of
working with Ulysses Kay. . . ." Includes photos of Kay and of the Mu
Phi Epsilon composer-in-residence studio at Brevard Center (NC).

B279.   Scholes, Percy, ed. *The Oxford Companion to Music*. Oxford: Oxford
University Press, 1970, p. 549.
Brief biographical sketch of Kay's life to the late 1960s. Mentions
education, naval career, and compositional forms.

B280.   Schonberg, Harold C. "Exchange Composers." *New York Times*,
September 21, 1958, section X, p. 11.
Notes the exchange of U.S. composers, Ulysses Kay, Roy Harris,
and Roger Sessions with Russian composers, Aram Khatchaturian,
Dmitri Shostakovich, and Dmitri Kabalevsky. Comments by Kay
reflect his wish "'to see a new production in rehearsal . . . to see how
the composers produce, in terms of what is expected of them.'" *See*:
K1, K4, K7

B281.   "Settling a Score." *New York Age*, May 16, 1953, p. 7.
Photo of Kay with Oliver Daniel, CBS Radio Director of Music,
1953, examining score for "Schottische," which received its premiere
on the CBS program "String Serenade" on May 10. *See*: W53

B282.   Shackelford, Rudy. "Yaddo Festivals of American Music, 1932-1952."
Perspectives of New Music 17 (Fall/Winter 78): 92-125.
Shackelford provides a chronicle of the nine Yaddo festivals (1932-
1952), detailing plans for a "'series of efforts toward the improvement
of the economic and artistic status of the American composer.'" The
author describes evolutionary changes by dividing the period into
three groups: "[1] 1932 and '33, when Aaron Copland was the
presiding presence; [2] 1936, '37, and '38, when the experiment was
made of integrating contemporary music with works from the
Baroque and Classical eras; [3] 1940, '46, '49, and '52, marking a
return to the practice of presenting only modern compositions."
Kay's *[Suite from] The Quiet One* was performed during the 1949
festival, along with compositions by Alvin Etler, Eugene Weigel,
Bernhard Heiden, Jacob Avshalomov, and Vincent Persichetti—all
reported as successful representations of a period of common practice.
Arthur Berger defines the properties of this practice as "'a sonority,
recognizably modern yet rarely biting; a few rhythmic formulas
assuring a constant, almost willful, motoriness verging at times on
the 'Brandenburg' manner; and fairly predictable fugatos.'" *See*:
W35

B283.   Siegmeister, Elie, ed. *The New Music Lover's Handbook*. Irvington-on-Hudson, NY: Harvey House, 1973, pp. 549-50.
          Reprint of article, "Ulysses Kay," by Nicolas Slonimsky in the *ACA Bulletin* (1957). Includes, also, an update of Kay's "more important compositions" to 1972: *The Boor, Concerto for Orchestra, A Lincoln Letter, A New Song, Choral Triptych, Markings, Symphony, The Juggler of Our Lady, The Capitoline Venus*, and *Five Portraits. See*: W32, W49, W57, W59, W60, W82, W100, W105, W110, W115; B286

B284.   Slonimsky, Nicolas. *Music Since 1900*.   New York: Charles Scribner's Sons, 1971, pp. 787, 912, 1176, 1223, 1254.
          A chronological listing of music since January 1, 1900, with reference to premiere performances of Kay's *Of New Horizons, Symphony in E, Umbrian Scene, Markings*, and *Stephen Crane*. Includes a brief description of each composition. *See*: W20, W44, W91, W100, W104

B285.   ____. *Supplement to Music Since 1900*.   New York: Charles Scribner's Sons, 1986, pp. 21, 90, 101, 115.
          An update of chronological listings of music to 1976. Includes premiere information for Kay's *The Capitoline Venus, Quintet Concerto, Southern Harmony*, and *Jubilee. See*: W110, W123, W124, W127

B286.   ____. "Ulysses Kay." *American Composers Alliance Bulletin* 7, no. 1 (1958): 3-11.
          Complete biography to 1957 highlighting Kay's education, teachers, awards, grants, and fellowships.   Style analysis and accompanying musical examples provide insight into Kay's use of melody, form, instrumentation, rhythm, and other elements. Includes catalog of works, arranged chronologically, with descriptive information by duration, publisher, medium, premiere performance data, and selected quotes from critical reviews.

B287.   Smythe, Mabel M., ed. *The Black American Reference Book*. Englewood Cliffs, NJ: Prentice-Hall, 1976, p. 820.
          In the section entitled, "The European Stream," Kay is noted as one of the best known Afro-American composers "to come to prominence after World War II. . . ." Others included are Howard Swanson and Margaret Bonds. This reference book was sponsored by the Phelps-Stokes Fund.

B288.   Sommers, Pamela. "Black American Composers." *Washington Post*, May 27, 1985, p. C11.
          Review of concert sponsored by the National Museum of American History's Program in Black American Culture, May 24, 1985. The concert featured music of black composers, Mark Fax, George Walker, John Carter, Howard Swanson, Dorothy Rudd Moore, Frederick Tillis, James Furman, and Ulysses Kay. "The high point of this long

evening was the world premiere of Ulysses S. Kay's *'Tromba'*, a haunting and lyrical suite for trumpet and piano, sensitively interpreted by Fred Irby III and Ronald Tymus." *See*: W135

B289.   "'Song of Ahab' to be done by Lyric Chamber Theater June 8 Y.M.H.A." *New York Age*, June 7, 1958, p. 19.
         Announcement includes names of soloists, conductor, time, and place of performance of *Song of Ahab*. *See*: W45a

B290.   Southern, Eileen. "America's Black Composers of Classical Music." *Music Educators Journal* 62 (November 1975): 34, 46-53.
         Historical discussion of Afro-American composers of the twentieth century. Kay, among the many composers discussed, is cited and referred to as one of the composers whose reputation had been established before he became a college professor. Southern affirms that for these composers "there has been no pressure on them to write music specifically for performance by black artists and groups. For the first time in history, a generation of black composers—this generation—has moved into the professional world in the same way their white colleagues do. Obviously, sociological changes in the United States allowed this to come about." Photo included.

B291.   _____. *Biographical Dictionary of Afro-American and African Musicians*. The Greenwood Encyclopedia of Black Music. Westport, CT: Greenwood Press, 1982, pp. 226-27, 422, 428, 438, 440.
         Provides biographical sketch and brief discussion of Kay's works. Includes a catalog of compositions from 1939 to 1974, arranged by medium. Appendices list musical occupation, place, and date of birth. Short bibliography provided.

B292.   _____. "Book Reviews." *Black Perspective in Music* 6 (Spring 1978): 100-101.
         Review of *The Black Composer Speaks* by David Baker, Lida Belt, and Herman Hudson which includes an interview with Kay and a catalog of his works to 1976. Extensive bibliography provided. "A special strength of the book is that the composers themselves tell their stories; there is no narrative other than the biographical sketches. To be sure, writers have long used oral-history techniques in dealing with jazz and folk music, but this may the first time classical composers have been allowed 'to speak.' This publication will be particularly welcomed by the black-music scholar and will be thoroughly enjoyed by the general reader." *See*: B27

B293.   _____. "Conversation with Clarence E. Whiteman." *Black Perspective in Music* 6 (Spring 1978):181.
         An interview with Clarence E. Whiteman, Professor of Organ and Theory at Virginia State College, reveals a list of organ music by black composers in his personal library. Among the holdings is *Two Meditations* by Kay. *See*: W46

B294.   [____]. "In Retrospect . . . a Pictorial Survey." *Black Perspective in Music* 3 (May 1975): 207-34.
Includes photographs of William Grant Still with family and associates, and reproductions of three musical works by leading black composers, written in dedication to Still on the celebration of his eightieth birthday—*Visions* (Kay); *For One Called Billy* (Hale Smith); and *Eclatette* (Arthur Cunningham). Also includes facsimile of flyer announcing Opera/South's production of *The Juggler of Our Lady* and Still's *Highway 1, U.S.A.* with photos of principal singers. *See*: W60; W125

B295.   ____. "Kay, Ulysses (Simpson)." In *The New Grove Dictionary of American Music*, Vol. 2. Edited by H. Wiley Hitchcock and Stanley Sadie. London: MacMillan Press, 1986. pp. 615-16.
Biographical sketch provided. Includes list of works to 1984, a short bibliography, and a partial listing of recorded compositions.

B296.   ____. "Kay, Ulysses (Simpson)." In *The New Grove Dictionary of Music and Musicians*. Vol. 9. Edited by Stanley Sadie. London: MacMillan Publishers, 1980, pp. 834-35.
Concise biographical sketch provided; includes catalog of works to 1975 and bibliographic sources.

B297.   ____. *The Music of Black Americans: A History.* 2nd ed. New York: W. W. Norton, 1983, pp. 510, 518, 524-29, 543.
Includes biographical sketch with highlights of Kay's career and lists of selected compositions. Mentions Kay's composition, *Markings*, as one that is "perennially popular." Includes score and analysis. *See*: W100

B298.   Standifer, James A. and Barbara Reeder. *Source Book of African and Afro-American Materials for Music Educators.* Washington: Contemporary Music Project, Music Educators National Conference, 1972, pp. 82-83, 123-24.
Selected discography includes Kay's *A Short Overture, Fantasy Variations, Sinfonia in E*, "Round Dance" and "Polka," *Concerto for Orchestra*, and *Suite* (string orchestra). Appendix A "includes lists of Afro-American musicians whose names and musical contributions should be familiar to music educators." The author maintains that "any disagreement with details of selection or categorization should not be allowed to obscure the basic purpose of this presentation, which is to demonstrate to the reader the scope of successful, creative participation by black musicians in the music profession." Kay is included among the sixty-five composers listed. *See*: D3, D4, D12, D15, D16, D17

B299.   Steinfirst, Donald. "Trigon." *Pittsburgh Post*, June 19, 1962. (reprinted in the *ACA Bulletin* 10, no. 3 (1962): 19).
Review of the June 18 performance of *Trigon* by the American

Wind Symphony, Robert Boudreau, conductor. "The piece has a quiet strength. For me, the second movement, marked 'Canticle' was the most rewarding. It is lyric in content, imaginative and often noble in its originality." *See*: W80; B88

B300.   Still, William Grant. "Fifty Years of Progress in Music." *Pittsburgh Courier*, November 11, 1950, p. 15.
          Still discusses the plight of the serious composer who happens to be black, mentioning Kay in this context.

B301.   Stucky, Steven. "Orchestral Music." *Notes, The Quarterly Journal of the Music Library Association* (December 1985): 390-92.
          Review of *Chariots: Orchestral Rhapsody*. "The work's rather traditional style and practical instrumental writing, and the fact that it is demonstrably 'about' something listeners can quickly apprehend, suggests that it will be heard again. The 'chariots' . . . are symbolic of 'a person's aspirations and being'. . . a more specific key to the work, though, is provided near the end when the solo horn quotes the first phrase of 'Swing Low, Sweet Chariot.'" *See*: W132

B302.   "The Symphony." *Virginian-Pilot and the Ledger-Star*, February 8, 1988, p. 6.
          Announcement of concert to be given by Yehudi Menuhin in Ogden Hall, Hampton University, which will include music of Bach, Chausson, Beethoven, and Kay's *Reverie and Rondo*. *See*: W94

B303.   "Things You Should Know." *Music Journal* 28 (January 1970): 12.
          Notes the world premiere of *Once There Was a Man: A Covenant for Our Time*, which was commissioned by the Detroit Symphony and the Worcester Chorus for the 110th Worcester (MA) music festival, with William Warfield, narrator. *See*: W111; B42

B304.   _____. *Music Journal* 26 (February 1968): 18.
          Notes the premiere performance of *Stephen Crane Set* (February 4) which was commissioned by the Chicago Musical College for its one hundredth anniversary. *See*: W104

B305.   _____. *Music Journal* 29 (May 1971): 13.
          Brief notice of the premiere of *Aulos* at the Indiana University School of Music, with John Solum, soloist, and Wolfgang Vacano, conductor. *See*: W103

B306.   _____. *Music Journal* 30 (January 1972): 60.
          Notes that twenty works received world premieres during the Eastman School of Music's fiftieth anniversary. Kay's *Facets* was among them. *See*: W113

B307.   "3 Composers Off to Soviet." *New York Times*, September 18, 1958, p. 37.

Brief note of the departure of Kay, Roy Harris, and Roger Sessions, from the United States to go to the Soviet Union.

B308.   "Tully Hall." *Music Journal* 32 (May 1974): 54.
Review of the New York premiere of Kay's *Symphony No. 1* (Juilliard Theater Orchestra, directed by James Conlon). "The work in 4 movements had a strong beginning with declamatory statements from the percussion and brass sections. The 2nd movement displayed a fresh, free-spirited type of writing. . . . The Largo entered into smooth, sensuous writing, which then was followed by a contrasting 4th movement. The symphony is fast moving and easy to listen to; the composer 'intended to compose an affirmative and communicative work'—and he succeeded." *See*: W105a

B309.   "2 Students Share $1,000 Music Prize." *New York Times*, January 29, 1947, p. 30.
Notes that Kay and Earl George were named winners of the Third Annual George Gershwin Memorial Contest, conducted by the Victory Lodge of B'nai B'rith. Kay's award-winning composition, *A Short Overture*, was presented at the Brooklyn Academy of Music on Monday, March 31, 1947. *See*: W27

B310.   "U.S. Composers Hailed." *New York Times*, October 31, 1958, p. 34.
Article reveals Soviets' pleasure upon successful completion of American composers' concert. This was expressed in a cable sent by Tikhon N. Khrennikov, general secretary of the Union of Soviet Composers to Herman D. Kenin, president of the American Federation of Musicians. The cable was signed by five Soviet composers including those who were participants in the U.S. - Soviet Cultural Exchange Program.

B311.   "U.S. Composers Reach Soviet." *New York Times*, September 18, 1958, p. 62.
Although Kay's name is not mentioned, the article informs readers that the four composers in the U.S. - Soviet Exchange Program have arrived in the Soviet Union.

B312.   "Ulysses Kay." In *Compositores de América: datos biográficos y catálogos de sus obras*. Washington, DC: Unión Panamericana, Secretariá General, Organización de los Estados Americanos 7 (1961): 34-45.
Biographical data and catalog of Kay's works, with descriptive information by date, medium, instrumentation, duration, publishers, and recording companies. Notes commissions and awards; photo included. In Spanish and English.

B313.   *Ulysses Kay*. New York: Pembroke Music Co. 1976.
Publisher's brochure contains brief biography and complete catalog of works published by Pembroke/Fischer to date. Compositions are

arranged by performance groupings, e.g., "Band Music," "Choral Music," "Solo Music," "Works Requiring a Narrator," "Orchestral Music," etc.

B314.   "Ulysses Kay Appointed to Endowed Chair of Composition." *Triangle of Mu Phi Epsilon* 73 (1979): 2.
Kay is cited as "the second composer to fill the Mu Phi Epsilon Endowed Chair of Composition at Brevard Center." Brief biographical information provided. Photo.

B315.   "Ulysses Kay Conducts Symphony in Ariz. Hometown." *Jet* 5 (March 18, 1954): 57.
Notes Tucson performance of *Of New Horizons*. Includes photo. *See*: W20b

B316.   "Ulysses Kay to Compose Score for TV 'Special.'" *Afro-American*, National Ed., March 10, 1962, p. 15.
Notes commission by Reuben Frank to Kay to create music for the "Westinghouse Presents" series segment, *The Land*. Also includes biographical sketch noting the USSR trip, his naval career, education, honors, and awards. *See*: W85

B317.   "Ulysses Kay Wins Sixth Music Prize." *New York Times*, May 25, 1947, p. 55.
Account of first prize of $700 awarded to Kay for *Suite for Orchestra* in contest, sponsored by BMI, involving members of the American Composers Alliance. *See*: W21

B318.   Vrionides, Christos, sel. "Music for the Community Orchestra." *American Composers Alliance Bulletin* 3, no. 1 (1953): 28-29.
The author "has long felt the need of bringing to the attention of conductors of small symphony orchestras many works which seemed particularly adaptable to their needs." He has selected *Brief Elegy*, among other compositions in the ACA library, as "works . . . 'that will give the orchestra a sense of constructive achievement, and give the audience something new to talk about.'" *See*: W22

B319.   Ware, John. "Classical: Yehudi Menuhin." *Port Folio Magazine*, February 9, 1988, p. 29.
In what "promises to be one of the season's best concerts," Yehudi Menuhin, world-famed violinist and conductor, will perform on February 19, 20, and 21, 1988, in Chrysler Hall (Norfolk, VA) and in Ogden Hall (Hampton University, VA). His program includes Bach's *Concerto No. 1*, Chausson's *Poème* (violin and orchestra), and Beethoven's *Symphony No. 8*, preceded by Kay's *Reverie and Rondo*. The author refers to Kay as "one of this country's best-known black composers." *See*: W94

B320.   Waters, Edward N. "Variations on a Theme." *Quarterly Journal of the Library of Congress* 27 (January 1970): 61.
Among the recent acquisitions to the library's music division, is the manuscript of *Two Madrigals*, which was presented to the Library of Congress by the composer, Ulysses Kay. *See*: W54

B321.   "What's New." *American Composers Alliance Bulletin* 11, nos. 2-4 (1963): 18-20.
Notes extensive performances of Kay's works during the 1962-63 season: *Suite for Strings* (ten performances); *Of New Horizons* (two performances); *Six Dances* (Canadian Broadcasting Corporation); premiere performances of *Fantasy Variations* (Portland [ME] Symphony), and in New York (Brooklyn Philharmonic); *Forever Free* (Fort Dix Army Band); *Umbrian Scene* (New Orleans Philharmonic); *Inscriptions from Whitman* (premiere and four repeat performances); and *Choral Triptych* (New York). Southern Illinois University has invited Kay to be guest composer at a special winter seminar. *See*: W20, W31, W53, W82, W83c, W89, W89a, W90, W91

B322.   White, Evelyn Davidson. *Choral Music by Afro-American Composers: A Selected Annotated Bibliography*. Metuchen, NJ: Scarecrow Press, 1981, pp. 136, 148.
Includes biographical sketch, discography, and annotated list of four choral works by Kay: *Choral Triptych*, "How Stands The Glass Around?," *Two Folk Song Settings*, and "What's In a Name?." Provides descriptive information by voicing, vocal range for women and men, range of difficulty, instrumentation, publisher, and catalog number. *See*: W51, W55, W82, W128; D20

B323.   ____, comp. *Selected Bibliography of Published Choral Music by Black Composers*. Washington, DC: Howard University, 1975, pp. 27-29.
Includes titles of published choral compositions of sixty-three composers, providing descriptive information by copyright date, number of pages, voicing and solo requirements, vocal ranges, range of difficulty, a cappella, type of accompaniment, publisher, and catalog number. Includes a catalog of Kay's choral works among the lists of choral music by selected black composers.

B324.   *Who's Who Among Black Americans*. Edited by Iris Cloyd, with William C. Matney, Jr., consulting ed. 6th ed. Detroit: Gale Research, 1990/91, p. 725.
Biographical sketch includes Kay's career, education, names of family members, honors, grants, awards, membership activities, military service, and home/office address. No works list provided.

B325.   *Who's Who in America*. 46th ed. Vol. 1. Wilmette, IL: Marquis Who's Who, 1990, p. 1738.
Biographical information includes mention of Kay's fellowships,

awards, honors, memberships, and commissions.   Provides home/office addresses.

B326.   *Who's Who in American Music: Classical.* Edited by Jaques Cattell Press. New York: R. R. Bowker Co., 1983, p. 228.
Biographical sketch highlights Kay's study, works, teaching positions, awards, and professional society memberships.

B327.   "Wins Fellowship at Rome." *N.Y. Herald Tribune*, May 30, 1949, p. 20.
Brief announcement of the "Fellowship in Musical Composition" awarded to Kay by the American Academy in Rome for the period of one year. The award, valued at three thousand dollars, includes transportation to Rome.

B328.   "World Premiere Set for Negro Composer's Opera." *Norfolk Journal and Guide*, December 30, 1961, p. 14.
Provides summary of libretto of *The Juggler of Our Lady*. Includes brief biographical information, with mention of Kay's awards, honors, prizes, and education. *See*: W60

B329.   Wright, Josephine, comp. "New Music." *Black Perspective in Music* 7 (Fall 1979): 264.
Notes publication of "Prologue" and "Parade" by Carl Fischer, 1978. *See*: W130

B330.   ____. "New Music." *Black Perspective in Music* 8 (Fall 1980): 240.
Notes publication and premiere performance of *Chariots, an orchestral rhapsody* (Carl Fischer), 1979. *See*: W132

B331.   ____. "New Music." *Black Perspective in Music* 10 (Spring 1982): 101.
Notes publication and premiere information of *Jersey Hours* (voice and three harps; also arranged for voice and piano or voice and solo harp). *See*: W131

B332.   ____. "New Music." *Black Perspective in Music* 11 (Spring 1983): 89.
Notes publication and premiere information of *Chariots*. *See*: W132

B333.   ____. "New Music." *Black Perspective in Music* 12 (Fall 1984): 140, 141, 143.
Notes publication of new works by Kay: *Suite for Trumpet and Piano* (1983); *Festival Psalms* (1983-1984); and *Frederick Douglass* (1983). *See*: W133, W134, W135

B334.   ____. "New Music." *Black Perspective in Music* 13 (Spring 1986): 197, 199.

Notes publication of new compositions: *Five Winds* (Divertimento for Woodwind Quintet) and *Guitarra* (Suite for Solo Guitar). *See*: W119, W136

B335.   "Writer Kay Named Professor of Music at Hunter College." *Billboard*, June 8, 1968, p.40.

Announces Kay's appointment to Hunter College as Professor of Music, leaving his position at BMI, as music consultant of contemporary music projects. "Kay . . . has been involved in many BMI projects in the concert music area, including Student Composers Awards and editorial supervision of the annual BMI Orchestral Program survey." The article provides list of CRI recordings: *Fantasy Variations*, "How Stands the Glass Around?", "What's In a Name?," *Sinfonia in E*, and "Round Dance" and "Polka." Mentions also the Louisville Orchestra recording of *Serenade for Orchestra*, the Cambridge recording of *Choral Triptych*, and the Folkways recording of *Brass [Quartet]*. *See*: D1, D2, D4, D12, D14, D16, D20

B336.   Wyatt, Lucius. "The Mid-Twentieth-Century Orchestral Variation, 1953-1963: An Analysis and Comparison of Selected Works by Major Composers." Ph.D. dissertation, The Eastman School of Music of the University of Rochester, 1974.

A technical analysis and comparison of fourteen orchestral variations of contemporary composers—Kay, Dallapiccola, Ginastera, Copland, Luening, and Ussachevsky, among others—with a view toward the delineation of significant techniques used in the variations process. Includes discussion of Kay's *Fantasy Variations* with emphasis upon thematic elements, its presentation and elaboration, musical form, melodic style, harmony and tonality, rhythm, meter, and orchestration. The author notes "the composers on the whole reflected sensitivity to the organization of rhythm and treatment of orchestral color in achieving contrasts between variation movements." *See*: W89

B337.   ____. "Ulysses Kay's Fantasy Variations: An Analysis." *Black Perspective in Music* 5 (Spring 1977): 75-89.

Discusses the structure of the composition in terms of thematic materials, form, melodic style, harmony, tonality, and orchestration. The author refers to *Fantasy Variations* "as one of the most successful American works of the mid-twentieth century utilizing the theme and variations idea." He concludes that "while the listener perceives the total effect of the piece as an entity, he also is able . . . to perceive the individual variations as a series of musical events in which each event espouses a distinct character." Wyatt adds, further, that "listening to the *Fantasy Variations* is an exciting experience!" Musical examples provided. *See*: W89; B33, B176

B338.   "Xavier U. to Stage New Opera by Kay." *Afro-American*, National Ed., December 30, 1961, p. 15.
Notes that Xavier University will present the world premiere of Kay's *The Juggler of Our Lady*, a one-act opera. *See*: W60

B339.   Yuhasz, Marie Joy. "Black Composers and Their Piano Music." *American Music Teacher* 19 (February/March 1970): 24-26.
Includes biographical sketch; brief summary of works; and analysis of two works for piano by Kay: *Ten Short Essays* and *Four Inventions. See*: W25, W63

ADDITIONAL RESOURCES

This section contains entries from general sources (e.g. encyclopedias, dictionaries, catalogs, and library holdings, etc.) which are included to guide the researcher to other research references.

GENERAL RESOURCES

B340.   Adkins, Cecil and Alis Dickinson, eds. *Doctoral Dissertations In Musicology*. Seventh North American Edition/Second International Edition. American Musicological Society, International Musicological Society, 1984, pp. 344, 351.
This combined edition of the American-Canadian publication and the international publication classifies musicological dissertations by topics: General, Miscellaneous, Antiquity, Middle Ages, Renaissance, Baroque Era, Classical Era, Romantic Era, and Contemporary. The volume provides descriptive information by author, title, type, place, date of publication, pagination, contents, and source numbers of dissertation abstract (RILM and UMI microfilm). Dissertations about Kay, by Laurence Hayes and Richard Hadley are identified in the "Contemporary" section. *See*: B156, B161

B341.   Basart, Ann P. *Perspectives of New Music: An Index, 1962-1982*. Berkeley, CA: Fallen Leaf Press, 1984, p. 87.
An index citing Kay in an article by Rudy Shackelford. "The Yaddo Festivals of American Music, 1932-1952." *See*: B282

B342.   Bohle, Bruce, ed. *The International Cyclopedia of Music and Musicians*. 11th ed. New York: Dodd, Mead & Co., 1985, pp. 1144-45.
Narrative includes biographical sketch with emphasis upon major events in Kay's career. A catalog of works, arranged by genre, is complete to 1969.

B343.   Brooks, Tilford. "A Historical Study of Black Music and Selected Twentieth Century Black Composers and Their Role in American

Society: A Source Book for Teachers." Ed.D. dissertation, Washington University, 1972. 795 pp.

Historical treatise on black music and black contributors. Provides an excellent biography of Ulysses Kay, a catalog of his works, and a complete analysis of Kay's *Fantasy Variations*. Musical examples included. *See*: W89; B33, B176, B337

B344.   Butterworth, Neil. *A Dictionary of American Composers*. New York: Garland Publishing, 1984, pp. 260-61.

Includes short biographical sketch of Kay and a summary of selected compositions written between the years 1941 and 1979. Arranged by genre.

B345.   Claghorn, Charles E. *Biographical Dictionary of American Music*. West Nyack, NY: Parker Publishing Co., 1973, p. 248.

Includes names of "5,200 individuals encompassing . . . lyricists, librettists, and hymnists as well as composers, musicians, and singers." Provides biographical sketch of Kay, citing fellowships, scholarships, and prizes, as well as a partial list of works to 1968.

B346.   "Composer Articles in the Bulletin." *American Composers Alliance Bulletin* 11, nos. 2-4 (1963): 20.

An index of bulletin editions highlighting individual ACA composers. Kay's career and a catalog of his works are featured in an extensive article by Nicolas Slonimsky in vol. 7 [sic], no. 1 (1957). *See*: B286

B347.   De Lerma, Dominique-René. "A Concordance of Black-Music Entries in Five Encyclopedias." *Black Perspective in Music* 11 (Fall 1983): 203.

Includes entries related to black music interests in *Baker's Biographical Dictionary of Musicians*, 6th ed., completely revised by Nicolas Slonimsky, New York: Schirmer Books, 1978; *Musicians Since 1900: Performers in Concert and Opera*, compiled and edited by David Ewen, New York: H. W. Wilson, 1978; *The New Grove Dictionary of Music and Musicians*, edited by Stanley Sadie, London: Macmillan Publishers, 1980; *Die Musik in Geschichte und Gegenwart: Allgemeine Enzyklopädie der Musik*, edited by Friedrich and Ruth Blume, Kassel: Bärenreiter, 1949-1979; and *Who's Who in Opera*, compiled by Maria Rich, New York: Arno Press, 1976. Kay's biography and a selected list of his compositions are located in MGG, v16, p926-27 (written by Dominique-René de Lerma); in Baker's, 867-68 (Slonimsky); and in Grove's, v9, p834-35 (Southern). *See*: B28, B113, B296

B348.   Edmunds, John and Gordon Boelzner. *Some Twentieth Century American Composers: A Selective Bibliography*. Vol. 2. New York: New York Public Library, 1960, p. 48.

Selective bibliography of American composers. Appendix I,

"Composers in Standard Reference Works," cites Kay and directs readers to bibliographical sources relating to him: *Baker's Biographical Dictionary of Musicians*, 5th ed., Gilbert Chases' *America's Music*, David Ewen's *American Composers Today*, Sir George Grove's *Dictionary of Music and Musicians*, Claire Reis' *Composers in America*, and A. N. Marquis's *Who's Who in America*. *See*: B28, B48, B267, B296, B325, B349

B349.   Ewen, David. *American Composers Today: A Biographical and Critical Guide*. New York: H. W. Wilson Company, 1949, pp. 136-37, 366-68.
          Includes definitive biography with a catalog of principal works to 1979. Provides a brief bibliography and an appendix, "An Index of Programmatic Titles." Early photo.

B350.   Greene, Frank, comp. *Composers on Record: An Index to Biographical Information on 14,000 Composers Whose Music Has Been Recorded*. Metuchen, NJ: Scarecrow Press, 1985, p. 267.
          Indexes reference and other sources for research. Kay is included among the 14,000 entries.

B351.   Hadley, Benjamin, ed. *Britannica Book of Music*. With consulting editors, Michael Steinberg and George Gelles. Garden City, NY: Doubleday/Britannica Books, 1980, p. 431.
          Brief summary of Kay's life and career includes mention of compositions, *The Quiet One, An Essay on Death, Song of Jeremiah, The Boor*, and *The Juggler*. Notes also that Kay has composed works for organ and piano, band, orchestra, chamber ensemble, and chorus. "Kay's music is characterized by melodic lyricism and tonal orientation supplemented by chromaticism. In his later works he also uses quartal harmony, or chords built of tones a fourth apart." A list of recordings includes *Fantasy Variations, Markings, Short Overture*, and *Six Dances for Strings*. *See*: W30, W34, W57, W60, W93; D4, D7, D15, D17

B352.   Heintze, James R. *American Music Studies: A Classified Bibliography of Master's Theses*. Detroit: The College Music Society Information Coordinators, 1984, p. 73 (Bibliographies in American Music, no. 8).
          A compilation of masters' theses in American music. Includes thesis by Dora Jan Wilson, "Selected Piano Compositions in America," Washington University, 1970, which discusses works by John E. Price, Ulysses Kay, Howard Swanson, George Walker, Arthur Cunningham, and Hale Smith.

B353.   Jackson, Richard. *United States Music: Sources of Bibliography and Collective Biography*. I.S.A.M. Monograph, No. 1. Brooklyn, NY: Institute for Studies in American Music, Department of Music, Brooklyn College of the City University of New York, 1973, pp. 63-64.

Provides bibliographic sources as a "practical aid to students engaged in American music studies." Kay is included in volume 7 of *Compositores de América: Datos biográficos y catálogos de sus obras* (*Composers of the Americas: Biographical data and catalogs of their works*) published by the Cultural Affairs Department of the Pan American Union. "In addition to the title, date of composition, duration of performance and the name of the publisher, each catalog includes biographical data, a photograph and a facsimile of a page of the composer's manuscript." *See*: B312

B354.   Kay, Ernest, ed. *International Who's Who In Music and Musician's Directory*. 7th ed. Cambridge, England: International Who's Who in Music, 1975, p. 466.

Brief biographical sketch provides information of Kay's birthdate, education, occupation, family, awards, hobbies, and address. Includes also a partial list of recorded compositions.

B355.   "Kay, Ulysses (Simpson)." In *Enciclopedia della Musica*. [Edited by Claudio Sartori]. Milano: G. Ricordi & Co., 1964, p. 524.

Brief biographical sketch of Kay, with partial catalog of works to 1961 and bibliographic sources in *ACA* (Slonimsky) and *Boletin Interamericano de Musica*. In Italian. *See*: B286, B369

B356.   "Kay, Ulysses Simpson." In *The New Encyclopaedia Britannica*. 15th ed. Micropaedia. Vol. V. Chicago: Encyclopaedia Britannica, 1984, p. 737.

Biographical sketch describes Kay as a "mid-20th-century composer, a prominent U.S. representative of the Neoclassical school. . . ." Includes brief style analysis; summary of his compositions; and makes special mention of *Essay on Death, Symphony, Song of Jeremiah, The Boor*, and *The Juggler of Our Lady*. *See*: W30, W57, W60, W93, W105

B357.   "Kay, Ulysses Simpson." In *Entziklopedichesky Muzükalnüi Slovar*. Edited by B. S. Sheinpress and I. M. Yampolsky. Moscow: Izdatelstvo "Sovetskaya Entziklopediya," 1966, p. 221.

Dictionary of musicians includes brief biographical information on Kay and an abbreviated list of his compositions to 1959. In Russian.

B358.   "Kay, Ulysses Simpson." In *Encyclopedie van de Muziek*. Edited by L. M. G. Arntzenius, H. H. Badings, J. B. Broeksz, Flor Peeters,

E. E. Schallenberg, and Jos. Smits van Waesberghe. Amsterdam: Elsevier, 1957, p. 217.

Short biography of Kay includes birth date, his study with Hindemith, and mentions that he has composed for orchestra and other media. In Dutch.

B359.   "Kay, Ulysses Simpson." In *Musikkens Hved Hvad Hvor*. Edited by Ludvig Ernst Bramsen, Jr., Vol. A-L (Biografier). Copenhagen: Politikens Forlag, 1961, p. 846.

A revision of the 1950 edition containing approximately six thousand biographies emphasizing contemporary musicians. Brief biographical sketch of Kay includes information relating to his education and career at BMI. A selected catalog of compositions from 1939 to 1956 is provided, with descriptive information by title, date, and genre. Danish text.

B360.   Mapp, Edward. *Directory of Blacks in the Performing Arts*. Metuchen, NJ: Scarecrow Press, 1978, pp. 202-3.

". . . A compendium of biographical and career facts on over 850 black individuals . . . who have earned a degree of recognition for their work in the performing arts." Information concerning Kay includes details of his education, interests, compositions, and recorded works. Current address is provided.

B361.   Mead, Rita H. *Doctoral Dissertations in American Music: A Classified Bibliography*. I.S.A.M. Monograph, No. 3. Brooklyn, NY: Institute for Studies in American Music, Department of Music, Brooklyn College of the City University of New York, 1974, pp. 12, 13, 27, 28.

Lists dissertations of Richard Hadley, Laurence Hayes, Donald Armstrong, Carl Harris, and Tilford Brooks as resources relating to Kay and other contemporary composers. *See*: B20, B33, B156, B159, B161

B362.   Ploski, Harry A., comp. and ed. (With Ernest Kaiser and Otto J. Lindenmeyer). *Reference Library of Black America*. Book 3. New York: Bellwether Publishing Co., 1971, p. 88.

Kay's name appears in list of "Other Negro Performing Artists," that is included in chapter entitled, "The Black Entertainer in the Performing Arts."

B363.   Vinton, John, ed. *Dictionary of Contemporary Music*. New York: E. P. Dutton, 1974, p. 392.

Biographical sketch highlights Kay's musical accomplishments in chronological order and mentions his noted instructors. Provides, also, a catalog of published works to 1970, arranged chronologically, and a bibliography.

B364.   *Who's Who in Music and Musicians*.   International Directory.
         London: Burke's Peerage, 1962, p. 116.
         Includes abbreviated sketch with information on Kay's honors,
         compositions, festivals, colleges, and societies.

B365.   *The World's Encyclopedia of Recorded Music*.   Third Supplement
         1953-1955.   Compiled by F. F. Clough and G. J. Cuming.   London:
         William Clowes and Sons, 1957, p. 233.
         Lists three recordings of Kay's compositions: *Concerto for
         Orchestra*, "Round Dance" and "Polka," and *Serenade for Orchestra*.
         See: D3, D12, D14

CATALOG RESOURCES

B366.   Balchin, Robert, ed. *The Catalogue of Printed Music in the British
         Library*. Vol. 32. London: K. G. Saur, 1984, p. 231.
         Catalog lists thirteen works by Kay, with descriptive information
         by title, medium, duration, and publisher.

B367.   *Catalog of the American Music Center Library*.   Vol. 3, *Music for
         Orchestra, Band and Large Ensembles*. New York: American Music
         Center, 1982, p. 86.
         Catalog of twenty-three hundred works of American composers
         includes sixteen orchestra, band, and other compositions by Kay, with
         descriptive information by title, instrumentation, publisher, duration,
         and notes concerning commissions and contest winners, where
         applicable.

B368.   *Catalog of the E. Azalia Hackley Memorial Collection of Negro Music,
         Dance and Drama in the Detroit Public Library*. Boston: G. K. Hall,
         1979, pp. 131-32, 342, 344, 365, 369, 372, 374-76.
         This source which includes an introduction by Jean Currie Church
         provides a brief biographical information with mention of seven
         compositions by Kay, with cross references, and a copy of an article
         by Nicholas Slonimsky reprinted in the *American Composers Alliance
         Bulletin* 7 [sic], no. 1 (1957). *See*: B286

B369.   "Catálogo Cronológico Clasificado de las Obras del Compositor
         Estadounidense, Ulysses Kay." *Boletin Interamericano de Música* 28
         [Washington, DC: División de Música del Dept. de Asuntos
         Culturales de la Unión Panamericana] (28 Marzo de 1962): 41-50.
         A chronology of works from 1939 to 1960.   Provides descriptive
         information by year, title, duration, publisher, and comments.
         Includes publishing houses and recording companies. In Spanish and
         English.

B370.   "Catalogue of ACA Facsimile Editions."   *American Composers
         Alliance Bulletin* 2, no. 3 (1952): 25.
         Lists availability of *Suite for Brass Choir* (chamber music for brass

instruments) and *Duo for Flute and Oboe* (chamber music for woodwind instruments). *See*: W16, W17

B371.   ____. *American Composers Alliance Bulletin* 2, no. 4 (1952-1953): 24.
Lists *Little Suite for String Orchestra* and *Sonatina for Two Violins*. *See*: [W9], W31

B372.   ____. *American Composers Alliance Bulletin* 3, no. 3 (1953). 24.
Title and cost of available scores by Kay include: *Concerto [for Orchestra], Danse Calinda: A Ballet in Two Scenes, Danse Calinda* (piano reduction), *Danse Calinda: Suite from Scene II, Evocation, Five Mosaics,* J. Weldon Johnson's *Lift Every Voice and Sing* (arr.), *Of New Horizons, The Quiet One* film score, *Suite from The Quiet One, Portrait Suite, A Short Overture, Sinfonietta,* and *Suite [for Orchestra].* See: W1, W5, W7, W19, W20, W21, W27, W29, W32, W33, W34, W35

B373.   ____. "From the Catalogue of the Composers Facsimile Edition." *American Composers Alliance Bulletin* 3, no. 4 (1953-54): 22.
Among titles and composers listed in the catalog are Kay's *Allegro for Oboe and Strings, Ancient Saga, Brief Elegy, Concerto for Oboe and Orchestra, Pietà, Scherzo [Suite for Orchestra], Song of Ahab,* and *Three Pieces After Blake. See*: W4, W13, W21, W22, W28, W42, W45, W48

B374.   "A Catalogue of Works by American Composers on LP Records." *American Composers Alliance Bulletin* 4, no. 3 (1955): 20.
Notes *Concerto for Orchestra* (Remington) in the catalog of LP recordings by American composers. *See*: D3

B375.   "CRI Catalog." *American Composers Alliance Bulletin* 11, no. 1 (1963): 26.
Notes recording release of "How Stands the Glass Around?" and "What's In a Name?" (The Randolph Singers). *See*: D20

B376.   De Lerma, Dominique-René. *Concert Music and Spirituals: A Selective Discography. Black Music Research Occasional Papers, No. 1.* Nashville, TN: Fisk University Institute for Research in Black American Music, 1986, pp. 20-21.
Occasional paper which the author offers as a "provisional reference" for teachers and repertoire selectors of black music. "Coverage is limited, however, to those recordings in my personal library." Includes some fifteen of Kay's commercially-available recordings, with descriptive information by record company and number, name of performing group and conductor, title, date, and, where available, contents, and duration. The author notes that "not all may be currently in print."

B377.   ____. "A Concordance of Scores and Recordings of Music by Black Composer s." *Black Music Research Journal*, 1984, pp. 60-140.

Lists published and recorded compositions by Kay to be found in author's private collection. Holdings, after 1950, include classified list of fourteen works, with descriptive information by publisher, record company, performer, date of composition, publication and recording, record number, and duration.

B378.   *Dictionary Catalog of the Music Collection, Boston Public Library.* Vol. 9. Boston: G. K. Hall, 1972, p. 416-17.

Catalog includes fifteen Kay scores which are housed in the library.

B379.   *Dictionary Catalog of the Negro Collection of the Fisk University Library, Nashville, Tennessee.* Boston: G. K. Hall, 1974, p. 156.

Card catalog includes article about Kay, written by Nicolas Slonimsky in the *American Composers Alliance Bulletin* 7 [sic], no. 1 (1957). *See*: B286

B380.   Eagon, Angelo. *A Catalog of Published Concert Music by American Composers*. 2nd ed. Metuchen, NJ: Scarecrow Press, 1969, p. 82.

A catalog of compositions for mixed chorus, including descriptive information by composer, title, publisher, solos, accompaniment, and author of text. Choral works of Kay cited are: *Choral Triptych, Flowers in the Valley, Grace to You, and Peace, Hanover*, "How Stands the Glass Around?," "Like As a Father," *A Lincoln Letter*, "O Praise the Lord," "Sing Unto the Lord," *To Light That Shines*, and "What's In a Name? " *See*: W49, W51, W55, W58, W59, W71, W78, W82, W87

B381.   ____. *Catalog of Published Concert Music by American Composers*. Second supplement to the second edition. Metuchen, NJ: Scarecrow Press, 1974, pp. 27, 51, 57, 114, 117.

Reference source "for the extensive repertory of concert music by American composers," arranged by genre. Includes Kay's *Parables* ("The Old Armchair," "The Hell-Bound Train"), *Triple Set*, and *Scherzi Musicali* in classified sections. *See*: W108, W112, W114

B382.   Famera, Karen McNerney, comp. *Catalog of the American Music Center Library*. Vol. 2. *Chamber Music*. New York: American Music Center, 1978, pp. 12, 32, 58, 63.

Catalog of instrumental and vocal/instrumental chamber music in the center's library for solo instruments through large ensembles. Also includes classification by number of players and an index of composers. Provides descriptive information by composer, instrumentation, publisher, date, physical format, and duration. Included are Kay's *Brief Elegy, Suite for Flute and Oboe, Fanfares for Four Trumpets*, and *String Quartet No. 3*. *See*: W17, W22, W79, W107

B383. Finell, Judith Greenberg, comp. *Catalog of Choral and Vocal Works*. Vol. 18. New York: American Music Center Library, 1975, pp. 97-98.
Ten choral works by Kay are available in the center's library. The catalog includes descriptive information by composer, title, voicing, and accompaniment. Publisher or manuscript information is also provided.

B384. Hall, David. "CRI: A Sonic Showcase for the American Composer." *American Composers Alliance Bulletin* 11, nos. 2-4 (1963): 26.
Lists four CRI recordings: "How Stands the Glass Around?," "What's In a Name?" "Round Dance" and "Polka," and *Sinfonia in E* in the "CRI Catalog 1963." *See*: D12, D16, D20

B385. *Katalog der Abteilung Noten: Informationszentrum für zeitgenössiche Musik*. Darmstadt: Internationales Musikinstitut, 1966, p. 139.
Alphabetical list of published contemporary compositions includes Kay's *Suite for Orchestra*. In German. *See*: W21

B386. *"Kay, Ulysses." The Edwin A. Fleisher Collection of Orchestral Music In the Free Library of Philadelphia: A Cumulative Catalog, 1929-1977*. Boston: G. K. Hall, 1979, pp. 455-56.
Works are listed, with descriptive information by performance, duration, medium, instrumentation, date of composition, and first performance dates. Included are Kay's *Ancient Saga, Brief Elegy, Concerto for Oboe, Danse Calinda, Five Mosaics, Portrait Suite, Serenade for Orchestra, A Short Overture, Sinfonia in E, Sinfonietta for Orchestra, Suite for Brass Choir*, and *Suite for Orchestra*. *See*: W1, W4, W5, W7, W16, W21, W22, W27, W28, W33, W44, W52

B387. Laster, James, comp. *Catalogue of Choral Music Arranged in Biblical Order*. Metuchen, NJ: Scarecrow Press, 1983, pp. 16, 20, 95, 102, 131.
"Designed as an aid for the church musician and/or pastor seeking to plan unified worship services." Provides information tracing biblical references, and additional scripture. Other descriptive information includes composer, arranger, title, voicing, solos, accompaniment, name of publisher, most recent date of publication, and the octavo number. Includes seven works by Kay: "How Long Wilt Thou Forget Me, O Lord?," "Like As a Father," *O Worship the King*, "O Praise the Lord," "Sing Unto the Lord," "Give Ear To My Words," and *Grace to You, and Peace*. *See*: W58, W59, W71, W82

B388. ____. *A Discography of Treble Voice Recordings*. Metuchen, NJ: Scarecrow Press, 1985, p. 70.
According to the source, this discography lists voice recordings of music for "either choirs of unchanged male voices, choirs of girls' voices, or for choirs of women's voices." Kay's *Christmas Carol* is

included in a private pressing of a recording by the University Treble Choir (Illinois State University, Donald Armstrong, conductor). *See:* W12

B389.   Library of Congress. *National Union Catalog: A Cumulative Author List Representing Library of Congress Printed Cards and Titles Reported by Other American Libraries 1968-72.* "Music and Phonorecords." Vol. 2. Ann Arbor, MI: J. W. Edwards, 1973, p. 343.

Catalog, compiled and edited by the Library of Congress, with the cooperation of the Resources Committee of the Resources and Technical Services Division of the American Library Association, lists the following Kay scores: *The Birds, Choral Triptych, Six Dances, Emily Dickenson Set, Forever Free,* "How Stands the Glass Around?," "What's In a Name?," *Madrigals, Markings, Parables, Scherzi Musicali, Serenade, Theater Set,* and *Triple Set. See:* W51, W52, W53, W54, W55, W82, W83, W92, W99, W100, W108, W109, W112, W114

B390.   _____. *National Union Catalog: A Cumulative Author List Representing Library of Congress Printed Cards and Titles Reported by Other American Libraries 1937-77.* "Music, Books on Music, and Sound Recordings." Vol. 3. Totowa, NJ: Rowman and Littlefield, 1978, pp. 455-56.

Catalog, compiled and edited by the Catalog Publications Division of the Library of Congress, lists the following Kay scores: *Choral Triptych, Epigrams and Hymn, Fantasy Variations, Flowers in the Valley, Forever Free, Markings, Parables, A New Song, First Nocturne, Five Portraits, Prelude for Unaccompanied Flute, A Short Overture, Four Silhouettes, Sinfonia in E, Stephen Crane Set, Organ Suite No. 1, Umbrian Scene,* and *A Wreath for Waits. See:* W14, W27, W44, W56, W59, W67, W78, W82, W83, W89, W91, W100, W104, W116, W118, W126

B391.   *Library of Congress Catalogs. Music, Books on Music and Sound Recordings.* Vol. 1. Washington, DC: Library of Congress, 1986, p. 672.

Catalog includes Kay's *Aulos, Guitarra, Southern Harmony, Organ Suite No. 1,* and *Tromba,* with descriptive information by medium, publisher, parts, duration, and movements, where applicable. *See:* W103, W119, W127, W135

B392.   *The Research Libraries Dictionary Catalog of the Music Collection.* 2nd ed. The New York City Public Library. Boston: G. K. Hall & Co., 1982, pp. 222-23.

Card catalog listing of Kay's compositions available in the library.

LIBRARIES AND RESOURCE CENTERS

B393.   Center for Black Music Research,   Columbia College Chicago. Chicago, IL.
Holdings include the following scores: *A Lincoln Letter, First Nocturne, Of New Horizons* (photocopy), *Parables, Stephen Crane Set*, and *Suite for Orchestra*. Available also are recordings of *Fantasy Variations* and *A Short Overture*. Biographical notes and composer brochures from Pembroke and BMI are also available. *See:* W20, W21, W49, W104, W112, W118; D4, D15; B105, B313

B394.   Center for Ethnic Music Collection, Moorland-Spingarn Research Center, Howard University. Washington, DC.
Holdings include biographical notes, and scores of: *A Lincoln Letter, First Nocturne, Of New Horizons, Stephen Crane Set, Suite for Flute and Oboe, A Short Overture, Fantasy Variations, Scene and Song [Incidental Music], Duo for Flute and Clarinet*, and *Serenade*. Pembroke and BMI brochures provide titles of published music. *See:* W17, W20, W27, W49, W70, W89, W104, W118; B105, B313

B395.   Chicago Public Library, Music Division. Chicago, IL.
Card catalog of scores housed in the library includes: *Brass Quartet, Flowers in the Valley, Of New Horizons, Parables, Three Pieces After Blake, Serenade for Orchestra, Ten Short Essays*, and *Umbrian Scene*. *See:* W20, W39, W48, W52, W63, W78, W91, W112

B396.   The E. Azalia Hackley Collection of Negro Music, Dance and Drama, Detroit Public Library. Detroit, MI.
Card catalog lists a manuscript of *Partita*, an article by Nicolas Slonimsky reprinted from the *ACA Bulletin* 7 [sic], no. 1 (1957), and the following scores: *Aulos, Choral Triptych, Epigrams and Hymn*, "Had I a Heart", *Four Inventions, First Nocturne*, "Ode: To the Cuckoo", *Partita, Thirteen Pieces for Children* (holograph), *Pietà, Five Portraits, Scherzi Musicali, Sinfonia in E, Southern Harmony, Stephen Crane Set*, and "A Toast". The collection also includes programs, correspondence, interviews, newspaper articles, documents, and other memorabilia relating to Kay. Of particular interest are copies of the programs of concerts in Russia (1958 U.S.-Soviet Exchange Program) that were donated by Kay. Also included are clippings from the Soviet newspapers and press releases upon Kay's return to the United States. Contains copies of Kay's evaluation of the trip, which was submitted to the Information Center Service; announcement of a lecture by the returning composers for the Juilliard faculty and students; and an invitation to a lecture, sponsored by the Italo-American Association and the U.S. Information Service (October 1958), with a copy of Kay's paper which was presented on the occasion. The paper, entitled, "An American Views the Soviet Musical Scene," is in Italian. Among other letters, travel documents, maps, etc., is one from Dwight D. Eisenhower, then

President of the United States, affirming that Kay and his colleagues "'represent us all in bringing assurance to the people you meet that the United States is a friendly nation and one dedicated to the search for world peace and to the promotion of the well-being and security of the community of nations.'" *See*: W3, W25, W41, W42, W44, W82, W103, W104, W108, W114, W115, W118, W126, W127; K1, K4, K7

B397.   The Joseph Regenstein Library, The University of Chicago. Chicago, IL.
         The Music Collection of the Library includes the following printed compositions, with descriptive information by date and publisher: *The Birds, Brass Quartet, Brief Elegy, Choral Triptych, First Nocturne, Parables, Serenade for Orchestra, Serenade No. 2, Stephen Crane Set,* and *Triple Set.* Available sound recordings are: *A Bicentennial Celebration, The Black Composer in America, Six Dances for String Orchestra, Fantasy Variations, Four Contemporary Choral Works, Markings,* and *Sinfonia in E. See*: W22, W39, W52, W62, W82, W99, W104, W112, W114, W118; D2, D4, D7, D13, D15, D16, D17

B398.   The Moorland-Spingarn Research Center, Howard University. Washington, DC.
         The Music Department holdings include a manuscript of *Thirteen Pieces for Children* and scores of *Two Meditations* and *Suite for Orchestra.* The Vertical File holdings include data relating to Kay from *Baker's Biographical Dictionary of Music*; the *Groves Dictionary*; the *International Who's Who Among Black Americans 1977-1978*; and Raoul Abdul's *Blacks in Classical Music.* Also contains an article written by Hope MacLeod from the *New York Post* ("Maker of Music," closeup section, Thursday, June 13, 1968); an article from *Vogue Magazine* (September 1, 1947); and a flyer announcing the world premiere of *Choral Triptych* on Thursday, March 21, 1968. *See*: W3, W21, W46, W82; B1, B28, B225, B296

B399.   Music Division, Library of Congress. Washington, D.C.
         Automated catalog lists the following unpublished recordings: *Five Portraits for Violin and Piano,* a performance by the Juilliard String Quartet at Coolidge Auditorium, Library of Congress, April 22, 1988; and an interview by Harold Boxer of Voice of America, which took place in Birmingham, Alabama, March 22, 1976 (copied from Voice of America, 7 in. tape no. 639). *See*: W115

B400.   Northwestern University Library, Northwestern University. Evanston, IL.
         Card catalog lists Kay's *Pentagraph, Ten Short Essays, Of New Horizons, Southern Harmony,* and *Suite for Strings. See*: W20, W31 W63, W117, W127

Appendix I: Alphabetical List of Compositions

This is a list of titles, alternate titles, and retitles of compositions including parts or sections of works which have been published separately. Numbers following each entry, e.g., W39, refer to the "Works and Performances" section of this volume.

Admiral Byrd (1960), W75
Allegro for Oboe and Strings (*see* Brief Elegy)
Alleluia (1962), W81 (*see also* Choral Triptych)
American Dances (*see* Six Dances for String Orchestra)
Ancient Saga (1947), W28
As Joseph Was A-Walking (1943), W11
Aulos (1967), W103
The Birds (1966), W99
Bleeker Street Suite (1968), W106
Blow, Ye Winds in the Morning (*see* Two Folk Settings)
The Boor (1955), W57
Brass Quartet (1950), W39
Brief Elegy (1946), W22
The Capitoline Venus (1969), W110
Chariots (1978), W132
Choral Triptych (1962), W82
Christmas Carol (1943), W12
City of Magic (*see* New York: City of Magic)
Come Away, Come Away Death (1944), W18
Concert Sketches (1965), W95
Concerto for Oboe and Orchestra (1940), W4
Concerto for Orchestra (1948), W32
A Covenant For Our Time (*see* Once There Was a Man)
Danse Calinda (1941), W7
Danse Calinda Suite (1947), W29
Dedication (1946), W23
Duo for Flute and Oboe (1943), W17

Eight Inventions (1946), W24
Emily Dickinson Set (1964), W92
The Epicure (1959), W68 (*see also* Phoebus, Arise)
Epigrams and Hymn (1975), W126
Essay on Death (1964), W93
Evocation (1944), W19
Facets (1971), W113
The Fall of China (1959), W69
Fanfare for Three Trumpets (*see* Heralds II)
Fanfares for Four Trumpets and Four Trombones (*see* Heralds I)
Fantasy Variations (1963), W89
FDR: From Third Term to Pearl Harbor (1958), W65
Festival Psalms (1983), W134
First Nocturne (1973), W118
First Suite for Organ (*see* Organ Suite No. 1)
Five Mosaics (1940), W5
Five Portraits (1972), W115
Five Winds (1984), W136
Flowers in the Valley (1961), W78
Flute Quintet (1943), W13
Forever Free (1962), W83
Four Hymn-Anthems (1965), W96
Four Inventions (1946), W25
Four Pieces for Male Chorus (1941), W8
Four Silhouettes (1972), W116
Frederick Douglass (1985), W133
Fugitive Songs (1950), W40
Give Ear To My Words, O Lord (*see* Choral Triptych)
God, The Lord (*see* Four Hymn-Anthems)
Going Home (1962), W84
Grace to You, and Peace (1955), W58
Guitarra (1973), W119
Had I a Heart (*see* Triple Set)
Harlem Children's Suite (1973), W120
The Hell-Bound Train (*see* Parables)
Heralds I (1968), W107
Heralds II (1974), W122
How Long Wilt Thou Forget Me, O Lord? (*see* Choral Triptych)
How Stands the Glass Around? (1954), W51 (*see also* Two Madrigals)
Hymn-Anthem on the Tune "Hanover" (1959), W71
Incidental Music to "Scene and Song" (1959), W70
Inscriptions from Whitman (1963), W90
Jersey Hours (1978), W131
Jubilee (1974), W123
The Juggler of Our Lady (1956), W60
The Land (1962), W85
Like As A Father (*see* A New Song)
A Lincoln Chronicle (*see* Forever Free)
A Lincoln Letter (1953), W49

The Lion, the Griffin and the Kangaroo (1951), W47
The Little Elf-Man (*see* Two Songs for Children)
Little Suite for String Orchestra (*see* Suite for Strings)
Lo, the Earth (*see* Four Hymn-Anthems)
Love Divine (*see* Four Hymn-Anthems)
Lully Lullay (*see* A Wreath for Waits)
Markings (1966), W100
A New Song (1955), W59
New York: City of Magic (1958), W66
Noel (*see* A Wreath for Waits)
Nosotros (1962), W86
O Come Emmanuel (*see* Four Hymn-Anthems)
O Praise the Lord (*see* A New Song)
O Worship the King (*see* Hymn-Anthem on the Tune "Hanover")
Ode: To the Cuckoo (*see* Triple Set)
Of New Horizons (1944), W20
The Old Armchair (*see* Parables)
Once There Was a Man (1969), W111
Organ Suite No. 1 (1958), W67
Pantomime (1986), W137
Parables (1969), W112
Partita in A (1950), W41
Pentagraph (1972), W117
Phoebus, Arise (1959), W72
Piano Quintet (1949), W36
Piano Sonata (1940), W6
Pietà (1950), W42
Portrait Suite (1948), W33
Prelude for Unaccompanied Flute (1943), W14
Presidential Suite (1965), W97
Prologue and Parade (1977), W130 (*see also* Concert Sketches)
Promenade and Galop (*see* Six Dances for String Orchestra)
Quartet for Two Trumpets, Tenor and Bass Trombones (*see* Brass Quartet)
The Quiet One (1948), W34
The "Quiet One" Suite (*see* Suite from "The Quiet One")
Quintet Concerto (1974), W124
Quintet for Piano and Strings (*see* Piano Quintet)
Reverie and Rondo (1964), W94
The Rope (1946), W26
Round Dance and Polka (*see* Six Dances for String Orchestra)
Sally Anne (*see* Two Folk Settings)
Scherzi Musicali (1968), W108
Schottische (*see* Six Dances for String Orchestra)
Second Nocturne (1973), W121
Second String Quartet (*see* String Quartet No. 2)
Serenade for Four Horns (*see* Serenade No. 2)
Serenade for Orchestra (1954), W52
Serenade No. 2 (1957), W62
The Shape of Things (1960), W76

A Short Overture (1946), W27
Short Suite (1950), W43
Short Suite for Band (*see* Short Suite)
Sinfonia in E (1950), W44
Sinfonietta for Orchestra (1939), W1
Sing Unto the Lord (*see* A New Song)
Six Dances for String Orchestra (1954), W53
Solemn Prelude (1949), W38
Sonatina for Two Violins (*see* Sonatina for Violin and Piano)
Sonatina for Violin and Piano (1942), W9
Sonatine for Viola and Piano (1939), W2
Song of Ahab (1950), W45
Song of Jeremiah (1947), W30
Southern Harmony (1975), W127
Stephen Crane Set (1967), W104
String Quartet No. 1 (1949), W37
String Quartet No. 2 (1956), W61
String Quartet No. 3 (1961), W79
String Triptych (1987), W139
Submarine! (1959), W73
Suite for B♭ Trumpet and Piano (*see* Tromba)
Suite for Brass Choir (1943), W16
Suite for Flute and Oboe (*see* Duo for Flute and Oboe)
Suite for Orchestra (1945), W21
Suite for Solo Guitar (*see* Guitarra)
Suite for Strings (1947), W31
Suite from the Ballet "Danse Calinda" (*see* Danse Calinda Suite)
Suite from "The Quiet One" (1948), W35
Suite in B (1943), W15
Symphony (1967), W105
Symphony in E (*see* Sinfonia in E)
Symphony No. 1 (*see* Symphony)
Tears, Flow No More (1959), W74 (*see also* Phoebus Arise)
Ten Pieces for Children (1939), W3
Ten Short Essays (1957), W63
Theater Set (1968), W109
A Thing of Beauty (1966), W101
Thirteen Pieces for Children (*see* Ten Pieces for Children)
Three Fanfares for Four Trumpets (1942), W10
The Three Musketeers (1960), W77
Three Pieces After Blake (1952), W48
Three Psalms for Chorus (*see* A New Song)
To Light That Shines (1962), W87
A Toast (*see* Triple Set)
Trigon (1961), W80
Triple Set (1971), W114
Triptych on Texts of Blake (1962), W88
Triptych for Voice and Three Harps (*see* Jersey Hours)
Triumvirate (1953), W50

Appendix II: Classified List of Compositions

The "W" number following each title, e.g., W40, refers to the "Works and Performances" section of this volume.

BAND
Concert Sketches, W95
Evocation, W19
Forever Free, W83
Four Silhouettes, W116
Prologue and Parade, W130
Short Suite, W43
Solemn Prelude, W38
Trigon, W80

CHAMBER
Brass Quartet, two trumpets and two trombones, W39
Duo for Flute and Oboe, W17
Facets, piano and woodwind quintet, W113
Five Mosaics, chamber orchestra, W5
Five Portraits, violin and piano, W115
Five Winds, woodwind quintet, W136
Heralds I, brass octet, W107
Heralds II, three trumpets, W122
Incidental Music to "Scene and Song," W70
Partita in A, violin and piano, W41
Piano Quintet, piano and string quartet, W36
Quintet Concerto, solo brass quintet, W124
Scherzi Musicali, chamber orchestra, W108
Serenade No. 2, four F horns, W62
Sonatina for Violin and Piano, W9
Sonatine for Viola and Piano, W2

String Quartet No. 1, W37
String Quartet No. 2, W61
String Quartet No. 3, W79
Suite for Brass Choir, four trumpets, four horns, three trombones/tubas, W16
Three Fanfares for Four Trumpets, W10
Triptych on Texts of Blake, high voice, violin, violoncello, piano, W88

CHILDREN'S WORKS
Bleeker Street Suite, elementary orchestra, W106
Harlem Children's Suite, elementary orchestra, W120
Ten Short Essays, solo piano, W63
Two Short Pieces, piano, four hands, W64
Two Songs for Children, voice and piano, W102

CHORUS
Alleluia (SATB), orchestra, W81
As Joseph Was A-Walking (SATB), a cappella, W11
The Birds (SA), piano, W99
Choral Triptych (SATB), string orchestra, W82
Christmas Carol (SSA), a cappella, W12
Come Away, Come Away Death (TTB), a cappella, W18
Dedication (SATB), a cappella, W23
Emily Dickinson Set (SSA), piano, W92
The Epicure (SATB), soprano and bass soli, orchestra, W68
Epigrams and Hymn (SATB), organ, W126
Festival Psalms (SATB), solo baritone, piano, W134
Flowers in the Valley (SATB), a cappella, W78
Four Hymn Anthems (SATB), organ, W96
Four Pieces for Male Chorus (TTBB), a cappella, W8
Give Ear To My Words, O Lord (SATB), string orchestra or piano/organ, W82
Grace to You, and Peace (SATB), organ, W58
How Long Wilt Thou Forget Me, O Lord (SATB), string orchestra
            or piano/organ, W82
How Stands the Glass Around? (SSATB), a cappella, W51
Hymn-Anthem on the Tune "Hanover" (SATB), piano/organ, W71
Inscriptions from Whitman (SATB), orchestra, W90
Like As a Father (SATB), a cappella, W59
A Lincoln Letter (SATB), solo bass, a cappella, W49
Lully Lullay (SATB), a cappella, W56
A New Song (SATB), a cappella, W59
Noel (SSATB), a cappella, W56
O Praise the Lord (SATB), a cappella, W59
Once There Was a Man (SATB), narrator, orchestra, W111
Parables (SATB), chamber orchestra, W112
Pentagraph (SSA), a cappella or piano, W117
Phoebus, Arise (SATB), soprano and bass soli, orchestra, W72
Sing Unto the Lord (SATB), a cappella, W59

Song of Jeremiah (SATB), solo bass-baritone, orchestra, W30
Stephen Crane Set (SATB), instrumental ensemble, W104
Tears, Flow No More (SSA), piano, W74
A Thing of Beauty (SATB), percussion, W101
To Light That Shines (SAB), piano/organ, W87
Triple Set (TTBB), a cappella, W114
Triumvirate (TTBB), a cappella, W50
Two Dunbar Lyrics (SATB), a cappella, W98
Two Folk Settings (SATB), a cappella, W128
Two Madrigals (SSATB), a cappella, W54
Welcome Yule (SATB), a cappella, W56
What's In a Name? (SSATB), a cappella, W55
A Wreath for Waits (SATB), a cappella, W56

DANCE
The Rope, solo dancer and piano, W26

FILM SCORES
Going Home, W84
The Lion, the Griffin and the Kangaroo, W47
Nosotros, W86
The Quiet One, W34
A Thing of Beauty, W101

OPERAS
The Boor, one act, W57
The Capitoline Venus, one act, W110
Frederick Douglass, three acts, W133
Jubilee, three acts, W123
The Juggler of Our Lady, one act, W60

ORCHESTRA
Alleluia (SATB), orchestra, W81
Ancient Saga, piano and string orchestra, W28
Aulos, solo flute, two horns, string orchestra, percussion, W103
Brief Elegy, oboe and string orchestra, W22
Chariots, W132
Choral Triptych (SATB), string orchestra, W82
Concerto for Oboe and Orchestra, W4
Concerto for Orchestra, W32
Danse Calinda, theatre orchestra, W7
Danse Calinda Suite, W29
The Epicure (SATB), soprano and bass soli, orchestra, W68
Fantasy Variations, W89
Five Mosaics, chamber orchestra, W5
Flute Quintet, flute and string orchestra, W13
Give Ear To My Words, O Lord (SATB), string orchestra, W82

How Long Wilt Thou Forget Me, O Lord (SATB), string orchestra, W82
Incidental Music to "Scene and Song," W70
Inscriptions from Whitman (SATB), orchestra, W90
Markings, W100
Of New Horizons, W20
Once There Was a Man (SATB), narrator, orchestra, W111
Parables (SATB), chamber orchestra, W112
Phoebus, Arise (SATB), soprano and bass soli, orchestra, W72
Pietà, English horn and string orchestra, W42
Portrait Suite, W33
Presidential Suite, W97
Reverie and Rondo, W94
Round Dance and Polka, W53
Scherzi Musicali, chamber orchestra, W108
Serenade for Orchestra, W52
A Short Overture, W27
Sinfonia in E, W44
Sinfonietta for Orchestra, W1
Six Dances for String Orchestra, W53
Song of Jeremiah (SATB), solo bass-baritone, orchestra, W30
Southern Harmony, W127
Stephen Crane Set (SATB), instrumental ensemble, W104
String Triptych, string orchestra, W139
Suite for Orchestra, W21
Suite for Strings, string orchestra, W31
Suite from "The Quiet One," W35
Symphony, W105
Theater Set, W109
Three Pieces After Blake, dramatic soprano and orchestra, W48
Trigon, wind orchestra, W80
Umbrian Scene, W91
The Western Paradise, narrator and orchestra, W129

ORGAN
Organ Suite No. 1, W67
Two Meditations, W46

PIANO
First Nocturne, W118
Four Inventions, W25
Piano Sonata, W6
Second Nocturne, W121
Ten Short Essays, W63
Two Impromptus, W138
Two Short Pieces, four hands, W64
Visions, W125

SOLO INSTRUMENT WITH ORCHESTRA
Ancient Saga, solo piano and string orchestra, W28
Aulos, solo flute, two horns, string orchestra, percussion, W103
Brief Elegy, oboe and string orchestra, W22
Concerto for Oboe and Orchestra, W4
Flute Quintet, flute and string orchestra, W13
Pietà, English horn and string orchestra, W42

SOLO VOICE
Fugitive Songs, medium voice and piano, W40
Jersey Hours, voice and three harps, W131
The Little Elf-man, voice and piano, W102
Song of Ahab, baritone and ten instruments, W45
Three Pieces After Blake, dramatic soprano and orchestra, W48
Triptych on Texts of Blake, high voice, violin, violoncello, piano, W88
Two Songs for Children, voice and piano, W102
Where the Boats Go, voice and piano, W102

SOLO VOICE WITH CHORUS AND PIANO OR ORCHESTRA
The Epicure (SATB), soprano and bass soli, orchestra, W68
Festival Psalms (SATB), solo baritone, piano, W134
A Lincoln Letter (SATB), solo bass, a cappella, W49
Phoebus, Arise (SATB), soprano and bass soli, orchestra, W72
Song of Jeremiah (SATB), solo bass-baritone, orchestra, W30

STRING
Five Portraits, violin and piano, W115
Guitarra, solo guitar, W119
Jersey Hours, voice and three harps, W131
Partita in A, violin and piano, W41
Sonatina for Violin and Piano, W9
Sonatine for Viola and Piano, W2

TELEVISION
Admiral Byrd, W75
Essay on Death, W93
The Fall of China, W69
FDR: From Third Term to Pearl Harbor, W65
The Land, W85
New York: City of Magic, W66
The Shape of Things, W76
Submarine!, W73
The Three Musketeers, W77

TRUMPET
Tromba, trumpet and piano, W135

WOODWIND
Duo for Flute and Oboe, W17
Pantomime, solo clarinet, W137
Prelude for Unaccompanied Flute, W14
Suite in B, oboe and piano, W15

WORKS WITH NARRATOR
Once There Was a Man, narrator, (SATB), orchestra, W111
The Western Paradise, narrator and orchestra, W129

Index

Numerals alone refer to page numbers in the "Biography" section. Numerals preceded by "B," "D," "K," and "W," refer to citations in the "Bibliography about Kay and His Music," "Discography," "Bibliography by Kay," and the "Works and Performances" sections of this volume, in that order. Cross references are indicated by "see" and "see also" notations. The asterisk (*) denotes African Americans and others of African descent.

Barbacci, Rodolfo, W201
Barber, Samuel, D10
Barnett, John, W97a
Barone, Marcantonio, 23; B13; W138
Barron, David, W110
Barron*, Sharon, W25b
Bartók, Béla, 6; B191, B275
Barzin, Leon, W29
Basart, Ann P., B30, B341
Basie*, "Count" (William); "Bill," 7
Baxter, Elsa, W40
Baylor University Golden Wave Band
   (Waco, TX), W38, W43
Bazemore*, Raymond, 19; W123
Beeson*, Mary, W3
Beethoven, Ludwig van, B97, B271, B302,
   B319
Bell, Glen, D19
Bell, Michael D., B229
Bellagio Study Conference Center (Italy),
   24
Belt, Lida M., B27, B292
Benjamin, Edward B., 13, 17; W91
Bennett, Grena, 10
Berezowsky, Nicolai, D4
Bergen, Harry von, W30
Berger, Arthur, 11; B282
Berkshire Music Center at Tanglewood
   (Lenox, MA), B87; W71; *Festival*, 8;
   Symphony Orchestra, B252; W94a; *see
   also* Tanglewood Festival
Berlin Radio Orchestra, D3b
Bernstein, Leonard, 12; B154; W9, W27
Bicentennial (U.S.A.), 22; B31, B222,
   B253; W129
A Bicentennial Celebration, B397; D13
Bickerstaffe, Isaac, W117
Biggs, E. Power, B262, B265; W46a
Billings, William, 22
Binkerd, Norman, D16
The Birds, B118, B209, B389, B397; W99
Birmingham Symphony (AL), B210; W91e,
   W100c
"The Bixby Letter" (Abraham Lincoln),
   W49
Blacher, Boris, B232
"Black American Music Symposium"
   (University of Michigan), 24; B32;
   W103a
Black Arts Center (Houston, TX), B56,
   B98
"The Black Composer" (TV), 18; B211,
   B256
"The Black Composer in America"
   (Oakland, CA), B5
The Black Composer in America (Desto),
   B5, B122, B189, B229, B245, B397; D15

The Black Composer Series (Columbia),
   24; B54, B55, B100, B115, B121, B134,
   B142, B143, B174, B226, B275; D7
Black Fête *see* Celebration of Black
   Composers
"The Black Man in American Music"
   (Virginia State University), B59
The Black Music Center *see* Indiana
   University
Black Music Symposium *see* AAMOA
Black Music Symposium (Spelman
   College), B226
Black Renaissance, B228
Black Studies in Music Chorale *see* Fisk
   University
Blackwood, Easley, B24
Blake, William, W48
Bleeker Street Suite, 21; W106
Bley, Carla, B57
Bloch, Ernest, 22
Blossoming (Lipchitz), 12; W33
"Blow, Ye Winds in the Morning," 22;
   B243
Blume, Friedrich, B347
Blume, Ruth, B347
Boatwright, Howard, B24
Boelzner, Gordon, B348
Bohle, Bruce, B342
Bolshoi Theater, 16
Bomhard, Moritz, W52b
Bonds*, Margaret, B159, B287
The Boor, 14; B41, B130, B196, B259,
   B283, B351, B356; W57
Booth, Alan, W15a
Booth, Thomas, D19
Born, Harrison, B90
Boston Public Library, B378
Boston University (MA), 18
Boudreau, Robert, B299; W80, W80a,
   W80b
Boxer, Harold, B399
Brahms, Johannes, B97
Bramsen, Ludvig Ernst, B359
Brandeis Commission, 16
"Brandenburg" style (Bach), B282
Brant, Henry, 24; D3b
Brass Quartet, 13; B51, B75, B81, B89,
   B120, B126, B193, B197, B200, B251,
   B256, B265, B270, B395, B397; D1; W39
Brass Quintet see Music for Brass Quintet
Brazeal Dennard Chorale, W98a
Brevard Music Center (NC), 23; B278,
   B314; W43; *Festival Orchestra*, W20m;
   Opera Workshop, W60b
Brice*, Eugene, W30a, W40a
Brice*, Jonathan, W40a
Brick Presbyterian Church (New York,

About the Compilers

CONSTANCE TIBBS HOBSON, Professor Emerita, Department of Music, Howard University, is a performer, author, and consultant. Her biography (with Jean Cazort) of the late Hazel Harrison, *Born to Play*, was published by Greenwood Press in 1983. Along with Hortense R. Kerr, she initiated the Hobson-Kerr Piano Duo, which focuses attention on the two-piano literature of African American composers.

DEBORRA A. RICHARDSON is an Archives Specialist with the Duke Ellington Collection, Smithsonian Institution, Washington, D.C. She has been in the field of Information Science since 1980. Introduced to this at the Moorland-Spingan Research Center, Howard University, her work experience has included African American music collections. She has also published articles on African American music.